"This book lifts up one of the most important feminists in the last fifty years. Through it we can trace how Letha Dawson Scanzoni challenged evangelicals' established and theologically legitimated roles for women and perspectives on LGBTQ persons, and then helped foster significant social change. It's not only the biography of a long neglected history changer, but a description of how one biblically literate scholar helped the church to think in new ways."

—Tony Campolo, Author of *Red Letter Christians: A Citizen's Guide to Faith and Politics*

"*Building Bridges* displays biography at its best, fully encompassing one life, yet written larger than life. The authors deftly set the narrative of Letha Dawson Scanzoni and her pioneering writings on sex and gender to showcase her pivotal challenge to the reigning contours of American evangelicalism. Scanzoni stands tall and courageous in this book, a prophet calling the American church to the biblical stance of justice for all."

—Priscilla Pope-Levison, Associate Dean and Professor at Perkins School of Theology, Southern Methodist University

"Many think of Letha Dawson Scanzoni above all as a feminist, and that is no doubt legitimate. But I think of her first and foremost as a courageous biblical interpreter, because when I was a young evangelical, I watched her take the same biblical texts that the (white male) evangelical gatekeepers used to oppress others and instead use them to liberate. I admired her courage to differ from the gatekeepers, having no idea that I would eventually walk that same path. This book tells Letha's story and celebrates her impact. I highly recommend it."

—Brian D. McLaren, Author of *The Great Spiritual Migration*

"If time travel were possible, I'd set the dial back two thousand years and place this book in the hands of the early church. Then I would roll the dial forward, stopping every decade to make sure its lessons were remembered. Alas, now I can only hope its prophetic witness is not too late."

—Philip Gulley, Author of *If the Church Were Christian*

"Kendra Weddle and Jann Aldredge-Clanton's book *Building Bridges* provides an informative and inspirational story of the life and work of Letha Dawson Scanzoni. Letha's life paves a pathway for a new generation of feminist theologians. This thoughtful biography will stimulate future generations of feminist thinkers in their work and witness."

—Grace Ji-Sun Kim, Author of *Embracing the Other*

"Kendra Weddle and Jann Aldredge-Clanton provide a deeply personal portrait of the pioneering life and work of evangelical feminist Letha Dawson Scanzoni. Breaking boundaries as she built bridges, Scanzoni fails to fit any of our conventional categories. And this is precisely the point. Her work and witness demand that we rethink our categories and consider instead a paradigm shift when it comes to what it means to embrace an evangelical faith. By telling Scanzoni's story, this book offers intimate glimpses into the evolution of Christian feminism and of an inclusive faith tradition over the past half century."

—Kristin Kobes Du Mez, Author of *A New Gospel for Women: Katharine Bushnell*

"Great read! This book shows some of the best of the work of the Christian feminist movement and the importance of building bridges and of Letha's work for a very diverse and broad group of folks! Feminist thought is a joint project, drawing people together to work toward justice. *Building Bridges* illustrates that truth through tracing the life and work of one of Christian feminism's most important thinkers and activists. Scanzoni's Christian feminist publications deeply influenced me while in seminary in the late 70's. Turns out, I'm not alone. This book shows her influence on thousands. An excellent history and an excellent, must read for both Christians and others!"

—Mark McLeod-Harrison, Professor at George Fox University

"Thanks to Weddle and Aldredge-Clanton for sharpening the lens on the groundbreaking work of Letha Dawson Scanzoni. *Building Bridges* documents an often-overlooked revolution in American evangelicalism. Christians seeking to build bridges today on pressing questions of gospel liberation and justice will find here a treasure trove of biblical resources and promising vision."

—Amy Oden, Professor at Saint Paul School of Theology

"I have known Jann Aldredge-Clanton and Kendra Weddle for many years, but I have not met Letha Dawson Scanzoni. After reading the book, I wish I knew her. *All We're Meant to Be* had a profound influence on my life, moving me toward Christian feminism at a time when that stance was not 'cool' on evangelical Christian university campuses. Reading this book reminded me of the journey Letha helped equip me for, and the journeys many women have taken into a worldview that sees people for who they are and values them regardless of race, ethnic identity, gender identity or color. Jann and Kendra have produced a fitting homage to Letha and an excellent review and analysis of the Christian feminist movement. As a church historian, I value their insight into and accurate interpretation of the pilgrimage of Christian women toward equality. I encourage anyone interested in the story of the intertwining of Scanzoni's life with the development of twentieth-century Christian feminism to read this book. Anyone searching for a good historical presentation of the development of Christian feminism should read this book. It is a fine addition to Christian feminist scholarship."

—Rosalie Beck, Associate Professor at Baylor University

"I am so honored to endorse *Building Bridges: Letha Dawson Scanzoni and Friends*, by Jann Aldredge-Clanton and Kendra Weddle. This important book places Letha Dawson Scanzoni where she belongs—as a founder of Christian feminism. The authors acknowledge her true context—the history of American religion, women in religion, and a branch of Christian feminism that dared to take on homophobia. This is a neglected story of personal and theological courage that helps us understand our current religious and theological struggles. I appreciate that the authors included some of Scanzoni's most important essays so that we can hear her voice afresh. Thank you also for lifting up her role as a mentor and friend to so many women theologians, expanding their horizons and multiplying their impact. As a leader in Metropolitan Community Churches for over four decades, I can personally attest to the powerful influences of Scanzoni and her friends, such as Nancy Hardesty and Virginia Mollenkott, on more than one generation of women and men of faith. We are ever in her debt."

—Nancy Wilson,
    Former Global Moderator of Metropolitan Community Churches

Building Bridges

Building Bridges

Letha Dawson Scanzoni and Friends

KENDRA WEDDLE &
JANN ALDREDGE-CLANTON

CASCADE *Books* · Eugene, Oregon

BUILDING BRIDGES
Letha Dawson Scanzoni and Friends

Cascade Books
An Imprint of Wipf and Stock Publishers
199 W. 8th Ave., Suite 3
Eugene, OR 97401

www.wipfandstock.com

PAPERBACK ISBN: 978-1-5326-3188-7
HARDCOVER ISBN: 978-1-5326-3190-0
EBOOK ISBN: 978-1-5326-3189-4

Cataloguing-in-Publication data:

Names: Weddle, Kendra, author. | Aldredge-Clanton, Jann, author. | Scanzoni, Letha Dawson, author.

Title: Building bridges : Letha Dawson Scanzoni and friends.

Description: Eugene, OR: Cascade Books, 2018. | Includes bibliographical references.

Identifiers: ISBN: 978-1-5326-3188-7 (PAPERBACK). | ISBN: 978-1-5326-3190-0 (HARDCOVER). | ISBN: 978-1-5326-3189-4 (EBOOK).

Subjects: LCSH: Scanzoni, Letha Dawson. | Feminist theology. | Feminism—Religious aspects—Christianity. | Women–Religious aspects—Christianity.

Classification: BT83.55 B86 2018 (print). | BT83.55 (ebook).

Contents

Introduction

The room was packed. An all-star speaker held everyone in rapt attention as she spoke about the intricate turns her life has taken—contours of a Christian feminist. She finished her speech to a rousing ovation and posed for multiple selfies, which were widely shared, extending her reach beyond the four walls of the 2014 Gathering of the Evangelical & Ecumenical Women's Caucus–Christian Feminism Today.[1] Her plenary address, "It Just Keeps Rollin' Along: Christian Feminism, Equality, and Justice—Our Part in the Ongoing Story," exemplified her lifelong goal of bringing people together. By recounting the shape of her life, she reminded seasoned Christian feminists of where they've come from, and educated newer members on the history they most likely have not known. Holding the liminal space between multiple generations who have seldom understood one another, she encouraged those gathered to join hands, to draw encouragement from each other and to extend the message of God's liberation for all.

From the hallowed halls of Moody Bible Institute to the heady heyday of being a heralded speaker and writer, Letha Dawson Scanzoni has done it all. An evangelical darling of the early 1970s and an evangelical outcast today, Letha has been loved and reviled by Christians of every ilk even as scant attention is paid to her extensive influence. This oversight, this looking past such an important figure, is due in part to the transitional space she has courageously occupied. It is a margin to which neither evangelicals nor mainline Christians gravitate. But Letha has lived her life here, building bridges between people, especially between people with differing religious convictions. In a time when social media, newspapers, television, and films foster animosity and distrust, many people exist in bubbles of division. Entrenched in ideological and religious presuppositions, many remain

1. Highlights from the Gathering can be located here, including one such selfie (https://eewc.com/conference-2014/).

content to seek reinforcement of their beliefs. Letha's life, however, offers an opportunity to consider a more meaningful and transformative approach. It entails the diligent and difficult work of helping people understand each other, of moving beyond difference to cooperation. It is the process of taking down barriers and building bridges.

A believer in the power of faith to move mountains, Letha did just that. She moved two mountains in particular: barriers that have barred Christians from, in her phrase, "being all we're meant to be." In 1974 she, along with Nancy Hardesty, published *All We're Meant to Be: A Biblical Approach to Women's Liberation*. It was a clarion call for Christians to acknowledge and reject sexism as a legitimate position of Christian faith. While some were thrilled with the book's liberating message, finding within its pages new insights about gender and the Bible, others responded with ire, even writing to Letha and urging her to remove the book from bookshelves. For these critics, the book represented all that was wrong with the world, especially as it challenged what they saw as divinely ordained patriarchy.

Despite such backlash, Letha remained confident in her convictions because she grounded her beliefs in solid biblical exegesis. While turning her attention to a book on ethics, Letha experienced another epiphany, one that would deal a final blow to her position within American evangelicalism. Collaborating with Virginia Ramey Mollenkott, Letha examined what the Bible really said about same-sex relationships, expanding their understandings of God's justice until they arrived at a fully orbed theology of LGBTQ persons.[2] The result was *Is the Homosexual My Neighbor? A Positive Christian Response*, now considered by many to be a classic on the subject.

Even though *All We're Meant to Be* and *Is the Homosexual My Neighbor?* provided new perspectives on previously held evangelical positions, Letha did not intend to blaze any particular trail or challenge any specific theology. Looking back on these accomplishments, Letha says that she sees herself as a reluctant prophet, someone who has felt a persistent call to speak into the gaps where the church's theology has not accurately reflected the justice of God.

Those who see feminism at odds with Christianity might have difficulty understanding the relationship between gender and LGBTQ justice, but to Letha they are interconnected, a relationship woven by interlacing parts that cannot be separated. For Letha, the clarion call to feminism

---

2. We use *LGBTQ* throughout, although when Letha wrote about this subject beginning in the 1970s, the term *homosexual* was preferred.

emerged because of her understanding of the Bible in general and of Jesus in particular. If people—all people—are created in the image of God, then no one is more fully or less fully a reflection of God's character. Those who assert women are a little less than men, designed to fulfill supporting roles, do not take the Bible's claims about humanity seriously.

Once Letha became solidly rooted in her convictions that feminism and Christianity were not at odds but rather that gender justice derived from the Bible's core message of liberation, she soon came to realize that this same insight applies to all people, including LGBTQ persons. God's justice is not dependent upon human gender or opposite attraction. Either God's grace and justice extend to all people, or they fail to be just. Letha realized her commitment to gender justice was at its core no different from a commitment to justice for LGBTQ people. In hindsight it is easy to make such arguments, to be on what many say is the "right" side of history. But making these claims, which Letha initially did in the 1970s, came at a high personal cost. To raise questions about equality, first for women, and then for LGBTQ people, meant she no longer had the acceptance she formerly enjoyed as a public figure within the evangelical community. Her choice to explore views that were out of step with mainstream evangelicals significantly diminished her presence among them even as her work has likewise not been widely acknowledged by progressive Christians.

Holding the marginal space of justice, the hinterlands between evangelicalism and mainline American Christianity, Letha is overlooked by people on both sides of the theological divide. Most histories of religion in America, including of American evangelicalism, make little or no mention of Letha, nor of the organization she helped found: the Evangelical & Ecumenical Women's Caucus–Christian Feminism Today (EEWC-CFT).[3] It is as though Letha's legacy is a blip, of someone who wrote a couple of books and then receded from the public eye. Given her considerable presence in American religious life via Internet articles and blogs, given her role within EEWC-CFT (including as longtime editor of the organization's newsletter, and as website manager), and given her extensive correspondence from coast to coast, it is difficult to assess this oversight.

---

3. This organization has had many names, including the Evangelical Women's Caucus (EWC), the Evangelical Women's Caucus International (EWCI), the Evangelical & Ecumenical Women's Caucus (EEWC), and the Evangelical & Ecumenical Women's Caucus–Christian Feminism Today (EEWC-CFT). Unless otherwise noted, we use Evangelical & Ecumenical Women's Caucus–Christian Feminism Today (EEWC-CFT) because this is the current name.

On the other hand, Letha does not fit neatly under labels or in boxes. Historians looking to place her voice in the midst of others may find that her contributions slip out of focus because of her fluidity and prophetic edge. Those focused on the majority will not find Letha there. Her work has drawn her to the margins and beyond neatly defined boundaries.

A recent article illumines Letha's theological acumen and illustrates as well why she is difficult to categorize. In 2015 an image of a dress took the Internet by storm because people realized they saw the dress in different colors. This difference could not be justified by computer or technological glitches but was due instead to "visual perception and human cognition."[4]

While most would make no more about the dress, Letha saw it as a teaching opportunity. Using the varying perceptions of the dress as an illustration of cognitive dissonance, she suggested that when people realize that someone truly sees the world differently, sometimes they react by rejecting the other person's perspective along with the person. So, she offered a counter approach, one that builds bridges between people based upon listening, learning, and discerning.

Such an ability to think creatively and to weave in and out of several different worlds and viewpoints is one of Letha's gifts. Her approach to others is to draw no boundary but instead to think deeply, using all of the latest discoveries, in the fields of not only biblical hermeneutics but also sociology, psychology, science, and history. As a result, she routinely connects diverse people in her steady work of liberation and justice.

The 2016 U.S. presidential election is but one illustration of the continued need for Letha's work on justice and building bridges. The majority of evangelical Christians voted for a person whose campaign rhetoric denigrated women, immigrants, those with physical limitations, and a host of other marginalized groups. Prominent evangelical leaders too lined up to campaign for and provide ongoing support to this person, whose ethics are diametrically opposed to those Jesus taught. While many mainline Christians and others are baffled by this evangelical loyalty for such a figure, instead of seeking to understand the reasons for this loyalty, they either dismiss or malign those they find puzzling. At the same time, those within evangelical churches, many who feel society has abandoned their worldview, do not seek to explore the theology and politics of progressive or mainline Christians, striving instead to guard themselves against thinking

---

4. Scanzoni, "Mystery Dress," para. 11. See part 3, pages 175–84, of this volume for the full text of this article.

that is outside of their comfort zones. Add to this mix people with faith traditions outside Christianity and those with no faith perspective at all, and the challenge comes into sharper focus. Just as dismissive and disrespectful public rhetoric has grown louder, the dividing lines between groups have deepened.

Given this divisive cultural context, *Building Bridges* is more important today than ever. People of faith, especially, need to see figures who know how to cross social divides and how to do so while taking the Bible and Jesus's life and teachings seriously. While this book is about Letha's liberating writings and life, the focus is much larger than any one person. Biographies are meant to spotlight a person, bringing into clear view the contours of a person's life. Such books bridge the gap between readers and subject by examining a life with precision. Providing context and nuance, geography and genealogy, biographies illumine a person often through elevation.

While Letha Dawson Scanzoni is certainly a worthy subject of such a book, her life also suggests a different kind of consideration, an approach we have provided here. Letha's work—as activist, author, speaker, organizer, and friend—can be best understood, we believe, through the lens of those whom she has influenced and those who are continually being transformed because of her. Therefore, part 1 provides an examination of Letha's life, of her groundbreaking works on biblical feminism and LGBTQ justice, and of her cofounding EEWC-CFT. Part 2 builds upon this foundation with narratives of people who have been transformed through Letha's writing and mentorship, and through their participation in EEWC-CFT. We are among these people. The transformations we have experienced inspired us to coauthor this book. Part 3 illustrates Letha's writing, which continues to bring transformation by building bridges of liberation, justice, and peace.

Kendra's Transformation

I was teaching in an almost entirely all-male religion department at an evangelical university in the Pacific Northwest when I first met Letha. She was the editor of *Christian Feminism Today*,[5] and I had submitted an article for publication because I saw EEWC-CFT as the alternative to CBE (Christians for Biblical Equality), a group I identified as illustrating

---

5. *Christian Feminism Today* was the print newsletter of EEWC-CFT at the time.

the kind of hermeneutical prison I was beginning to feel from every angle within my particular evangelical cocoon.

Letha was not the editor I expected, not that I knew what to expect since this was early in my academic career, before I had published much. Not only was she the most thorough and gifted editor, someone who could spot an error a page away and whose research abilities are second to none, she also welcomed my continued input. Her excising skill was not the final say. She actually invited communication. She cared about what I had written and wanted to ensure that what I meant was conveyed by what I had written. This perspective resulted in much more interaction than I expected to have with someone I did not really know.

But Letha quickly became more than an editor. She seemed to know instinctively that I was on a journey that went beyond needing to have a few articles and book reviews published to fulfill professional development expectations as a new academic. Every so often, she would drop me an e-mail, suggesting I might want to consider a certain book to review. Her suggestions were always ones that met my spiritual and academic hunger. When I look back on the books I reviewed for EEWC-CFT, I can see Letha's insight at work: *Leaving Church*, by Barbara Brown Taylor; *Her Story*, by Barbara J. MacHaffie; *A People's History of Christianity: The Other Side of the Story*, by Diana Butler Bass; and *An Altar in the World*, by Barbara Brown Taylor. These authors were charting my journey, showing me the potential of a vibrant faith possible on the other side of what I had come to experience as confining and personally damaging evangelical doctrine.

These books and Letha's encouragement probably undergirded me more firmly than I realized at the time. While my graduate work in the history of Christianity prepared me for a teaching career, I had not estimated the extent to which being in an evangelical environment would challenge me in the classroom, with my colleagues, and spiritually. Conservative students immediately resisted me, especially in Bible classes. They had been instructed, after all, that women should not teach the Bible and yet there I was, standing in front of them, hoping to teach them about historical context and literary criticism, topics out-of-bounds according to their youth pastors and church leaders.

Colleagues, too, were wary of having a woman in the religion department. In my office, I noticed they seldom looked at me, drawn instead to examine the books on my shelves, their furtive glances revealing judgment. It always felt like being undressed in a public space. One time a peer asked me if I struggled with Jesus being a man. We'd not had any significant theological conversations before that, and so it felt as if he were fishing for something, hoping perhaps to find a reason to report me to the dean or provost.

This "gotcha" environment in which I spent my days receded only at home when I curled up with books whose authors felt more like friends than those whose offices surrounded mine. Reading books by women who were thinking similar things was especially helpful in the midst of what felt like an antagonistic environment. Barbara Brown Taylor's writings, given her and my shared teaching experience and her decision to loosen her connection to a specific faith community in lieu of a more sustained attentiveness to the divine in the world, worked as balm for my raw wounds.

I had wanted so badly to fit into this evangelical world I had chosen, but from the first moment of the faculty retreat where the exclusive language hit me like a ton a bricks, I knew that my difference was going to be problematic. Letha understood my challenge; she knew the depths of my anguish because she had been there. She, too, had experienced the power of revivalistic faith. She, too, had known the exhilaration of academic study. She, also, knew all too well the scorn of being outside the fold, of going too far, of moving beyond "sacred" boundaries.

Letha's sound guidance did not come, however, from countless hours of talking (although we do often enjoy long telephone conversations), and she has always been somewhat reluctant to speak too much of her own experiences. Rather, Letha's support of me came through her encouragement for me to read books she knew would provide excellent companionship for my emerging feminist understanding and to give me space to write about what I learned. She, as editor and mentor, would accommodate my need for professional development, tying it to what I was yearning for personally and spiritually as well.

Expansive and progressive thinking is often derided by those who draw stark boundaries around authoritative doctrines and decrees, and yet Letha made no such claims as she encouraged me from afar. I initially was wary of Letha and EEWC-CFT not because of its appearing to be "liberal" with its "ecumenical" nomenclature. Instead, I was being scorned so routinely by the evangelical culture in which I worked that I wanted nothing to do with any other organization that even remotely might be seen as evangelical. So, to work and speak with Letha, who claims the term "evangelical" in its historical context, caused me some ideological dissonance, despite the fact that during my PhD program I had studied the developments of the evangelical movement in the United States and knew that its early proponents were women—women who claimed rights to preach and teach, to go into the world spreading the gospel with no limits based upon gender. I knew this historical reality and yet had not really known a woman who identified as evangelical and feminist. This was new territory.

I am grateful for Letha's strong example and wise guidance on this journey.

Jann's Transformation

In 1976, when I was teaching English at Dallas Baptist University, my husband, David, gave me a copy of *All We're Meant to Be: A Biblical Approach to Women's Liberation*. David had not read the book, and neither of us could have imagined the revolutionary effect it would have on me. The words from "Amazing Grace," which I had long sung—"was blind but now I see"— became reality for me. Although I had claimed my professional vocation, I had never questioned biblical interpretations that prescribed the subordination of women at home and at church. I hadn't objected to designations of David as the "head" of the house, nor had I questioned the "divine right" of men as church leaders. As I read *All We're Meant to Be*, I discovered more than enough biblical support for gender equality in the home and in church leadership. Although Betty Friedan's *The Feminine Mystique* had come out in 1963, I'd never heard of the book or raised any questions about women's traditional roles. The call to gender justice could reach me only through the Bible. *All We're Meant to Be* transformed my life with new revelations from the Bible. Letha and Nancy gave thorough, convincing biblical support for gender equality in all areas of life; I became an instant convert and passionate evangelist for these new truths. I bought copies of *All We're Meant to Be* and gave them to the leaders, all men, at our Baptist church. I believed the copious scriptural evidence and the clear theological reasoning that had so thoroughly convinced me of the rightness of gender equality would persuade them as well. But I soon discovered strong resistance to equality.

Growing up, I never saw a woman in the pulpit, except a missionary to Nigeria. Of course, what she did was "speaking," not "preaching." The messages I got from my church and culture were that women could be missionaries, teachers, or nurses, but certainly not pastors. When I read *All We're Meant to Be*, a new world of possibilities opened for me. Because I found in this book such compelling biblical support for women as church leaders, my self-perception began to change. Even though I delighted in my teaching vocation and viewed it as a ministry, now I could see myself in other kinds of ministries as well. So I was receptive when the call came to pastoral ministry that soon included social justice activism and writing on gender equality. *All We're Meant to Be* inspired me to follow the challenging yet rewarding path of Christian feminism.

The more I tried to live out my call, the more I realized that the resistance to gender equality is part of a larger culture that gives greatest value to white, heterosexual, able-bodied, financially privileged males. I came to understand that at the foundation of this culture is an image of a male God, sanctioning patterns of dominance and submission. The suggestion in *All We're Meant to Be* that God could be more than male planted a seed that would bloom into persuasive writing on expanding divine imagery and then into hymns, liturgies, and stories that include female names and images of Deity. As I mined Scripture for inclusive divine images and social justice themes, *All We're Meant to Be* provided a model of sound biblical hermeneutics.

In 2011 when I interviewed Rev. Rebecca (Becky) L. Kiser for my book *Changing Church: Stories of Liberating Ministers*, she talked about Letha's profound influence on her. Becky asked me if I knew Letha. I told Becky of the epiphany I'd had through *All We're Meant to Be*, but that I didn't know Letha personally. Becky strongly recommended that I contact Letha because of our shared advocacy for gender justice. When Letha responded immediately and enthusiastically to my e-mail, I felt honored and a little surprised. I expected her to be like some other authors whose work I've admired, but who remain aloof. A few weeks later Letha called me. I felt more excited than if the president of the United States had called! I was amazed to actually be talking to the woman whose work had changed my life. And I was delighted and honored that she knew about my work and affirmed it.

Shortly after I read *All We're Meant to Be*, I joined the organization called at the time EWC. After a few years I let my membership lapse because of my busy schedule. In my phone conversation with Letha in 2011, she encouraged me to come back into the organization, which was now even more inclusive. Letha not only gave me a warm invitation to EEWC-CFT, but also asked me to serve on the Executive Council, to write articles for the newsletter, and to give a plenary at an annual Gathering. Even before I met Letha, she challenged me to grow as a writer through her expert editing.

She is one of the best editors I've ever worked with, both meticulous in catching errors and collaborative in making revisions.

When I met Letha in person at the 2012 EEWC-CFT Gathering in Indianapolis, I found her to be just as warm and engaging as she had been in phone conversations and in e-mail interactions. Also amazing was this annual Gathering of the organization that Letha had helped create. In fact, it was the most inclusive large gathering I had ever attended: the language of songs, presentations, sermons, and liturgies included female images of the Divine, and people of various sexual orientations, gender identities, and races were included in leadership.

Working with Letha in the EEWC-CFT Executive Council meeting that followed, I appreciated her administrative gifts and learned how generously she has contributed her gifts of writing, editing, and leadership to the organization. At the 2013 Executive Council meeting in St. Louis, I had the joy of doing a video interview with Letha. Tiana Marquez, a member of EEWC-CFT who is an actor and storyteller, came to our St. Louis meeting to interview council members. Preferring collaboration as in her coauthoring of two major books, Letha asked if I would join her in this interview. I was grateful for this opportunity to cocreate with Letha. As we went back and forth, weaving our stories together, I could clearly see the guiding hand of Sophia ("Wisdom"), connecting us at pivotal points in our journeys.

An Invitation to Readers

We invite you to join us in a discovery of Christian liberation through the life and work of Letha as well as those who also have been transformed by her witness. Letha's 2014 plenary address to EEWC-CFT inspired her listeners to continue the work of expansive justice. *Building Bridges* reinforces the foundation from which such vital outreach extends. It is our hope that in learning more about Letha and friends, many will be empowered and inspired to pick up new tools and cross divisions with hope-filled bridges.

PART 1

Birthing Christian Feminism

Letha Dawson Scanzoni is a founding mother of Christian feminism. In this part of *Building Bridges* we explore how Letha changed American evangelicalism, giving birth to a movement through her groundbreaking books, advocacy, and organizing. These chapters also examine Jesus's liberating message to women and ways that message extends to all marginalized groups, including to those of various sexual identities.

1

Changing Evangelicalism

In 2015 Letha wrote about her longtime correspondence with missionary Elisabeth Elliot, who worked with her husband in eastern Ecuador and who stayed even after her husband was killed.[1] Elisabeth later returned to the United States where she was lauded for her courage, for her missionary zeal, and for showing women that although they could not embrace leadership opportunities in their churches, they could follow in her steps and work as a missionary overseas. Even though Elisabeth and Letha's career paths took very different shapes in terms of gender assumptions, they share in the sad reality that while their presence within evangelicalism is undeniable as people who influenced scores of the faithful, they rarely are recognized for doing so.[2]

Of course this paradox is not unique to Letha or Elisabeth. As Ann Braude illustrates in her groundbreaking essay, "Women's History *Is* American Religious History," women, while being central to the life of the church, have seldom been included in historians' accounts because scholars have not seen women's participation as important, focusing instead on the power of the pulpit.[3] In sharing parts of Letha's story here, we contribute to a fuller recognition of women in the church.

1. Scanzoni, "A Christian Feminist Remembers Elisabeth Elliot."

2. The most recent example of ignoring the contributions of women can be seen in FitzGerald, *The Evangelicals.*

3. Braude, "Women's History *Is* American Religious History."

The contours of Letha's life in some ways mirror the rise of evangelicalism in America, and in other ways diverge. As a movement, evangelicalism is built upon a foundation of experiential faith—having a personal relationship with Christ—and seeing the Bible as the way to inform one's life. Letha's faith, too, is steeped in a steady friendship with Christ, bolstered by a lifelong study of the Bible. Where evangelicalism and Letha diverge is over belief systems as litmus tests for belonging. Evangelicals use certain beliefs as boundaries for determining who is in and who is out. In contrast, Letha believes that persons and relationships are more important than ideas and doctrine. This divergence of beliefs versus persons has resulted in evangelical leaders rejecting Letha as one of their own while Letha continues to identify not only as evangelical but also as ecumenical.

Letha's early identification within evangelicalism correlates to evangelicalism's rise to prominence within American culture, sparked by the social upheaval of the 1960s. Evangelicalism in America began, however, with the series of religious awakenings in the late eighteenth and early nineteenth centuries. Broadly speaking, evangelicals subscribe to the authority of the Bible, salvation through the person and work of Christ, the priority of evangelization, and the importance of a transformed life.[4] Early in the twentieth century, the movement experienced a setback with the Scopes Trial, which caused its leaders to retreat from public view due to the derision they experienced during the trial. Even though they had won, negative publicity drove them underground. It was then that they mobilized to create a subculture that served as astute training ground for their reemergence some thirty years later.

Mid-twentieth-century evangelicalism has often been referred to as neoevangelicalism because of its cooperating tenor, a tone distinguishing it from American fundamentalism on the one hand and mainline or progressive Christian tradition on the other because it hoped to strike a balance between them. Robert Ellwood suggests evangelicalism in the 1950s featured several characteristics: it was friendly to science and intellectual investigation, rational in its apologetics, tolerant of nonessential doctrine, willing to examine itself, and responsible for social engagement.[5] At the same time, evangelicalism's need to draw lines of demarcation, and a corresponding necessity to attack a person or idea—an antichrist—resulted in

4. See Marsden, *Understanding Fundamentalism and Evangelicalism*.
5. Ellwood, *1950*, 187.

a separatist spirit that abates and returns based upon the current cultural milieu.

In its 1950s expression, the burgeoning movement drew heavily from all kinds of people desiring an experientially based relationship with Christ and wanting to put that faith into action. Letha, like many other women and men of that era, was readily welcomed into this fold where her personal contributions to a reemerging community on the cusp of bigger and better things could be utilized.

In later years, however, as will become evident in Letha's writings and contributions, the boundaries that evangelicalism requires eventually work to exclude those whose faith was birthed within the movement. This is true even among those whose understandings and experiences of God are still largely experiential and, indeed, evangelical in the historical sense of the movement.[6]

Letha's own expulsion from the evangelical fold is an example of how crossing ideological boundaries is not tolerated by the group even as she continues to self-identify as an evangelical and works within this framework. In 1973 she wrote *Sex Is a Parent Affair: Help for Parents in Teaching Their Children about Sex*, and James Dobson, an academic psychologist at the time, heartily endorsed it, even writing its foreword. Asserting it provided a "biblical basis for morality and decency without making sex dirty and distasteful," Dobson commended Letha for writing a "timely book" that spoke to Christian families in a helpful and sensitive way.[7] While at the time, Dobson did not yet hold the influence he later came to possess, he was a figure of substantial import within evangelicalism, and his endorsement confirmed Letha's position within the burgeoning movement.

Ten years later, however, Letha had crossed the ideological line and was subsequently pushed to the margins as someone who was no longer considered an insider. In those ten years, she had written other books, including *All We're Meant to Be* and *Is the Homosexual My Neighbor?* According to Letha, the withdrawal of Dobson's endorsement for a new edition of *Sex Is a Parent Affair* was not a result of anything she specifically wrote in that book, but rather was due to her published views on gender equality and

6. A contemporary example is Rob Bell. Early in his ministry he was seen as a rising star within American evangelicalism, but he was eventually shunned for crossing theological lines with his *Love Wins* book, which called into question eternal damnation, and his willingness to work with people like Oprah reinforced an evangelical assumption that all things Hollywood are hopelessly secular. See, for example, Corey, "Rob Bell."

7. Dobson, "Foreword."

positive views of LGBTQ issues, positions at odds with the evangelical majority. Upon hearing of plans for a revised and updated version of *Sex Is a Parent Affair*, Dobson contacted its publisher, Bantam Books, to ensure his name would not be associated with Letha in its 1982 release.[8]

Despite her outsider status today, Letha is evangelical, holding firmly to her experiential faith and working diligently for social justice precisely because of—not in spite of—her decision to follow Jesus. Her dedication to Bible study and prayer—also hallmarks of an evangelical—is immediately evident to any who know her: Friday evenings are spent with two friends committed to Bible study over the phone; and prayer, too, is a normal part of her busy schedule.

Those quick to negatively assess her evangelical muster might claim Letha no longer attends church on Sunday, opting instead to participate in her local movie theater community, viewing a film and engaging in a talk-back session. But such accusations fail to examine the deeper spiritual life of a faithful Christian. Those who take the time to listen will find that Letha is fully steeped in her faith, a person who dedicates not just Sundays but every day to following Christ.

Women in American Evangelicalism

The foundation of American evangelicalism lies in an earlier era of revivalism, the 1720s, in what has been called the First Great Awakening, and extends through the 1860s, including the Second Great Awakening. This era of revivalism and its democratizing impulse heralded people for making public declarations of their conversions. Public meetings often included personal testimonies: individuals spoke about how faith in Christ had changed their lives; because of their decision to follow Christ, they were transformed.

Revivalism, including the early camp meetings that dotted the plains and prairies, as an American phenomenon fostered spiritual experiences and encouraged people to testify about them. No doubt, women benefitted from the loosening reins of religious authority. As they bore unrestricted

---

8. Scanzoni, "When Evangelicals Were Open," para. 13. Based upon a conversation with a friend on staff at Regal Books at the time, Letha learned more about Regal's decision to take her book out of print in 1980. Dobson may have used his power within evangelicalism to pressure Regal Books to do so. Scanzoni, phone interview with coauthor Kendra Weddle on January 15, 2016.

witness to their faith, they learned they could speak in public, that they did have a voice, that God could indeed work through them.

No history of evangelicalism is complete without noting the scores of women who because of their faith transgressed social norms that otherwise may have confined them. From Phoebe Palmer (1807–1874) and her Tuesday Meetings for Holiness, which inspired countless other women to organize similar prayer meetings, to Frances Willard (1839–1898), who founded and directed the Woman's Christian Temperance Union (WCTU) and later openly called for churches to grant women equal roles, women worked as activists, not in spite of their faith, but because of it. Writing to Mrs. D. L. Moody, Willard expressed the connection of following God and equal rights:

> All my life I have been devoted to the advancement of women in education and opportunity. I firmly believe God has a work for them to do as evangelists, as bearers of Christ's message to the ungospeled, to the prayer-meeting, to the church generally and the world at large, such as most people have not dreamed. It is therefore my dearest wish to help break down the barriers of prejudice that keep them silent.[9]

The experience of conversion shifted religious authority from pastors and leaders to individuals. As women embraced their own voices as reliable expressions of faith, they also looked to the Bible, seeking within it confirmation—of their experiences, but also of their experiences *as women*.

Phoebe Palmer, for example, used the book of Joel to assert that in the "last days" young men and women would prophesy. Believing she was living in these "last days," Palmer asserted that this passage provided the justification she needed to transgress gender norms because of her faith. How could someone doubt her or his own actions if they derived from the call of God and not one's own desires? Despite what her culture said, God would gladly receive her work as evidence of faithful living.

Frances Willard similarly justified her activism with the Bible. By turning traditional assertions upside down, Willard claimed that in order to protect the family, a God-given responsibility, women needed to work to change their world, especially because their society had become too enamored with alcohol and irresponsible men. "While alone on my knees one Sabbath," Willard claimed, "in the capital of the Crusade state, as I lifted my heart to God, crying, 'What wouldst Thou have me to do?' There was born

9. Tucker and Liefeld, *Daughters of the Church*, 274.

in upon my mind, as I believe from loftier regions, this declaration, 'You are to speak for woman's ballot as a weapon for protection for her home.'"[10]

Palmer, Willard, and countless other women understood the relationship between their faith and activism in a way that scholars, including secular feminists, have failed to acknowledge or realize. Some, however, including religious scholar Braude, rightly acknowledge the feminist movement has inspired new liturgical creativity, new inclusive-language Bible translations such as *The Inclusive Bible*, new developments in theology including critiques of male-centered assumptions about the cross and monarchical visions of God.[11] Too, the reverse has been true: women's faith commitments have influenced the broader feminist movement. But, for nineteenth-century evangelical women, faith preceded feminism.

Such is the case for Letha: faith led to feminism, and feminism illumined faith. It is an organic relationship, but its foundation is firmly established in following Christ.

Letha's Early Life

Letha Dawson Scanzoni spent her earliest years in rural Pennsylvania. She was born in 1935 in Pittsburgh, but grew up in small towns where her parents operated mom-and-pop restaurants and gas stations. The Depression era with its emphasis on conservation shaped Letha in ways that are still evident. Her apartment, for example, principally a library and working office, contains items that have been carefully collected and stored for years: post office envelopes and gently-worn shoes that might be useful to someone at some point. Or, coffee made each morning and the leftover transferred later to a carafe to be stored in the refrigerator for another day or an exceptionally late evening. Each speaks to the serious business of making the most of the smallest of things.

Time, too, is of the essence, not to be wasted but cherished. Letha's mother and father yearned for a child but were married eleven years before she was born. At the time, the Dawson family lived in a large house with her grandmother and other extended family members. One night Letha's uncle, a young man in his thirties, died suddenly during his sleep, leaving Letha's then-pregnant mother distraught about her own mortality and a fear she would not be around to care for the long-awaited baby. Letha recalls her

10. Quoted in ibid., 273.

11. Braude, "Women's History *Is* American Religious History," 102.

mother's subsequent confession that "I think I'm going to die," and her resultant nervous breakdown.[12] While not seemingly anxious about her own health, Letha is, however, keenly aware of the gift of time, a gift she sees as being full of potential: possibilities for writing, for contributing to the ongoing conversations about life and faith.

Even as the Depression and the evaporation of time left indelible marks on Letha, so too did her early experience of war, especially as it related to women's experiences. She was ten years old when World War II ended, just old enough to hear about and see social changes, including women working outside the home and then perhaps returning back to it. After women secured the right to vote in 1920, without a clear mandate to work toward, energy subsided, and there was a sense of falling back into what had previously been the normal way things were: men working to provide monetarily for the family while women kept the home-fires burning. When America entered World War II in 1941, another precipitating event called forth their activism, and women streamed into the workforce, changing not only the workplace, but also women's sense of autonomy and confidence. Following the war, despite the changed situation, women were encouraged by social forces to retreat to the home. And so they did, being told in part, this was their patriotic duty. Just as entering the job market to support the war-based economy was good for America, so too was leaving the job force following the war to make room for returning men who needed to support their families, holding up a romanticized version of familial happiness.

And yet this domestic trend isn't as clear as historians have earlier assumed, according to Stephanie Coontz. She notes that by 1947 women's employment grew; married women gained acceptance as they earned extra income for their families. Even in 1956 President Dwight Eisenhower urged Congress to require equal pay for equal work. During the 1950s more women went to college; they were featured in films even in working roles; they saw dramatic increases in their power. Still, as Coontz points out, society's image of women as exclusively wives and mothers did not change.[13]

The growing media, especially television, idealized an image of the white middle-class family happily living in suburbia. This "homogenized national culture" saturated the messages women received. "Prior to the 1940s and 1950s," Coontz writes, "a woman was condemned if she did not

12. Scanzoni, phone interview with coauthor Kendra Weddle on January 15, 2016.

13. Coontz, A Strange Stirring, 59–63.

do what was expected of her. In the 1950s, she was pitied if she did not want what was expected of her."[14]

The pressure to conform intensified in part due to McCarthyism and the fear of Communism. Anything or anyone who seemed different was suspect. Gail Collins notes that "the Cold War and anti-Communism overshadowed almost every other aspect of public life in the 1950s."[15] In this context, women who dared to think or act in ways out of sync with finding their fulfillment as wives and mothers would have experienced even more ostracism, an aspect of the fearmongering that had become part of the 1950s American context.

So, these social changes regarding women were evident as Letha was learning about her place in the world. Her mother, while not allowed by her husband to work early in their marriage because an employed wife was thought to indicate a man's failure as a provider, later essentially ran their family restaurant and store. As a young girl Letha witnessed both approaches to family life: her mother working within the home and her mother working outside it to help support the family. Likewise, when Letha married, she, like many women she knew within evangelicalism, forfeited graduating from college in order to follow her spouse. Explaining this situation, Letha wrote:

> In the spring of 1963, most people who didn't really know me would have thought of me as a highly unlikely candidate for challenging traditional notions of women's roles in the home, church, and society. On the surface, they would have seen a dedicated young Christian wife and mother, married to a graduate student at the University of Oregon, and mother of two young boys, one a two-and-a-half-year-old, the other a just-turned six-year-old, whom I was home-schooling as a kindergartner who would start public school in the fall.[16]

And yet, despite the ways in which Letha's life reflected American evangelicalism's assumptions about how women were to live, she noticed cracks in evangelical practice: differences between what the Bible said and practices in evangelical communities. Letha's dedication to Bible study and her relationship to God led her to question what she saw.

14. Ibid., 75.

15. Collins, *America's Women*, 412.

16. Scanzoni, "*The Feminine Mystique*: Then and Now," para. 11.

Part of Letha's challenge to evangelicalism lies in her critical thinking skills. Letha seldom finds a question she doesn't like: her approach to almost anything is to ask as many questions as she can. This is a skill she learned early in life, a natural response when explanations did not satisfy her. She wrote, for example, of when she first doubted that there is such a person as Santa Claus, at age six. Sitting in her tiny one-room school, one day after she had completed her assignment, she caught herself looking out the window realizing she faced a conundrum regarding Santa. Letha explained, "I remember the anxiety I felt as I thought about those words. If Santa knows when I'm awake or sleeping, he must know what I'm thinking! And right now I'm thinking that he doesn't exist! He must be very angry with me!"[17] Such contradictions seldom escape her observation, but instead of rejecting one idea in order to accept another, Letha keeps the opposites in tension, a skill few are able to cultivate.

As early as ten, Letha recalls being uneasy about what it would mean to grow into a young woman. Even though she says her parents taught her she could do anything, society pressured women to see themselves as less important than men, to curtail their aspirations to only a few acceptable occupations, such as teaching and nursing. One way Letha navigated the contradictory messages of society and family was to transgress gender assumptions. She began playing the trombone. Reflecting on how her music helped her find her way in the world of gendered realities, Letha wrote, "What I think made the difference for me rather than anything else during my teen years was my music. When I was 12 years old, I began playing the trombone and it became the love of my life. I practiced hours and hours and excelled. And I rather like the fact that the trombone was not considered a stereotypical 'feminine' instrument."[18]

Church was an important although not central aspect of Letha's youth. Since her parents were often busy running their business, Letha usually went to church with a friend. In fact, her best friend was a preacher's daughter. While Letha responded to an altar call at a church when she was eleven, it was at the urging of a preacher's wife, who walked Letha to the altar, telling her she needed to be confirmed and thereby overcome sin. What Letha, on the other hand, says she remembers most vividly was the feeling that God loved her and that the sky's vastness gave her a sense of awe for the grandeur and greatness of God. Her response to these feelings of love was a desire to

17. Scanzoni, "My First Encounter with Religious Doubt," para. 8.
18. Scanzoni, "Why Should Difference Make Any Difference?," para. 28.

11

develop her natural abilities to their fullest. This sense of responsibility was augmented when, as a senior in high school, Letha saw a remaindered copy of *In His Steps* by Charles Sheldon on a department store's bargain book table. She quickly paid the fifty cents to purchase the book.[19]

Inspired by a female musician in the book, Letha contemplated how she could similarly use her musical talents for God. At the same time, she knew doing so would be a departure from her previous dreams of having a dance band and the accompanying fame and fortune that would follow such success. Letha wrote, "At that point, almost without thinking, I reached over to the nightstand and picked up the pocket New Testament that the Gideons had distributed in my high school . . . The Bible fell open to John 12:43 in the King James Version: 'For they loved the praise of men more than the praise of God.'"[20]

Even though she didn't tell anyone at the time about this experience, Letha decided that she would shift her perspective from seeking personal recognition to using her talents in service to God. She didn't know then what that meant for her, but she knew that she loved God with an intensity that she needed to unleash, and that in order for her to know more about what this meant, she had to learn more from others who also loved God and wanted their lives to express this commitment.

In Letha's early religious experiences, one can readily see the evangelical influence at work. The Bible, personal conversion, and an active response were central to her early sense of self and calling.[21]

Letha graduated from high school early, having skipped the seventh grade. In order to continue developing her musical skills, she attended Eastman School of Music in Rochester, New York, where she studied trombone under the world-renowned master teacher Emory Remington. As a young woman away from home for the first time, and nurturing her nascent faith, Letha sought out others who "talked about prayer and Bible study and a personal walk with God."[22] Many of these were from fundamentalist and conservative evangelical groups.

In this environment, it didn't take long before she experienced more contradictions that, while not shaking her faith in God, certainly introduced her to the difference between God's love and the actions of Christian

19. Scanzoni, phone interview with coauthor Kendra Weddle on January 5, 2016.

20. Scanzoni, "Reflections of a Christian Feminist," para. 16.

21. See, Marsden, *Religion and American Culture*, 181.

22. Scanzoni, "Reflections of a Christian Feminist," para. 18.

people. At seventeen and while at Eastman, Letha became involved in Youth for Christ, a prominent organization.[23] One night the director, who was from Bob Jones University, kissed Letha without her permission. The experience offended Letha, causing her emotional and physical stress. Letha was also shocked by the anti-Semitic remarks he made to her Jewish roommate, as well as his racist comments about an African American fellow trombonist she had brought to a service to play a duet with her for a radio program. Too, she became aware of the judgmentalism and gossip some of her new friends engaged in. Letha's idealism about people from conservative groups who considered themselves to be the "real and true" Christians was beginning to break down.[24]

Given Letha's early questioning about the legitimacy of Santa Claus, it is easy to see that more important contradictions would weigh heavily on such a critical thinker. She realized that while God's love for her was firm, she was less convinced those around her were as holy as they claimed to be or as right about God as they would have her believe.

Another contradictory experience also occurred while Letha was in college at Eastman. Her newfound Christian friends while supporting her trombone playing at churches also told her she should not be speaking in churches, especially not about the Bible. Since she was a woman—despite her opportunities to share the gospel—it was not acceptable for her to teach it to others, especially if men were involved. Although this restrictive thinking did not make logical sense to Letha—hadn't she felt the spirit of God calling her to use all of her talents in service?—she accommodated her Christian friends, even as she also began her own more rigorous examination of the Bible. As Letha noted, "I was still not convinced that God saw things in the restrictive way I was being taught. But I was only 17 years old that first year, and it was hard to contradict those older than I and who, I thought, must surely know the Bible well."[25]

In some ways, Letha's early awareness of Christian hypocrisy is no different from what others learn. On the other hand, what perhaps sets Letha apart from many is that instead of removing herself from those who ignore their double standards or those who dismiss theological contradictions,

23. Growing out of World War II mass rallies, Youth for Christ International formed in 1945. Led by the young Wheaton College graduate Billy Graham, according to George Marsden, during its first year it sponsored about 900 rallies and had one million participants. Marsden, *Understanding Fundamentalism and Evangelicalism*, 69.

24. Scanzoni, phone interview with coauthor Kendra Weddle on January 5, 2016.

25. Scanzoni, "Reflections of a Christian Feminist," para. 24.

Letha opted for a middle way, seeking to understand what there was to be gained by exploring the challenges she faced.

It would be justified, given her early experiences of Youth for Christ and in other fundamentalist or conservative evangelical groups, for Letha to make her mark within the broader Christian stream of American mainline Christian expression. But, Letha didn't turn away from evangelical groups, despite the hypocrisy she knew existed. Her faith was birthed within the evangelical movement and owed much to evangelicalism's emphasis on a personal relationship with God, and she had committed herself to sharing this news, along with her musical talents, in any way that would be useful.

Of course the neoevangelicalism of the 1960s and 1970s is not the same as evangelicalism today. Emerging from divergence with fundamentalists over aggressive attacks on progressive theologies, leaders of neoevangelicalism often sought to engage in theological debate rather than lambast views they saw as not traditional enough. So, perhaps more than mere doctrine itself, the approach of neoevangelicals, as exemplified by Billy Graham, was to engage in educated dialogue with the goal of changing minds and hearts.[26]

In fact, writing some fifty years after her initial foray into public print, Letha explained why evangelical feminists must continue to have a voice in the ongoing conversation. She says that religion can be limiting or liberating with regard to gender.[27] As a young Christian she experienced firsthand how some leaders used religion to limit women. But Letha's trust in a loving God propelled her to examine more closely whether or not her teachers and preachers were reflecting the Bible or were instead using the Bible to defend their ideas about who women were supposed to be. Her questions drove her to the Bible, and what resulted was an emerging voice who shaped the very movement, even as it challenged, and continues to challenge, it.

Eternity Articles

In her early thirties and married for about ten years with two young children, Letha began writing more widely to educate others on the liberating message of the gospel. Her first major article was written as a response to a limiting vision provided by Charles C. Ryrie, the second author of a joint

26. Letha writes about this shift within evangelicalism in "When Evangelicals Were Open."

27. Scanzoni, "Why We Need Evangelical Feminists," 67.

essay published in *Eternity* in 1963. A quote from Ryrie's article served as an epigraph to Letha's piece and conveyed his sexist bias: "A woman may not do a man's job in the church any more than a man can do a woman's job in the home."[28] Finding the logic of Ryrie's perspective deeply flawed by personal opinion and proof texting, Letha ruminated on her response for a long time before she went public with her concerns. Her initial musings entailed a "letter to the editor," but after she exceeded three hundred words and had not finished her thoughts, Letha realized she had the beginnings of a larger project.[29]

As in many if not most of her writings, Letha began her article—"Woman's Place: Silence or Service?"—with personal knowledge, in this case the conflicting experience she and other women faced when they felt called by God to speak and yet were told that being a woman precluded them from doing so. Yet, Letha's use of this experience reveals a somewhat unique argument. Rather than claiming only the affirming Bible references as they apply to women and building a case from them, Letha, because of her early experiences, drew attention to how this conflict actually affects women. She wrote, "Inconsistency coupled with inflexibility produces many problems—one of which is that women feel forced to serve the Lord with guilt instead of gladness . . . Is it God's intention that they must feel they are sinning by serving?"[30]

While Letha briefly mentioned the typical "problematic" passages used to confine women to limited roles within the church (1 Corinthians 11 and 14; 1 Timothy 2), she didn't provide alternative interpretations to them but rather suggested those who invoked Scripture this way needed to take seriously the inconsistencies embedded in such an approach, especially in light of women becoming more educated. Without belaboring her point, Letha also suggested that the early Christians eventually departed from the way Jesus had treated women as conveyed in the Gospels. This reliance on Jesus as a hermeneutical lens would make it difficult for evangelical leaders to dismiss her arguments. By taking Jesus seriously, Letha demonstrated not only her christocentric theology, but also her alignment with one of evangelicalism's main requirements: a personal relationship with Christ.

At the same time, Letha challenged evangelicalism for its narrow understanding of the Bible. She used the Bible to challenge gendered dogma.

28. Kent and Ryrie, "Women in the Church," 13.
29. Scanzoni, "Backstory: Woman's Place—Silence or Service?," para. 16.
30. Scanzoni, "Woman's Place: Silence or Service?," 15.

Is not the Holy Spirit the one who distributes God's gifts, she asked? Or, what about Paul's advice to the Corinthians that all parts of the body of Christ are necessary?

Letha's questions would prove difficult to disregard.

A second pivotal article appeared in 1968 in *Eternity*. She had written to the editors, praising their editorial that had raised the question, "Is It a Sin for a Woman to Think?" After corresponding with the editorial's author, William J. Petersen, Letha agreed to write a second article, this time on the so-called roles of wives and husbands.

"Elevate Marriage to Partnership" reflected Letha's view that while marriage within many Christian circles had been seen as denigrating to women, this was not a true reflection of the Bible. Using her style of asking questions, Letha wrote, "In a day when young men and women are educated similarly and are seeing one another not in terms of sex stereotypes, but as individual *persons*, many are asking, 'Why must marriage be a dictatorship?'"[31]

Echoing her first *Eternity* article, Letha wondered if Christian women who had egalitarian marriages felt guilty when they heard sermons or teachings that taught otherwise. To counter such arguments, Letha made several propositions, staking out a stronger position, showing a firmer voice than she had in her first *Eternity* piece. She based her positions on the hermeneutic strategy of interpreting specific biblical passages within their contexts and of balancing each passage with others.[32]

While drawing on logic and science, experience and empathic understanding, Letha addressed each position often upheld by those using the Bible to subjugate women to men. She ended her argument saying, "Christian marriage should be a relationship in which each partner helps the other to grow in Christ, a relationship in which the fruit of the Spirit is clearly exhibited (Gal. 5:22–26)."[33] Who could argue with that?

Even though through this evangelical magazine Letha's voice was being heard and she was having a positive impact on her readers (and challenging some), in the editing process itself Letha experienced limitations, boundaries that marked the ideological scope she was not to transgress. If all we had access to were Letha's articles as they appeared in *Eternity*, this effort to keep her within the acceptable confines of evangelical borders

31. Scanzoni, "Elevate Marriage to Partnership," 11 (italics original).

32. Ibid., 12.

33. Ibid., 14.

would not be known. However, through Letha's later explanations and documents, she offers backstory information, shedding a useful light on evangelical culture. These editorial experiences would also shape Letha's own editing skills later when she became an editor, too.

In "Woman's Place—Silence or Service?" (her first *Eternity* article) Letha indicated that she did not aim primarily to make the case for women pastors. Instead, she brought to light inconsistencies in biblical arguments, unanswered questions, and practical problems emerging from the position that women should be silent in churches.[34] Letha's method of asking questions to encourage reflection can be seen in her original draft, in which she noted a contradiction: evangelicals rejected the idea that women could be church leaders whereas at the same time Pentecostal and Holiness groups (also considered evangelical) celebrated women in church leadership positions. Yet, as the article appeared in the publication, the context in which Letha pointed out this contradiction was excised, resulting in people subsequently thinking Letha was not supportive of women's ecclesial rights.[35]

More substantial editorial oversight occurred in Letha's second *Eternity* article. In making her case for egalitarian marriage, Letha had not examined the word "headship" in Ephesians 5. *Eternity* editor William Petersen asked Letha to address male headship as part of "divine order" in order to keep her readers from dismissing what she had to say.

Making such a revision perplexed her. Letha says that while her understanding of Ephesians 5 challenged traditional visions of marriage, the only message she had heard from sermons focused on female submission. To achieve her goal of helping readers think differently, she had opted for an alternative angle—one, it seemed, her editor was not ready to embrace. In the end, Letha made an acceptable revision, willing to "dilute" her message slightly if it meant she could establish that egalitarian marriage was biblical.[36] Even though Letha now says that if asked to accommodate similarly today she would refuse, her decision in 1968 illustrates her personal goal of building bridges with people, of working diligently to sustain community and a sense of relationship, even when it came at personal cost to her.

At the same time, Letha's initial articles for *Eternity* point to what George Marsden calls an ideological fault line, a widening and deepening

34. Scanzoni, "Woman's Place: Silence or Service?," 15.
35. Scanzoni, "Backstory: Woman's Place—Silence or Service?," para. 27.
36. Scanzoni, "Backstory: Elevate Marriage to Partnership," para. 30.

chasm evident in the second half of the twentieth century.[37] As an evangelical, Letha held fundamental commitments to the Bible and Jesus. As a woman, she felt acutely her role as a wife and mother, and she was careful to keep her work as an independent scholar and writer in balance with her domestic life. Too, because of her work, she was becoming well versed in psychology, sociology, and what came to be called situational ethics. Feminism also was challenging the construction of families and even the traditional notions of women's leadership in churches, especially as mainline churches began ordaining women in the 1950s.

Faith and Feminism

The questions Letha posed as an author of the two groundbreaking *Eternity* articles were questions born of her experience and her commitments. She was living the challenge of a working wife and mother and a Christian who wanted more than anything else to follow the way of Jesus, a way she understood, despite what she was often taught, that led to liberation not limitation.

Many contend feminism and Christianity are diametrically opposed. According to sociologist Robert Wuthnow, for example, feminism of the 1970s took flight among those who were better educated and generally ran counter to traditionalist values prominent in churches in the 1950s. To conservatives, feminism was too much aligned with the countercultural movement that included sexual experimentation, abortion rights, and poor moral standards.[38] Those who pitted feminism and faith against—or at least in tension with—each other fail to understand how feminist convictions might be birthed, not from a source outside one's faith, but instead from deep within one's faith.

This is Letha's experience. Her feminism springs from her understanding of Jesus and not despite him or the Bible. Such was also the case with early American feminists, those from the nineteenth and early twentieth centuries, who while working as activists to advance the antislavery movement, had epiphanies that the arguments they made for the full rights of blacks should also extend to themselves, not as something to hoard, but as a duty to use to its fullest potential.

37. Marsden, *Religion and American Culture*, 247.
38. Wuthnow, *The Restructuring of American Religion*, 227.

When, for example, abolitionist Sarah Grimké was attacked by the Congregational Ministerial Association of Massachusetts for public lecturing, she responded, not from a feminist position, but from one of deep religious conviction. "The motto of woman," she wrote,

> when she is engaged in the great work of public reformation should be,—"The Lord is my light and my salvation; whom shall I fear? The Lord is the strength of my life; of whom shall I be afraid?" (Ps. 27:1). She must feel, if she feels right, that she is fulfilling one of the important duties laid upon her as an accountable being, and that her character, instead of being "unnatural," is in exact accordance with the will of Him to whom, and to no other, she is responsible for the talents and the gifts confided to her.[39]

Well aware of the antislavery movement's activists, Letha drew on their approach to women's rights when she responded to the feminist movement of the 1960s and 1970s. "The image of women's lib is unfortunate," she wrote in a 1973 *Christianity Today* article, "it misses the whole point of the movement and encourages the widespread suspicion that Christianity and feminism are incompatible." She further explained, "For the most part, nineteenth-and twentieth-century feminists professed Christianity and took the Bible seriously. When critics hurled theological arguments against them, they sought to answer with well-reasoned rebuttals."[40] In focusing on how the early feminists responded to their critics, Letha not only educated feminists or those open to the possibility about the longer history of a happy relationship between feminism and Christianity, but she also demonstrated how such arguments could similarly be employed to counter 1970s antifeminism. "It is profitable to explore the message the early Christian feminists have left for us," she suggested. "The vision of men and women as co-sharers of God's grace and co-workers in Christ's kingdom is a timely message for the 1970s."[41]

To illustrate how 1970s feminists might respond to their critics (much as the early faith-centered activists did), Letha noted several key points. The book of Genesis points to women being made in God's image. The motif of Eve from Adam's rib does not require women's subordination to men. The more accurate meaning of "helper" connotes companionship. Or, when opponents used Paul's epistles to silence women, eschewing their historical

39. Quoted by MacHaffie, *Her Story,* 187.

40. Scanzoni, "The Feminists and the Bible," 10.

41. Ibid., 15.

contexts for their own gain, Letha pointed out how the early feminists used closer textual examination to illustrate the fault of such approaches, including Angelina Grimké's early assertion drawn from Gal 3:28: "'I recognize no rights but human rights—I know nothing of men's rights and women's rights; for in Christ Jesus, there is neither male nor female.'"[42]

Letha also commented that it was useful to look to women in the Bible as examples for 1970s women and to see an ethic for equality especially in how Jesus treated women. Such equality better reflected the shared humanity of women and men: these arguments Sarah and Angelina Grimké had made. Despite the hypocrisy that sometimes existed within the history of Christianity, 1970s feminists had good historical guides to assist them in working toward greater equality in their homes and churches, not less.

The women whom Letha drew insight from for her article were part of what is often called first wave feminism, a movement credited with achieving the right for women to vote in the United States (this movement also extended beyond American borders). And while this suffrage-seeking movement included women from across a broad spectrum of beliefs and convictions, those Letha drew insight from for her work in the 1970s were motivated by the imperative of following Jesus. Early feminists who helped gain suffrage for women knew, Letha remarked, that "Jesus Christ wanted his good news to spread and that he had clearly spoken against burying talents and hiding one's light under a bushel."[43]

An Emerging Author

Letha's formal education beyond music is in biblical interpretation and theology. She graduated with high distinction from Indiana University in Bloomington in 1972 with a BA in religious studies.[44] She also has extensive knowledge within the field of sociology.

As a young married professional writer, Letha assisted her husband in his professional work as a professor, which entailed research and writing in addition to classroom engagement. She not only edited his work, but also she became a partner in writing sociology textbooks. Too, she had earlier written three books geared toward young women and men: *Youth Looks at*

42. Ibid., 12.

43. Ibid., 15.

44. She also graduated with honors in religion and was elected to membership in Phi Beta Kappa.

Love (Revell, 1964), *Why Am I Here? Where Am I Going? Youth Looks at Life* (Revell, 1966), and *Sex and the Single Eye* (Zondervan, 1968).

Written in her late twenties and early thirties, these books offer a good glimpse into Letha's young writing career. She had routinely written Sunday school curriculum and various other articles for publication, but in these books she wrote for a young audience, teens starting to contemplate dating, marriage, and life.[45] *Youth Looks at Love* describes adolescence and the challenges involved in relating to one's family, the emergence of sexuality, the process of dating, and marriage. Given the time in which this book was written, there are few surprises about the kinds of insight Letha provides: family is a God-given gift; dating involves challenges, including sexual attraction; being "unequally yoked" is probably not the best idea.[46] At the same time, there is an easygoing, conversational tone that young readers probably appreciated. No idea was dismissed as unimportant but rather was given direct attention.

Too, perhaps drawing from her own sense of partnership with her husband, John, Letha encouraged a view of marriage that in 1964 conservative evangelical circles probably struck a progressive note. In her chapter called "Courtship and Engagement," she instructed couples contemplating marriage to practice good communication. To urge them in this, she listed several practical issues they should consider: money, sex, children, in-laws, housing, and leisure.[47] In this context, she said the couple should not take these lightly but talk through each aspect of a life together, so that clarity of intention is achieved. Letha also pointed out that in this process differences will emerge, especially if each partner is honest. Given that women in this period would have easily opted to be silent and submissive, Letha's guidance is important in understanding, not only her approach to writing, but also her expansive view of women as equal partners in marriages.

Urging couples to move beyond the idea of wives having no legitimate voice, Letha quoted Ruth Graham—Billy Graham's spouse—as saying, "If two people agree on everything, one of them isn't necessary." She also

45. Letha wrote for numerous Sunday school publishers, including Union Gospel Press, David C. Cook, the American Sunday School Union and the weekly *Sunday School Times*. She did this work while she was a student at Indiana University, and she used the payments, although small, to assist her parents (Scanzoni personal note).

46. Being "unequally yoked" was a common expression used among evangelicals primarily to denote dating and marriages between believers and nonbelievers. It was based on 2 Cor 6:14 in the King James Version.

47. Scanzoni, *Youth Looks at Love*, 96–97.

noted how "dull and lacking in spice" a marriage would be if women simply assumed their husband's position in all things.[48] Suggesting that a couple should see marriage not as happening haphazardly but as something that needs attentiveness and care, Letha relied on her musical background to strike an appropriate image. "Marriage," she said, "is somewhat like a musical composition—some passages may be in unison (all singing or playing the same notes); other parts may be in harmony (a pleasing blend of different notes); and there might even be a bit of dissonance (or discord) to add spice."[49] Such realistic, practical, and commonsense advice is a hallmark of Letha's writing. As a planner and deep thinker, she instructed young people on intentionality and not falling into the trap of doing something or being someone without a sense of purpose and planning.

Two short years later, when she was thirty-one, Letha expanded her attention beyond marriage to other aspects of life in her book *Why Am I Here? Where Am I Going? Youth Looks at Life*. In this call for attentiveness to life, Letha urged young people to think deeply about life as a gift from God: relationships as potential for cultivation and interest, work as vocation and service, even decisions as the gift of learning discernment. Her reflections again strike a practical key. She raises questions and uses examples to help her readers contemplate the hidden potential that each aspect of life entails, including its promise for great joy. Just as her earlier book had, so too this volume offered a perspective firmly rooted in evangelical culture but also conveying challenge. In her chapter "Life Is Vocation," Letha addressed the question of whether a Christian should consider attending a secular college or university, a popular query at the time due to the perceived threat of secularism.

Within the evangelical fold, Wheaton College, Gordon College, Moody Bible Institute, and other lesser known places were centers of up-and-coming figures who would take America by storm in the 1970s, including the massively popular Billy Graham. While many evangelicals held to the position of only going to Christian colleges, Letha encouraged her readers to think differently. "Many Christians fear that young people will be robbed of their faith if they attend a secular college," she said. "Actually, if you have a strong faith in the first place—if you're really committed to Jesus Christ and seeking His will—you needn't worry that you'll be shipwrecked

48. Ibid., 93.
49. Ibid.,115.

on intellectual icebergs of unbelief."[50] "True," she admitted, "you'll run up against some ideas that will really cause you to think through your beliefs and reevaluate many things you've always just taken for granted. But this can be healthy, and you can emerge a stronger Christian for the experience. God needs witnesses for Him on secular campuses."[51]

It appears Letha took this advice seriously, for by the time she wrote *Sex and the Single Eye*, just two short years later, her thoroughgoing investigation into the theological and philosophical currents was apparent. *Sex and the Single Eye: A Christian Philosophy of Sex* was Letha's response to what was called the new morality—a controversial subject begun by Bishop John A. T. Robinson's book *Honest to God* in 1963 and continued with Joseph Fletcher's *Situation Ethics* in 1966.

Letha's argument for writing the book, according to the first chapter, was that evangelicals could be too quick to criticize a position without examining it first. So rather than joining with the massive condemnation that was afoot, Letha studied the position, seeking to learn from the process. "True," she wrote, "some may feel that this is a bothersome and unnecessary effort—that it's far easier to hurl epithets at the new morality supporters. But others may find they have actually learned something by giving consideration, for example, to the warnings against exploiting other persons and the importance of looking not on overt behavior alone, but on motivation and meaning as well."[52]

Striking a balance, Letha quickly pointed out that there was important insight to be gained by studying new morality, including attentiveness to persons as opposed to rigid guides or rules, and focus on intention as opposed to mere behavior. At the same time, she noted that some—not all—new morality proponents did not give adequate focus to God's law, a subject she examines at great length in the book as an alternative perspective to what she sees as an anemic theology of sexuality endorsed by many historians and theologians throughout the church's history.

This measured approach is also evident in Letha's updated version of *Sex Is a Parent Affair*. Regarding abortion, one might expect Letha to make

50. Scanzoni, *Why Am I Here?*, 115.

51. Ibid. At this point, Letha still used exclusive language to refer to God. She later came to change her way of speaking of God, to include the Divine Feminine. See chapter 4 for more information on this aspect of her development.

52. Scanzoni, *Sex and the Single Eye*, 17.

an impassioned argument against it, but instead she calmly explained the 1973 Supreme Court ruling on abortion and added,

> There are sharp differences among Christians with regard to abortion. Some consider it murder; others say the operation might be an act of mercy. Some believe that the soul enters the fetus at conception. Others feel the zygote (fertilized ovum) is just a cell that may become a potential human being but it's not yet one at the moment and hence its removal is not "murder." The Bible is silent on the subject, although some Christians believe Exodus 21:22, 23 may indicate a developing embryo or fetus was not regarded as a full human being, since infliction of an injury on a pregnant woman which resulted in its loss was to be punished by a fine rather than by death, under the "life for life" law.[53]

Indeed, the way Letha portrayed the complexity about abortion is illustrative of her method on each subject, and it is useful to highlight that method here. Notice that she first recognized a variety of opinions on the given topic, a variety among Christians as well as scientists or other professionals. Too, she was careful to provide a clear explanation of the reasons for such variety. Then, when appropriate, she explored whether or not the Bible contains an opinion about it. In the case of abortion, she acknowledged that it doesn't, but with regard to another topic, such as masturbation, she goes to great lengths to explain the Bible's position, including how a passage may have been used incorrectly in the past.[54]

Letha's discussion of masturbation further illumines the deftness of her analysis, the clarity of her thought in placing biblical passages within their contexts, and her open-mindedness in responding to practical questions with transparency and honesty. She begins by recognizing the variety of opinions: masturbation is a sin; masturbation is wrong because it falls short of the ideal God had in mind; masturbation is morally neutral; masturbation is legitimate as a way to release sexual tension; masturbation is

---

53. Scanzoni, *Sex Is a Parent Affair*, 147.

54. In the case of masturbation, for example, Letha wrote, "It used to be thought the 'sin of Onan' mentioned in Genesis 38:8–10 was masturbation. That's why masturbation is sometimes called 'onanism.' It seemed like a good proof-text for parents to frighten their children, 'God will strike you dead if you "play with yourself."' Yet, Onan's sin was not masturbation. Rather, he failed to complete an act of sexual intercourse. Onan simply withdrew before emission of semen because he did not want to fulfill an Old Testament law that required the brother of a dead man to go to the man's widow and produce an heir in the name of the deceased brother. That was the sin for which he was punished" (ibid., 187).

a gift from God. Then, noting the Bible's silence on masturbation (once Gen 38:8–10 is understood in its context), Letha pointed out possible situations when masturbation might be useful—as a better alternative than extramarital sex, for example. But upon mentioning the potential goodness of masturbation, she also addressed the related issue of what occurs in people's minds during masturbation, suggesting one way to guard against illicit fantasies could be to "concentrate one's thoughts on the beauty of sex in the context of marriage."[55]

Letha continued by considering the possibility of sublimation, of channeling sexual energies into other activities, and she noted this could be accomplished by using a wide range of activities to keep teenagers, especially, from lapsing into unhealthy "preoccupations" with masturbation. Still, Letha quickly suggested considering differently the tendency to focus most specifically on the act of masturbation rather than on the state of mind driving the practice. She offered that considering all aspects—physical, mental, psychological, social, physiological—ensured that parents and children alike learn "God never intended that sex should control or use us; rather *we* are to use and control sex!"[56]

Midcareer Success and Midlife Grief

With the publication of *All We're Meant to Be* (1974) and various articles, in addition to her editing work, Letha Dawson Scanzoni had by all accounts become a well-established author. According to sociologist Sally Gallagher, *All We're Meant to Be* established Letha as well as Nancy Hardesty (her coauthor) as the two most prominent evangelical voices in second wave feminism, and the book garnered several awards, including recognition by *Eternity* in 1975 as the book of the year and by *Christianity Today* in 2006 as one of the top fifty books influencing evangelicals.[57] Finally, in 2010, *All We're Meant to Be* was listed as one of the top hundred books (besides the Bible) that "Have, Should or Will Create Christian Culture."[58] Pamela Cochran likewise suggests it was "the most influential work in helping launch the evangelical feminist movement."[59] Numerous speaking

55. Ibid., 189.
56. Ibid., 191 (italics original).
57. *Christianity Today*, "The Top 50 Books."
58. Gibson et al., *Besides the Bible*.
59. Cochran, *Evangelical Feminism: A History*, 25.

engagements followed its publication, including lectures at conferences, colleges, and theological seminaries.

Spreading the message of Christian feminism was not confined, however, to books and articles. A movement began emerging around the same time that Letha and Nancy were writing their book. In 1973 a group of socially active evangelicals met in Chicago to consider their response to various social issues. They later identified themselves as Evangelicals for Social Action (ESA). During their 1974 meeting, a task force formed to study the Equal Rights Amendment, women's ordination, and Bible translations, among other things, in order to make proposals at an upcoming ESA meeting. This task force developed into its own organization known as the Evangelical Women's Caucus (EWC).[60] Not only was Letha a founding member, but she has continued to provide steady guidance and inspiration to it for more than forty years.

In 1978 Letha, along with Virginia Ramey Mollenkott, published what turned out to be another monumental book within Christian circles: *Is the Homosexual My Neighbor?* Often noted as the first book to take an affirmative position on LGBTQ relationships, it was nevertheless the decisive work that resulted in Letha's further separation from the evangelical fold. More important, however, in this book Letha went beyond abstract theories and nonjudgmental assessments of the subject to an examination that was "up close and personally" related to her own faith and biblical understanding—because, as she learned while in the writing process itself, her coauthor was a lesbian Christian. Letha acknowledged in the updated preface of the 1994 edition that "she would at some point have to take an unpopular public stand that would be costly to her Christian writing and speaking ministry."[61] Despite this challenge, Letha would not have it another way: she followed the contours of her faith, trusting Christ's liberating presence and realizing that sometimes that message of liberation means the road will be rocky and few will travel it.

The path Letha had to walk alone that she did not choose, however, was the one that followed the breakup of her marriage. In the first years of her career and marriage, Letha was uniquely involved in her husband's career, writing textbooks with him and routinely hosting students in their

60. *Christian Feminism Today*, "Origin," para. 2. More about the origins and contemporary work of the Evangelical Women's Caucus (EWC) can be found in chapter 3. EWC has had several name changes, including its current Evangelical and Ecumenical Women's Caucus–Christian Feminism Today (EEWC-CFT).

61. Scanzoni and Mollenkott, *Is the Homosexual My Neighbor?* (1994), vii.

home for Bible studies and other gatherings. Too, they had reared two sons, Letha providing the majority of their care and oversight at the same time that she cultivated her own writing career.

What appeared to be a successful marriage, however, was not. Letha and John had been married twenty-five years when John reported to Letha he "was no longer in love" with her and that he "felt trapped and dying inside" and wanted out of the marriage.[62] She was forty-eight at the time of their divorce two years later and felt like her dreams shattered. Her self-esteem plummeted and her sense of security evaporated.[63]

In retrospect, Letha confides she often questioned her sanity as she realized in hindsight that the "equal partnership" they both espoused and which she believed their marriage embodied was a lie.[64] Later when she recalled their day-to-day interactions, she recognized they probably had never had that kind of relationship. Sure, John had perhaps been "better" than many men. When she asked him to help more around the house, this was his reply: he did so much more than other men of his generation, so she shouldn't complain. Truthfully, Letha had managed to sustain a career, something not many women did then. And, John had invited her to work with him on his books, respecting her scholarly research and writing abilities. So, she wasn't a wife who didn't have any life outside of her husband's. Still, she did the cooking and cleaning. She kept track of their busy schedules and provided most of the oversight of their sons. In fact, Letha once mentioned that John was most loving to her when she scrubbed their floors.[65]

Their divorce deeply affected Letha, in part because they had spent so many years crafting their view of what marriage should be and defending it in writing and speaking; nevertheless, their relationship crumbled, as well as her image of it. When Letha eventually wrote about the dissolution of her marriage, she revealed the extent to which her life had radically altered.

62. Scanzoni, "A Long Time Grieving," 15. For John's view, see Scanzoni, *Love and Negotiate*.

63. Ibid.

64. See, for example, their textbook where they identify four patterns: Owner-Property, Head-Complement, Senior Partner/Junior Partner, and Equal Partner. The goal of the Equal Partner marriage, they say, is "not to 'destroy' marriage but to *change* it so that both partners can fulfill individual aspirations unhindered by gender-role stereotypes and traditional ideas about the division of labor." Scanzoni and Scanzoni, *Men, Women, and Change*, 273.

65. Scanzoni, phone interview with coauthor Kendra Weddle on January 22, 2016.

Writing in the third person, Letha noted, "What the middle-aged woman had thought was settled for life—her feelings about herself, her relationship with her husband, her perception of her world—have become uncertain and chaotic. And it seems so late in life to have to rethink everything."[66]

Married twenty-seven years, she confessed that the uncoupling process was so complex and her feelings of rejection so intense that the grieving process simply could not be hurried.[67] Despite her deep personal pain, Letha turned to her writing career as part of her path back to her *self*. At fifty-three, Letha had the opportunity to move to a new city. It was an invitation to embrace the twist her life had taken and to concentrate on her writing again.

An analysis of her writing reveals, however, the lingering effect her divorce had. Letha's early life displays almost a frenetic amount of writing: numerous books and articles almost flying off of her typewriter, all while she maintained what she thought was a happy home and family. Once John asked for a divorce, however, and she was forced to face the reality of life after a so-called Christian marriage, the wind had in many ways been taken out of her sails.

She still wrote two more editions of the sociology textbook she had coauthored with John, writing the third edition almost entirely without his assistance, she says, because he had moved on to other projects and had seemingly lost interest in work on their book. And she wrote *Sexuality* (1984), worked on revised editions of both *All We're Meant to Be* (1992) and *Is the Homosexual My Neighbor?* (1994), and coauthored with psychologist David G. Meyers *What God Has Joined Together: A Christian Case for Gay Marriage* (2005, 2006). From 1994 through 2013, she was the editor of EEWC (the Evangelical & Ecumenical Women's Caucus, of which Letha was a founding member) publications, which included *Update*, a quarterly print magazine, and the online version called *Christian Feminism Today*. Due to Letha's encouragement, EEWC was one of the first religious organizations to have an Internet presence, beginning in 1998—the same year Google was established as a search engine. In addition to editing for EEWC, Letha managed content on the website from 1998 until she retired in 2013, including an annotated "Link of the Day" feature—and prior to that, "Web Explorations for Christian Feminists." Letha participated in two blogs hosted by the EEWC website: 72–27, a "cross-generational" conversation

66. Scanzoni, "A Long Time Grieving," 16.

67. Ibid.

with Kimberly G. George, and *FemFaith*, an "intergenerational" discussion with Melanie Springer Mock and Kendra Weddle.

Today, working as an independent scholar, writer, editor, and writing consultant, Letha specializes in feminism, relationships of love and friendship, marriage and family living, divorce, self-esteem, human diversity, aging and caregiving, sexuality and gender, sex ethics, and social justice.[68]

The Internet feeds Letha's intellectual curiosity and insatiable desire to learn. Having access to so much information at her fingertips, Letha spends much of her time online. The Internet is her personal academic library and is how she establishes and maintains contacts from all over the world. While her writing production—and certainly her economic security—suffered because of the divorce, in other ways Letha finally had an opportunity to develop her voice more clearly, to strike out on her own without the constraints she may have felt living in the shadow of John and his academic career. Too, because of her divorce, she could write more personally and persuasively to scores of women who had in one way or another experienced similar familial challenges.

Financial and professional accolades, while gratifying to some, have never been motivating factors for Letha or her work. She has not achieved status that many use to measure the influence of someone on religion in America. And yet, our consideration of her contributions suggests that she has changed the lives of many, she has modeled responsible and reasonable biblical interpretation, she has demonstrated how to engage new developments over time, and she exemplifies someone whose dedication to the way of Christ reflects an ever-widening understanding of and commitment to justice for all people.

Resources for Church Groups

In this first chapter we note that Letha always looks to the Bible for answers to life's questions, and she realizes how a person's unique experiences shape one's sense of self and convictions.

Throughout her life Letha never failed to take the Bible seriously. As a result, she is an astute student of the time and cultures from which it emerged. Here are a few questions to get you thinking about the Bible.

---

68. See www.lethadawsonscanzoni.com/.

» Make a list of technological changes you've witnessed throughout your lifetime. Imagine that as a group you were to write the Apostle Paul a letter describing your church, including your worship services. How many aspects of your church life would you need to "translate" for him?

» What do you know about the Jewish culture of Jesus's life? Use the Internet to learn more about Sadducees, Pharisees, Essenes, and Zealots, for example. Explore what synagogues were like.

» How did the Jews at the time of Jesus respond to their larger Greco-Roman society? Use the Internet to see how Greco-Roman religion differs from what we think religion involves today. What was the Greco-Roman system of government? What percentage of the Greco-Roman world was wealthy? What percentage was poor? What percentage of Greco-Roman people could read? How does this information about the Greco-Roman world help us to understand the biblical narrative?

» How might you contrast the time and cultures of the Old Testament (the Hebrew Bible) from those of the New Testament?

» Do you think your church or church group learns enough about the time and cultures of the Bible?

Letha also greatly values personal experience and sees our individual insights as important avenues for building bridges. In 2015 she wrote an article about what was then called the "mystery dress" phenomenon: people saw the same dress in different colors. Letha used the occasion to explore how people can look at the same thing and see it so differently, although she went beyond the dress itself to consider faith commitments. Consider reading the article together (located in part 3, pages 175–84).

» Identify an idea or perspective you have that differs from that of one of your friends or group members. We suggest you start with something like an ice cream flavor or favorite color.

» Identify something more significant that you think is a unique perspective within your group. (Here an option could be to have each person write their responses rather than share them with the group.)

» Identify an idea that would be a challenge for your group to "see." Letha says that we can become more empathetic listeners if we can try to understand why someone might "see" this idea as they do. Consider the following: what do I know about the person's background, including how they view God, the Bible, their religious experiences? What do I know about this person's stage of life, and how that might affect them? What do I know about this person's personality or disposition?

Thinking about all of the factors involved in how each of us "sees" our world, including our convictions, can help us be more in tune to our own perspectives and more compassionate toward others who "see" differently.

Bible Reading: Acts 9:1–19

Paul learns to "see" with new eyes.

» Explore the context of Paul's conversion experience by looking up some key words in online commentaries or Bible dictionaries. Start with Paul's Jewish background. Explore the ethnic divisions that existed. What can you discover about Tarsus?

» Put yourself in the shoes of Jesus's disciples who now are considering working with Paul. How do you justify trusting this person who previously sought to harm those who followed Jesus?

Implementing New Ideas

» Determine as a congregation to study the cultural context of the Bible with more diligence. Ask your pastor to dedicate more time in each sermon to examining the time and place of specific biblical narratives.

» Create times for people to share their faith experiences while others listen and affirm.

2

Gendering Justice

How often has the slippery slope argument been employed to stem the tide of justice?

Letha recalls this line of reasoning used against her by a "highly regarded evangelical leader from a conservative theological seminary" after she had written *All We're Meant to Be*. He'd told her, "When I saw you had published a book on the Bible and feminism a few years ago, I said to my wife, 'You just watch. Her next book will be on homosexuality.'"[1] Although he turned out to be right—she would go on to write about LGBTQ persons—the idea that her theological conviction derived from a slippery slope trajectory is inaccurate, even as the image continues to be widely used today to restrict Christian thinking about gender and gay marriage.

According to Letha, those who rely on the slippery slope metaphor do so to control people, to keep them from asking questions, exploring new theologies, or even reconsidering a biblical passage with a fresh perspective.[2] Using scare tactics—the image of falling into the abyss at the bottom of a slippery slope—is often dependent upon viewing the Bible as God's verbatim word and eschewing some ideas as simply so far out-of-bounds that there is no need to give them a second thought. Feminism is one such topic, and Christian conservatives see feminists on a particularly slippery slope indeed. The argument usually follows a predictable pattern beginning with an affirmation that the Bible contains no factual or historical

1. Scanzoni, "Christian Feminism and LGBT Advocacy," para. 1.
2. Scanzoni, "'Paradigm Lost' and Slippery Slope Panic," para. 9.

inaccuracies and that it is the only lens through which to understand truth. The Bible, without any historical or cultural markers, is seen as a collection of God's intentions—or rules—that can be accessed much like words and definitions in a dictionary. If someone has a problem, the Bible has the answer. Never mind the wide discrepancies of time and place, of cultural clues or historical complexities.

Those taking this approach to the Bible generally believe all biblical statements apply to all times and in all places. Any human element within the text is nullified by divine intention. When evidence of oppression occurs in the Bible, it points to God's design for the world and is not to be questioned. Interpretation of the garden narrative found in Genesis illustrates this position. Eve and Adam's fruit-eating episode is evidence of how evil takes over when women assert initiative over men. When Eve ate and encouraged Adam to eat with her, she demonstrated just how bad it is for women to be in charge. In a word, Eve was the first feminist, and the Bible's judgment on her is abundantly clear: for all time, she will have pain in childbearing and will desire her husband even as he rules over her. Women who follow in Eve's footsteps tread the dangerous slope she did. Seen from the safe hilltop, the terrain below is fraught with danger. Those who reject that the Bible is inerrant and who acknowledge the human fingerprints within the Bible's pages will obviously follow Eve as she gleefully tumbles down the slippery slope leading to feminism, which will result in women seeking individual rights rather than divine roles, and such rights for women will inevitably lead to other kinds of wrong decisions, such as granting ecclesial rights to women, supporting LGBTQ rights, even affirming the ordination of gays and lesbians. So goes the thinking of slippery slope advocates.

This slippery slope argument, however, does not take seriously the claims Letha Dawson Scanzoni and Nancy Hardesty illumined in *All We're Meant to Be: A Biblical Approach to Women's Liberation*, or the convictions Letha and Virginia Ramey Mollenkott expound in *Is the Homosexual My Neighbor? Another Christian View*. The foundation of both books is the liberating message of Jesus. In a rigorous and thorough examination of the life and teachings of Jesus, who turned the conventional thinking of his day on its head in order to show compassion to the "least of these," Letha and her writing companions establish a consistent biblical methodology—not a discounting of biblical material.

In this chapter we explore this interpretive method as it is employed in Letha's two groundbreaking books: *All We're Meant to Be* and *Is the Homosexual My Neighbor?*

All We're Meant to Be

Much like earlier Christian feminists before them, Letha and Nancy developed their convictions from the life and work of Jesus, which necessitated a rigorous study of the Bible. Because they understood Jesus's message as one of liberation for all, including and especially those on the margins, this idea of freedom from bondage served as a lens through which to examine all other biblical narratives.[3] By the time they updated the third edition of their book, they more pointedly critiqued the evangelical reliance on gender roles, seeing them as an oppressive regression from Jesus's teachings. They wrote: "We became convinced that Jesus Christ came to set us free from restrictive roles."[4]

Situated on the person of Christ, their work and methodology remained distinctly at home within evangelicalism even as many of their conclusions diverged from most previous assumptions. They were not, however, seeking to endorse a Christian approach to the women's movement that was gaining steam in American culture. Rather, they explain, "In speaking of liberation for the Christian woman, we are not thinking of an organization or movement, but rather a state of mind in which a woman comes to view herself as Jesus Christ sees her—as a person created in God's image."[5]

Having established their christocentric methodology, Letha and Nancy also explain the necessity of understanding what the Bible says by its cultural and historical settings, the intention of the author, and insights to be gained by archaeology, science, and psychology. Such open-ended inquiries reflect the ongoing nature of a relationship between Jesus and a discerning reader. Within the search for deepening meaning and faithful living, the presence of Christ serves as the steady foundation and illumining guide as all knowledge is brought to bear on the text. This process is no

3. Scanzoni and Hardesty, *All We're Meant to Be* (1974), 11. The revised edition changed the sentence slightly. "Jesus Christ came to set us free, to make us whole." *All We're Meant to Be* (1986), 17.

4. Scanzoni and Hardesty, *All We're Meant to Be* (1992), ix.

5. Scanzoni and Hardesty, *All We're Meant to Be* (1974), 11.

haphazard slippery slope falling away from God, but rather is a courageous adventure of being connected to God even as one treads unknown or uncharted regions, trusting God to be one's partner in the quest to understand the message of the Bible.

Asking historical and contextual questions Letha and Nancy say is not an attempt to reduce the value of the Bible but rather is an effort to understand what it says.[6] Further, attention to individual passages requires evaluation about how to approach them, whether they are intended, for example, to be taken allegorically, figuratively, or literally. Letha and Nancy point out that even a Christian who says she takes the Bible literally, unless she views wearing jewelry or braiding her hair to be a sin, is actually violating her claim. Further, men who pray without lifting up their hands rarely see this as problematic although the Bible says men should lift their hands when praying. In each of these cases, interpretive evaluation is required in order to understand what the Bible meant *then* and subsequently to determine how that meaning could be applied *today*.

After examining questions of historical and cultural context and literary analysis, Letha and Nancy outline a key principle they utilize to interpret the Bible: identifying the major theme or idea running throughout a text and using that as a light from which to consider various individual passages within it. This principle eliminates "proof texts," which have been "hurled at women to 'keep them in their place.'"[7] Letha and Nancy use the formative biblical principle to ascertain how to approach ideas that are more localized or specific. In other words, "passages which are theological and doctrinal in content are used to interpret those where the writer is dealing with practical local cultural problems."[8] They illustrate the results of this process by noting that the truth of the gospel (the major theme) is the liberating work of Jesus. So, any individual passage must be brought into the light of this conviction. When an individual passage adheres to a different message, it must be evaluated for its continuing application. Such interpretive analysis reveals the difference between ideas that pertained to a specific location, time, or both, and those that apply to all times and in all places. Letha and

---

6. Even though many of their critics claim they reject that the Bible is inerrant, Letha and Nancy do not specifically address this terminology. Instead, they point to the need to understand the Bible within its historical and cultural contexts.

7. Scanzoni and Hardesty, *All We're Meant to Be* (1974), 19.

8. Ibid., 18.

Nancy note, "any teaching in regard to women must square with the basic theological thrust of the Bible."[9]

An illustration of how they applied their methodology can be seen in how they addressed a pervasive evangelical meme: women should be silent in churches. This perspective is based upon 1 Cor 14:34 and 1 Tim 2:11–12. The question raised, of course, is, should this silence apply for all times and in all places, or was it specific to a place and time? Letha and Nancy begin their research by considering the way women experienced ancient Judaism and then investigated the way the early Christian movement empowered women rather than silencing them. From the resurrection to the evangelistic work of Paul, women were key figures spreading the gospel. Romans 16, for example, reveals ten women among twenty-nine listed who received specific recognition from Paul, including Junia, who is listed as an apostle. In the process of unearthing the numerous women whose contributions to the Christian movement are often buried by patriarchal preference, Letha and Nancy also use linguistic analysis to show how sexism has been embedded in translations. In the King James translation, for example, Phoebe is referred to as a servant rather than a deacon, a translating decision that supported a patriarchal vision of the church.

As Letha and Nancy work through passage after passage related to women (1 Cor 11:2–16 [11:13]; 1 Cor 14:34–35; Eph 5:3; 1 Tim 2:8–15 [2:10]; Titus 2:1), they clearly and steadily show how such passages do not speak in a vacuum but instead reflect notions emerging from a particular time and place. The limiting ideas that recur in these New Testament letters reveal the extent to which the early Christian community was establishing itself as a movement within the Greco-Roman world. Letha and Nancy write, "Into a very structured and restrictive society, the gospel of Jesus Christ came as a liberating, mighty rushing wind, overturning racial, social, and gender differences . . . But such freedom was not fully understood by those outside the church and even by some within . . . And so early church leaders offered some strong suggestions . . . Rule one was, don't rock the boat quite so hard!"[10]

Letha and Nancy's answer to the question of whether or not women are required to keep silent in churches is a resounding no. Yet this decision isn't established because of their presumed distaste for silence but rather because of their biblical analysis. Jesus demonstrated a preference for a

9. Ibid., 20.

10. Scanzoni and Hardesty, *All We're Meant to Be* (1992), 90–91.

gospel of liberation. The New Testament letters fail to maintain this message, leaving to contemporary Christians the challenge of deciding which message to follow.

The complexities involved in biblical interpretation, of relationship between readers and text, text and God, God and readers are often points for division and demarcation among Christians. How, for example, is the Bible authoritative? Or, for whom is it more or less authoritative? How does the Bible's authority relate to the authority of Jesus? Such questions have, and more to the point, how one answers such questions has, potential to result in varying interpretations of the Bible and therefore often create division among Christians. While Letha and Nancy identified as evangelical in part because of their commitment to Jesus, others saw their approach to the Bible as pushing beyond the so-called evangelical limits.[11] Ironically, of course, Letha and Nancy used the Bible to point people to God and to show them how to live in the world by fully embracing who God designed them to be.

As with any skill, if one practices diligently, one makes progress over time. So, Letha and Nancy's interpretive method develops and matures. Their fundamental approach does not change, but they do add important nuance and perspective with each subsequent revision of *All We're Meant to Be*. Rather than leave their readers to deduce these changes on their own, Letha and Nancy call attention to them. In these shifts, their movement is toward greater clarity and precision.

In the edition they wrote ten years after the book's initial publication, Letha and Nancy expanded their explanation of methodology by noting the importance of considering the Bible not as a collection of individual parts but as a whole. If the Bible's metanarrative is taken seriously, the Bible could not be used to justify assumptions and biases of any one group. Letha and Nancy add, however, a new nuance: "we must remember that the book was primarily written by men in patriarchal cultures; that the canon was defined by men, who left out many books now known to us to be more favorable to women; that Scripture has been interpreted for two thousand years by male exegetes and theologians in support of male supremacy."[12] Still affirming the Bible as foundational for their work and as inspirational for women, Letha and Nancy were becoming more cognizant of the patriarchal bias

11. Cochran, *Evangelical Feminism*, 29.
12. Scanzoni and Hardesty, *All We're Meant to Be* (1986), 26–27.

embedded in the Bible itself as well as the bias of subsequent interpreters, including contemporary theologians.

In the second edition Letha and Nancy also add three additional insights to their methodological explanation. First, under the heading of "Male and Female" they explain the problem of dualism, of conceptually defining something as over against the other. Throughout history, the notion of dualism (that reality is composed of two parts) is often used to label women as less than men, as secondary, whereas men are primary. Because they critiqued dualism and its justification of patriarchy as ordained by God (with its normative view of men and subordinate view of women), Letha and Nancy also recognized that dualisms of all kinds must be challenged, not just that of male versus female. Acknowledging Rosemary Radford Ruether, who claimed that all dualisms or polarities are evil, they elaborated, "We make such distinctions to put ourselves up and others down. We stigmatize and stereotype the 'other' in order to oppress. All distinctions between people—male and female, rich and poor, black and white, gay and straight, Western World and Third World, Christian and non-Christian—are attempts to deny our common humanity."[13]

Second, Letha and Nancy identify their theological method, an approach that is often called the Wesleyan Quadrilateral, where Scripture, tradition, reason, and experience are brought into conversation in order to make deductions about specific beliefs. Beyond this formalized method, Letha and Nancy share their presuppositions, convictions derived because of their faith in God. In stating these assumptions they reflect the influence of feminist theologians who criticize so-called orthodox theologians of confusing presuppositions with revelation. The presuppositions Letha and Nancy identify include the following: God is love, and there is nothing anyone can do to make God love us more or less; God created all people in God's image; the essence of sin is not pride but dualism and domination; and God's consistent stance is on the side of justice and mercy.[14]

The third and most important new development Letha and Nancy include in their later edition is attentiveness to language. They write, "The major reason we chose to revise this book rather than simply reissue it was because of our naïveté concerning the language issue in the first edition."[15] Acknowledging that they originally thought language was a trivial issue,

13. Ibid., 30.
14. Ibid., 31–32.
15. Ibid., 32.

they later realized it was at the heart of oppression, because language determines what people think. Admitting this would be seen as a "radical" move on their part; they, nevertheless, trusted their methodology that the whole trajectory of the Bible did in fact point to liberation, and this included understandings of God. When studied closely, the Bible conveyed numerous feminine images of God, and it was not, therefore, the ultimate defense of male supremacy and patriarchy that conservatives believed and promoted it to be. Too, they explained that masculine preference in language had resulted in the invisibility of women and that the arc of justice could not support such bias. They would no longer follow tradition that had excluded women. Employing inclusive language, they said, "is a matter of practicing what we say we believe—that women and men are both made in the image of God, redeemed by the blood of Jesus Christ, restored to wholeness by God's ever-healing love and grace."[16]

Despite being positively received by many evangelicals,[17] *All We're Meant to Be* had detractors who criticized Letha and Nancy usually for individual conclusions rather than engaging with and critiquing their hermeneutical method. Writing in 1988, for example, Van Campbell saw *All We're Meant to Be* as an excellent book that made a compelling case for feminism. Nevertheless, he was quick to point to what he saw as the errors in the second edition: a clear rejection of biblical inerrancy, the presence of too many questions without clear answers, a pro-choice point of view on abortion, and approval of sexual fantasy, sexual intercourse outside of marriage, and homosexual practice.[18] Campbell failed, however, to understand how Letha and Nancy arrived at the positions they took. In other words, given that Campbell, like many of their detractors, did not engage their approach to the Bible, his critiques revealed only his a priori biases.

Many conservative Christians refuse to consider making shifts in theology because they have been conditioned to see a certain set of beliefs as ordained by God, and are not willing to examine beliefs with a clear methodology. Conversely, *All We're Meant to Be*, written during a time of significant social change, demonstrated how to apply consistent analysis to specific challenges, including shifting cultural norms. Such analysis appears in the chapter on reproduction. Yet Campbell and others disavowed

16. Ibid., 34.

17. It was praised by *Vanguard, Eternity,* InterVarsity's *HIS* magazine, and *Christianity Today.* By 1978 it had seven printings.

18. Campbell, Review, 97.

Letha and Nancy's analysis here because the authors do not dismiss abortion out of hand.

Letha and Nancy begin their chapter by suggesting that women, more than any time in the past, had the opportunity to reflect carefully on who they are as persons and what their goals are related to children. They remind their readers that knowing the contours of the entire Bible helps people see how to deal with social change. In the Old Testament, where societies were agrarian, women were valued primarily for their childbearing potential. However, in the New Testament, where societies were clustered in cities, Jesus revealed a different approach toward women. He saw in them their potential to be evangelists. This, Letha and Nancy point out, signals a shift of emphasis in the New Testament. They write, "Seeing the total picture, rather than the Old Testament emphasis alone, can help the Christian woman rethink the matter of motherhood. She can come to see that being a physical life-bearer is not nearly so important as being a bearer of spiritual life—the kind of life-bearer Jesus was."[19]

Within the framework, then, of being a disciple of Christ, Letha and Nancy encourage women to contemplate their goals and dreams as opposed to going through life, including marriage and family relationships, without sustained attentiveness to how each action fits within an overall trajectory of spreading the gospel. Such reflection necessarily entails questions about contraception. Because of new medical advances, they point out that women have more options from which to choose how to be the best steward of their reproductive abilities.

It is within this context of stewardship that they examine abortion as one of the most difficult choices a woman may make. But instead of dismissing entirely the possibility of abortion, they consider specific cases in which an abortion might be considered a realistic decision, a moral option for a woman who nevertheless values life. Contemplating real-life situations (such as, "what about a couple who finds out their offspring will have a debilitating disease?") changes the angle on this topic: rather than an abstract scenario, the decision to have an abortion centers on a couple faced with two very difficult options. This personal approach, they say, negates easy answers and quick rebuttals. Having this perspective, they argue, enables a realization that "Christian love, compassion, and sensitivity demand that we recognize their struggles and their desire to do what they believed to be

---

19. Scanzoni and Hardesty, *All We're Meant to Be* (1986), 161.

the right thing, regardless of our own feelings about abortion."[20] Further they elaborate, "To support a woman's right not to be coerced into bearing a child is not to be against life."[21]

Such depth of perspective is seldom acknowledged in circles where people argue that "family values" means that Christians must oppose abortion. Instead, Letha and Nancy begin with the Bible, ascertaining that its metanarrative is about the justice and compassion of God—characteristics that should also be evident in people who see themselves as followers of God. When this perspective is employed, what becomes evident is that easy and trite answers are really no answers at all, and instead women are called to be more than machines that produce babies.[22] Further, Letha and Nancy point out that Christians do not have uniform thinking about abortion; neither have theologians agreed on when a fetus becomes a human being. Additionally, they make clear an important distinction between what is lawful based on the U.S. Constitution and what any individual woman may do within the framework of those freedoms.

Perhaps one of the most helpful ideas that Letha and Nancy present is that men have always had reproductive freedom in a way women have not enjoyed. They write: "To tell a woman that under no circumstances could she ever have an abortion is to place a burden on women that men have never had to bear. To brush over this fact by saying that she *chose* to become pregnant and now that the time of choice is over, she has no further options except to give birth is both unrealistic and unfair."[23]

Whereas their detractors simply point to Letha and Nancy's acknowledgement of the validity of abortion as a reason to exclude them from the circle of evangelicalism, in taking their affirmative position, they have maintained their hermeneutical method and have rightly included abortion within the larger concerns of reproduction, motherhood, and even adoption. They acknowledge, too, women who freely choose motherhood can find within it a life of fulfillment, and those who are not mothers—either by choice or circumstance—can also live lives of fullness and joy, knowing that God calls all persons as agents of compassion.

Social transformation often elicits fear, such as in those who saw *All We're Meant to Be* as dangerous and who argued against some of the

20. Ibid., 167.

21. Ibid., 166.

22. Ibid., 170.

23. Scanzoni and Hardesty, *All We're Meant to Be* (1992), 218–19.

positions offered in the book. Eager to push back against change, some people easily settle into the status quo, finding safety in how things used to be. Writing many years after the book's publication, Letha suggests that many Christians fear freedom because "they don't trust themselves or others to do the right thing without strict rules to follow."[24] Looking back on the social climate of the 1970s when *All We're Meant to Be* was initially released, she wrote, "to counter the changes happening in society, conservative Christians proclaimed, with more fervor than ever, an insistence on hierarchical order. In the home, the emphasis was on a wife's submission to her husband as her primary duty. It was even suggested that a wife might think of her husband in the way John the Baptist thought about Jesus. 'He must increase, and I must decrease.'"[25]

One review of *All We're Meant to Be* stated, "This book raised controversy among evangelical Christians as [Betty] Friedan's book had in society at large." Letha once mentioned that she and Nancy lost personal friendships over their book's publication, and one person wrote them demanding they buy back all the copies of it "before the devil" used it "to lead more women astray." "Someone else said she felt guilty about having read the book as though her mind had been contaminated."[26]

Despite the abundant critiques of *All We're Meant to Be*, especially from complementarians,[27] who hewed to an inerrant and literal interpretation of the Bible, Letha and Nancy also received much praise. According to Letha, "In 'letter after letter,' evangelical women confessed that, for so long, they had felt alone in their feminist inclinations. They celebrated the liberation the book had revealed and shared their resolve to attend college, to become pastors, to pursue their dreams."[28]

The freedom of Christ that Letha and Nancy had discovered through their Bible study and their work together, however, was too compelling to be applied to only one segment of people. This was a message meant for everyone. If the gospel was indeed good news, it needed to be good news for all people.

24. Scanzoni, "Ordered Order," para. 13.

25. Ibid., para. 15.

26. Scanzoni, "It Just Keeps Rollin' Along." The review was in *Evangelical Missions Quarterly* 21/4 (October 1, 1985).

27. *Complementarian* is a term identifying those who subscribe to the belief that people are to fulfill God-designed roles based upon gender. For example, women are to be primarily wives and mothers while men are to be husbands and breadwinners.

28. Quoted in Lee, *Rescuing Jesus*, 55.

Is the Homosexual My Neighbor?

Letha says she had the same presuppositions as most evangelical Christians in the 1970s: she thought homosexuality was a choice, and furthermore it was an immoral choice. Nevertheless, Letha recognized homophobia as a problem among many Christians, and she thought Christians instead had a responsibility to offer friendship to LGBTQ persons. Having made such a step in the direction of understanding the complexity of sexuality, Letha experienced three events that shaped her perspective more fully. The first involved corresponding with a woman who had at one point worked to help LGBTQ persons move away from their same-sex attractions and later changed her mind because she realized that the people she tried to change were some of the most devout Christians she had met. The second experience entailed Letha's friendship with Virginia Ramey Mollenkott, especially as they worked together on an ethics book that would become *Is the Homosexual My Neighbor?*, when Virginia shared with Letha her own same-sex sexual identity. The third experience was a controversy over gay rights in Bloomington, Indiana, where Letha lived at the time. When a city ordinance passed prohibiting discrimination against LGBTQ persons, conservative Christians galvanized in opposition to the measure. Letha studied the issue, interviewing several people involved on both sides of the controversy in order to write an article for the *Christian Century*.[29] From her study she realized at least three aspects had to be considered: civil rights, human rights, and theology. Her thinking going forward, she acknowledged, would embrace more complexity than before.[30]

As Letha continued to struggle with this issue, she could not shake the conviction that justice and freedom are foundational aspects of the gospel, intended for all people in all places. This liberating message of Jesus—indeed, the very question of who is one's neighbor—applied not only to women but also to people who had been marginalized by the church and society because of sexual orientation. This expansive conviction guided Letha as she took up the question of LGBTQ persons and their Christian faith. In fact, as she dug deeper into her work, Letha felt increasingly confident that she was called to do this work. Perhaps it is of little surprise that Letha consistently made the case that Jesus's countercultural actions mean that

---

29. The article is Scanzoni, "Conservative Christians and Gay Civil Rights."
30. Myers and Scanzoni, *What God Has Joined Together* (2006), 185–87.

in every instance where people are oppressed by social and faith-related structures, the work of justice must be done.

In *Is the Homosexual My Neighbor?* Letha and Virginia write that Jesus did not narrow the identity of one's neighbor to geography, race, or religion but only to need. They state, "Anyone who crosses my path and needs my help is my neighbor." This call to be a neighbor should also, they suggest, result in considering the following questions: Do I care about LGBTQ persons and their lives? Do I care about their struggle for self-acceptance? Do I care about how they have been rejected by Christians? Do I care about their parents and spouses and children? Do I care about how Christian communities build healthy understandings of human sexuality? Do I care enough to do something constructive in light of these questions?[31]

While many viewed the positive position Letha and Virginia held for LGBTQ persons as evidence of their faulty theological digression, they consistently reject this criticism. In a 2015 article, Letha argued that the "Slippery Slope Paradigm" is based upon "a simplistic image of the Christian faith as comprising an essential set of beliefs and rules, along with required stances on certain social issues."[32] The idea, of course, is if someone adopts one belief outside the accepted corpus, then that person is in danger of falling down the slippery slope and embracing other beliefs assumed also to be beyond the theological boundary.

In contrast, Letha advocates for what she calls the "Love Thy Neighbor Paradigm." She explains how this view is based upon empathy and relationships—between God and others—rather than upon rules or restrictions. This perspective requires more engagement with people, especially with those whose experiences and backgrounds differ from one's own. Too, it involves listening and seeking to understand. It is this kind of diligent relationship that led Letha, over time, to expand her thinking about LGBTQ experiences as she constantly worked to comprehend the message of the Bible more fully. Letha explained the contrasts between the two paradigms this way: "Whereas the Slippery Slope Paradigm focuses on a judgmental God and defines sin as the breaking of certain rules and requirements, the Love Thy Neighbor Paradigm focuses on *people*—human beings made in the divine image—and views *sin* as a failure to love others as God has loved us."[33]

---

31. Scanzoni and Mollenkott, *Is The Homosexual My Neighbor?* (1978), 10–11.

32. Scanzoni, "Christian Feminism and LGBT Advocacy," para. 26.

33. Ibid., para. 27 (italics original).

Such attentiveness to people and relationships informed Letha's journey and resulted in her commitment to neighbors over doctrine. Although in their first edition of *Is the Homosexual My Neighbor?* Letha and Virginia share only how they had developed admiration for each other through their respective writings prior to meeting, in their revised and updated edition they reveal their personal experiences of a friendship initially challenged and strengthened by the ethical question raised in the book itself.

In 1975 while they were already working on what they intended to be a book on ethics (including a chapter on homosexuality), Virginia divulged her identity as a lesbian to Letha for the first time. Virginia knew that before they went any further on the joint project, it was only right that Letha know this about her coauthor because of the ramifications for both of their lives as evangelical Christians. For Letha, Virginia's identity as a lesbian and as a friend meant their approach to the book was from that time on very personal. At the same time, Letha knew that taking a positive approach to LGBTQ Christians would affect her work as a Christian writer and speaker. On the other hand, while Virginia waited to see how Letha would respond to her, Virginia endured the agonizing question of how she would be received by her friend once her sexuality was out in the open. In the book, they both admit to having many difficult moments and days as they worked through their thoughts and feelings, acknowledging that only after a time of intense prayer and study did they emerge with greater clarity and understanding of each other. They write:

> Letha was helped to see through Virginia's eyes what it is like to live as a homosexual Christian experiencing the intense pain that society and church attitudes constantly inflict on God's gay and lesbian children. And by watching Letha's struggles, Virginia was able to see firsthand how difficult it can be to move from the safety of silence and the relative detachment of scholarly objectivity to the taking up of so unpopular a cause as homosexual personhood within a heterosexist church.[34]

After she came out to Letha, Virginia wrote to Letha, sharing her appreciation for Letha's steady support and empathy. "On the topic we discussed so much," she wrote, "has it occurred to you that you currently are at the place where many of the most humane evangelicals are about women—in practice, *acting* as if women were equals, *wanting* to see women as equals before God, yet unable to theorize that way because they feel the

---

34. Scanzoni and Mollenkott, *Is the Homosexual My Neighbor?* (1994), ix.

Bible says no? You wrote *All We're Meant to Be* chiefly for those people. Maybe a future book will offer the same liberating affirmation to another oppressed group of Christians and will help to break down some of the prejudice against them."[35]

Given the depth of their friendship and the subsequent challenge that their book would generate for Christians in general and evangelicals in particular, it is appropriate not only that Letha and Virginia ask the question of who is one's neighbor, but also that they acknowledge how moral growth is accompanied by risks and rejections. For each of them, these realities have been acutely present in their lives since publishing *Is the Homosexual My Neighbor?*

Integral to their thinking about the higher value of love over rules is the example of Peter noted in Acts 10–11. In this narrative, Letha and Virginia see the apostle Peter illustrating the challenge of an evolving understanding of morality. In the first century, the moral question for Christians revolved around whether or not non-Jews needed to convert to Judaism in order to become Christians, or if they could convert without first becoming Jews. This quandary was highlighted by distinctions about dietary laws. As a Jew who adhered to dietary restrictions, Peter agonized over how to resolve this challenge among members of a nascent movement when the movement's leader was no longer physically present. In the midst of this social turmoil, Peter had a vision in which he was instructed to move beyond the Jewish dietary laws. Peter was faced with a serious conundrum: disobey the voice of God conveyed in his vision, or disobey the rules of God he had been taught to obey his entire life. In the end Peter realized, of course, that the liberation of Jesus's good news transcended ethnic identity. According to Letha and Virginia, "Peter's story indicates that there are times when human beings are directed to transcend general laws of God and society because of the specific work God has chosen them to do. Gone is the certainty of assuming that all we need to do is simply cling to the rules handed down to us by decent people. Gone, even, is the simplistic use of Scripture . . . Attention to this story warns us that thoughtless obedience, even to a passage of Scripture, can be disastrous in its effects on our moral life."[36]

While Peter's visionary experience illustrates what Letha sees as the Love Thy Neighbor Paradigm, this explanation of how to live is rooted in Jesus's claim that the two greatest commandments are to love God with all

35. Ibid., x (italics original).

36. Ibid., 17.

of one's heart and soul and to love one's neighbor as oneself. This christo-centric foundation of their approach to LGBTQ questions situates Letha and Virginia, just like Letha and Nancy earlier, within an evangelical framework. At the same time Letha and Virginia strike a cautionary tone, one that acknowledges the unhealthy power of unthinking uniformity:

> If we are to seek scriptural guidance concerning our moral and ethical attitudes, we must be extremely careful in our interpreta-tions. When we assume that the Bible is perfectly clear on a moral issue—so clear that only a fool or a dishonest person could pos-sibly differ from our view of what it says—that overconfidence should alert us to the possibility that our egos are clouding our interpretations. Self-suspicion is especially in order when our view happens to coincide with the prevailing view, whether of a particular church or of the secular society. If and when such a cor-relation is present, we cannot reasonably doubt that we need to open our minds to careful reconsideration.[37]

For all of the controversy surrounding LGBTQ persons, the Bible has little to say about it, a point Letha and Virginia note. Nevertheless, they examine three passages: Sodom and Gomorrah (Genesis 19), the Holiness Code in Leviticus (chapters 17–26), and Paul's statements in his letter to the Romans (Romans 1). Additionally, they analyze two related Greek words found in 1 Cor 6:9–10 and 1 Tim 1:9–10. To conclude, they admit that un-answered questions remain, including same-sex orientation and long-term, committed love relationships between people of the same sex—both ideas not mentioned in the Bible. Since the Bible is silent on these questions, Letha and Virginia suggest more must be known from scientific perspec-tives, an insight that has come into sharper focus in recent years.

When the Bible Interprets Itself: Sodom and Gomorrah

The process of examining how the Bible reflects or illumines itself is part of Letha's hermeneutic in *All We're Meant to Be*, and it occurs in *Is the Homosexual My Neighbor?* as well. Allowing biblical narratives to shed light on other biblical passages can reveal important interpretive clues. Such is the case with the Sodom and Gomorrah narrative in Genesis 19. Multiple Old Testament passages refer to this well-known story. Letha and Virginia note that in Isaiah 1 the nation of Judah is rebuked for aligning itself with

37. Ibid., 19.

Sodom and Gomorrah. The reason for the rebuke, however, is not homo-sexuality, as is commonly suggested; rather, "the specific sins mentioned are greed, rebellion against God, empty religious ritual without true devo-tion to God, failure to plead the cause of orphans and widows, failure to pursue justice, and failure to champion the oppressed."[38] Likewise, Ezek 16:49–50 refers to Sodom because of its "abominable things." Again, the sin is not homosexuality but rather "lack of concern for the poor."[39] Jeremiah too uses Sodom and Gomorrah as examples of those who have gone astray. In this case the problems are "adultery, lying, and cooperating with evildo-ers rather than urging people to turn away from wickedness."[40] Jesus too mentions Sodom (once), but as Letha and Virginia note, "not in the context of sexual acts, but in the context of inhospitality."[41]

Despite the oft-cited Sodom and Gomorrah narrative as an indication of homosexuality being a sin, when Letha and Virginia employ the inter-pretive practice of allowing the Bible to illumine itself, their conclusion is instructive. "If, then, we decide to follow the time-honored principles of al-lowing the Bible to provide its own commentary and of interpreting cloudy passages in the light of clearer ones, we are forced to admit that the Sodom story says nothing at all about the homosexual condition." Further, Letha and Virginia claim, "The only real application to lesbian and gay people would have to be a general one: homosexual people, like everybody else, should show hospitality to strangers, should deal justly with the poor and vulnerable, and should not force their sexual attentions upon those unwill-ing to receive them."[42]

For All Times and in All Places? The Holiness Code

The two Old Testament passages that make explicit references to homo-sexual acts are found in what is called the Holiness Code, a series of in-structions for Israel's cultic practices (Leviticus 17–26). Letha and Virginia note that the Holiness Code with its list of commandments (including prohibitions against eating meat with blood, against being tattooed, and against engaging in bestiality) served a specific function in ancient Israel.

38. Ibid., 60.
39. Ibid., 61.
40. Ibid.
41. Ibid.
42. Ibid., 62.

According to Letha and Virginia, ritual purity was a means of separating the people from other groups, of pointing out Israel's distinctiveness. Three principal reasons for these various proscriptions existed: (1) to ensure separation from other nations or cultures, (2) to avoid idolatry and related practices, and (3) to deal with ceremonial impurity. So, it is within this context of purity that the list of prohibitions is stated. For readers looking back at this list seeking to understand it, Letha and Virginia argue that a distinction between ceremonial law (with its context of separateness) and moral law (practices that are morally acceptable) must be made. Ancient Israelites connected sexual practice and ceremonial purity. Semen and blood were both important because of their necessity for life, and for this reason, presumably, acts involving semen or blood were clearly specified. Respecting laws about semen or blood maintained ceremonial purity.

Nevertheless, to extrapolate sexual parameters for today from the Holiness Code does not make sense given the absence of ceremonial necessity today. Letha and Virginia point out, for example, the lack of congruence that shows itself when Christians on the one hand apply verses from the Holiness Code to LGBTQ persons today while on the other hand dismissing all other aspects of the code as no longer relevant. Consistency and fairness would mean that if we stipulate against same-sex sex marriage, then, too, all people should avoid "eating rare steak, wearing mixed fabrics, and having marital intercourse during the menstrual period."[43]

Social and Historical Contexts: Paul's Statement to the Romans

Romans 1:26–27 is the most specific reference to same-sex acts and the only place where such acts for women are mentioned in the Bible. Letha and Virginia consider how the historical milieu of Paul's letter may shed light on how to understand this passage. They note that in Greek and Roman culture, same-sex activity was an accepted custom, and Paul was not the only one of his time expressing concern about the misuse of sex. Additionally, they point out the context of the passage as a whole is idolatry and lust. The behaviors listed follow as the result of a people who are idolatrous. Referring to New Testament scholar Victor Paul Furnish, Letha and Virginia note that same-sex relations during first-century Roman civilization were undergirded by three beliefs: (1) same-sex acts were an avenue of lust; (2) same-sex acts were seen as evidence of lust and something that

43. Ibid., 65.

"rich men" did; and (3) same-sex acts involved exploitation.[44] These insights, Letha and Virginia argue, indicate that Paul is referring not to sexual activity between two loving and committed individuals but to the abuse of one person by another. "Homosexual people must certainly learn to cease from unloving abuses of sexuality, as heterosexuals must; and all of us must struggle against idolatry and other manifestations of the ego nature."[45]

Two additional New Testament passages have been used to condemn LGBTQ persons even though the evidence marshaling them is even more questionable than is Romans 1. Each passage involves the translation of a particular Greek word: in 1 Cor 6:9–10 the word is *malakoi*, and in 1 Tim 1:9–10 the word is *arsenokoitai*. Both words have been difficult to translate, and translations have varied widely, ranging from "homosexuals" to "sexual perverts," from "boy prostitutes" to "practicing homosexuals" to "male prostitutes" and "sodomites" and others as well. To understand what these words mean, Letha and Virginia turn to historical and literary contexts, finding that the most plausible suggestion is that the issue addressed in 1 Corinthians and 1 Timothy wasn't sexuality but rather exploitation, idolatry, or both. Letha and Virginia argue the "point of 1 Cor. 6:9–11 is that no unrighteous person will enter the kin-dom, no matter what his or her particular brand of unrighteousness may be." And, "similarly, in 1 Tim 1: 8–11 there is a contrast between condemnation of various sins under the law and the 'glorious gospel of the blessed God.'"[46]

When the revised edition of *Is the Homosexual My Neighbor?* came out in 1994, evangelical leader John Stott had begun using Gen 2:24 and Matt 19:4–6 to argue that God intended solely heterosexual monogamy, so Letha and Virginia used the opportunity to point out how such an argument violated good biblical hermeneutics by ignoring context. Noting that Genesis 2 is part of a creation narrative, they point out that it "in no way indicates that this first couple was to be considered normative for all sexual experience forever after. (If that were true, all childless marriages would have to be relegated to sinful status or, at best, to a status of sickness.)"[47] Similarly, Letha and Virginia conclude that using Jesus's statement about divorce in

44. Ibid., 74. See Furnish, *The Moral Teaching of Paul*, 65–66.

45. Ibid., 80.

46. Ibid., 79–80. Letha and Virginia explain their use of kin-dom: "we prefer to drop the *g* and speak of God's kin-dom in order to emphasize the nonsexist, nonclassist nature of that realm and to underscore our common kinship with God and one another" (79).

47. Ibid., 81.

Matthew as a rationale for heteronormative marriage dismisses the context of his saying, which was a response to a question from the Pharisees. Such violations of basic hermeneutic principles, they claim, is "dishonoring to the Scriptures."[48]

Conclusions

The tide is turning among evangelical Christians. Older factions are holding fast to their "love the sinner, hate the sin" mentality while younger groups are finding such binaries illogical and uncharitable. For millennials, a much broader sense of human sexuality has taken root, and they are notably diverging from their evangelical training that judges LGBTQ persons to be outside of the faith family.[49]

Too, as Christian colleges and other institutions find themselves increasingly in an unsustainable position between changing cultural realities on the one hand and old prejudices on the other, they are finding new solutions and theologies to support more welcoming positions toward LGBTQ persons.[50] Notable evangelical leaders also are changing their minds, finally coming to see what many, including Letha, have known for many years: there is no line in the sand determining who is one's neighbor and who is not.[51]

While these shifts are positive, there is a difference between their philosophical underpinnings and those of Letha and Virginia. Those moving toward a more inclusive view today are mirroring changes in social mores and realizing that reflecting that change is in their self-interest whereas Letha and Virginia stood by their convictions at a time when these convictions were in conflict with society. In other words, for those assuming a new, inclusive position, self-interest comes into play. In contrast, Letha and Virginia took their positions at significant cost to their livelihoods and influence, and indeed their membership within the faith communities they continue to claim as their own. They seemed to realize this potential sacrifice prior to the publication of *Is the Homosexual My Neighbor?* when they note "the high price of caring." They wrote, "those who dare to pioneer

48. Ibid.

49. For a broader understanding of gender, see Mollenkott, *Omnigender*.

50. See Wheeler, "LGBT Politics of Christian Colleges."

51. Tony Campolo, David Neff, and Jim Wallace, for example have recently changed their views. See Bailey, "Some Evangelical Leaders Splitting."

in such rethinking must be prepared to pay a price. Deeply ingrained attitudes toward taboo subjects do not disappear overnight. Even to suggest a reexamination of the subject can call forth charges that a person is guilty of heresy, of leaving Christian teachings and going against the will of God."[52]

Letha and Virginia point to the work of psychologist Gordon W. Allport (*The Nature of Prejudice*) to suggest that people often reform previously held beliefs if they are either continually open-minded or are met with a crisis of self-interest.[53] The position of being open-minded reflects the attitude of Jesus, Letha and Virginia say, when he refused to put limits on who is one's neighbor. Such openness today requires people to be constantly evaluating new information on human sexuality, psychology, sociology, even biblical scholarship, with the possibility that old convictions and opinions will need to be modified. This also means, of course, that an issue is never settled but instead is open to revision and change.

However, Letha and Virginia caution that people have a tendency to want everything settled. When something doesn't fit with the way we've constructed our world, we often either ignore the exceptions to our worldview or condemn those segments that simply do not fit with how we conceive things to be. Letha and Virginia challenge their readers, however, to resist either of these dichotomies for a more just position: to make space in our understandings for difference and diversity.[54] This space-making process allows LGBTQ persons to tell their stories, to move the majority from seeing them as deviants to knowing them as individuals with feelings and value, with the desire for love and intimacy. In other words, viewing them, quite alarmingly, very much like ourselves.

Letha and Virginia close *Is the Homosexual My Neighbor?* with this injunction: "You shall love your neighbor as yourself. Your own well-being is tied up in giving and receiving such love." In this, they say, there can be no limits or boundaries or classifications.[55]

There is no doubt, however, that such openness and uncertainty flies in the face of order and stability. Slippery slope analogies often work so effectively because they assuage people's insecurities about what-if scenarios. If everyone embraces a static view of social order, then the danger of a

52. Scanzoni and Mollenkott, *Is the Homosexual My Neighbor* (1978), 132–33.

53. *Is the Homosexual My Neighbor* (1994), 159.

54. Here the authors are drawing on the work of cultural anthropologist Mary Douglas, *Purity and Danger*.

55. Scanzoni and Mollenkott, *Is the Homosexual My Neighbor?* (1994), 198.

slippery slope is avoided. Questions do not need further examination or debate and everything stays in the same comfortable place. Further, to the extent that such order can be convincingly attributed to the will of God the potential for maintaining the status quo is reinforced.

Letha writes that "those who benefit from systems of power have long used their power to make sure that those in subordinate positions hear warnings about rebellion against God if they question the 'ordered order.'"[56] Whether the question is slavery or women's equality or LGBTQ rights, those who feel their power at risk rely on keeping others from questioning the validity of these movements, and they are largely successful because of their ability to stir up fears to the point the fearful retreat to safe positions of acceptance and compliance.

One of the related reasons this fear-based approach continues to be so successful is biblical illiteracy. Many Christians in America have little to no real knowledge of the Bible. They may be able to cite memorized verses learned long ago, but they have no understanding of when or how the Bible was produced; no clear knowledge of its historical backgrounds and contexts; no true framework within which to understand the founder of their faith, Jesus.[57] In lieu of these key elements, they rely on what they have been told from their pulpits and even more from social media. And the voices to whom people turn for their information are now more often than not untrained. Pastors and leaders of nondenominational churches frequently have little to no seminary education. They themselves do not know how to interpret the Bible, and they pass on this naiveté to the masses.

Without basic biblical knowledge, Christians are even more prone to accept slippery slope logic. Failing to know, for example, about the social upheaval during Jesus's day and how he responded to the chaos—not by accepting the status quo but by challenging it—today's Christians miss the parallels between the Greco-Roman world and contemporary American society. Without these key contextual clues, readers and hearers of Scripture react to social change with fear rather than responding with love.

An example of this kind of misunderstanding can be seen in the well-known parable of the Good Samaritan. Failure to grasp the politics of Jesus at work in this narrative results in readers or hearers viewing the Samaritan as simply a caring person who helped a stranger along a dusty and dangerous

56. Scanzoni, "Ordered Order," para. 9.

57. Consider, Mohler, "The Scandal of Biblical Illiteracy"; and Berding, "The Crisis of Biblical Illiteracy."

road. But upon deeper analysis of historical and cultural realities, the radical nature of the Samaritan-as-model begins to take sharper focus. A priest and a Levite (a member of the priestly family) were the two who passed by the injured man without stopping to lend aid; they were leaders within the Jewish system. They refused to help because doing so would likely mean they would become unfit to fulfill their religious obligations and duties until they had once again purified themselves, because touching someone who was bleeding—or worse, someone dead—would immediately have resulted in their uncleanness. The purity system put in place originally to maintain a sense of unity for the ancient Israelites had, over time, become a system of oppression. It had taken on a reality far different from its original design. The resulting system pushed vulnerable people—the sick, the outcasts, women, and ethnic outsiders—to the margins.

In Jesus's decision to tell a parable about a Samaritan helping a stranger, he subverted the Jewish purity system and offered in place of purity the act of compassion. Choosing a Samaritan—an ethnic and religious outsider—as the hero, Jesus told a story where this man willingly touched the injured man on the side of the road, resulting in his uncleanness. In this culture the Samaritan would have been reprehensible and unworthy. Jesus, however, held up the Samaritan as an example of someone who knew no limits to love.

For contemporary Christians who feel threatened by our current social situation, it would be useful to draw parallels between today and the social upheaval of the first century. Doing so would enable these Christians to see Jesus's teachings and actions within a context not so different from the challenges we face. This context, too, would perhaps give people greater clarity to see that following the way of Jesus does not lead to order, and in fact may lead in the opposite way entirely. Jesus created chaos because of the way he challenged the status quo, and this reality should shed light on how today's status quo should also be brought to scrutiny.

Few people have been as determined as Letha to follow the hard convictions that Jesus calls people to embrace. Yet she has done exactly that. Attacks on Letha, or complaints that she has simply landed on the slippery slope that starts with feminism and has no end, are entirely misguided. Letha's biblical interpretation is consistent and rooted in the conviction of God's expansive love. The sound methodology that guided her discovery and articulation of Christian feminism is the same methodology that enabled her to find room in Christian faith to accept LGBTQ persons as they are. Refusing to be daunted by troubling uncertainties, Letha time and again turns toward the Bible for guidance, keenly aware that it has the capacity to point always toward the expansive love of God.

Resources for Church Groups

In this chapter we focus on Letha's approach to the Bible, noting that she looks to the life of Jesus to help her understand what the Bible means for us today. Relying on Jesus and how he treated people ensures that we see the radical love of God, a love that extends to all people.

» Begin the conversation by each person sharing a favorite Bible story about Jesus.

» After people have shared their favorite story, invite people to write on a piece of paper what aspects of Jesus's character are evident in the story they have identified.

» Together as a group, explore one narrative that someone shared. Take time to refresh your memories about the social and political context of Jesus. Who was wealthy? Who was poor? What was daily life like for most people? In other words, what did they do, and how did they live? What did they eat?

» Imagine why Jesus would have attracted people in light of this social context you've identified.

Letha's commitment to Jesus as a lens for the rest of the Bible helped her to see the equality of women and the need for an affirmative position regarding LGBTQ persons.

» What are the risks that might keep others from accepting Letha's position?

» Consider using *All We're Meant to Be* to study the biblical passages related to women and *Is the Homosexual My Neighbor?* to study all of the biblical passages that mention homosexuality.

Bible Reading: Matt 15:21–28

Jesus's mission is expanded by the help of the Canaanite woman.

» Before reading the Bible passage, divide those present into three groups, asking each one to identify with a particular position represented in the narrative: some should align themselves with the woman, some with the disciples, some with Jesus.

» Read the narrative and then ask each group to reflect on their thoughts and feelings throughout the episode.

» Here are some questions to consider: Why was the woman willing to risk rejection? What is the importance of noting she is a Canaanite? Why does Jesus treat her as he does? Are you surprised by Jesus's initial response to her? Why do the disciples respond as they do? What does Jesus gain by this conversation?

Implementing New Ideas

» Ask your pastor to preach on the Canaanite woman.

» One of the insights that probably emerged from your discussion of the Canaanite woman was how it took someone—a woman who was an ethnic outsider—to teach Jesus that his mission was larger than he originally understood it to be. If it took this outsider woman to show this to Jesus, how much more do we need people who are different from us to help us understand our mission? Explore how your group might take initiative to hear from people who are different from yourselves.

3

Building the Evangelical & Ecumenical
Women's Caucus–Christian Feminism Today[1]

It was Wednesday morning, the day after the 2016 presidential election. Like many across America, we were astonished by the previous night's results. Reeling from our massive disappointment as well as from fitful sleep, we each logged onto our respective computers to find Letha had penned a note to our EEWC-CFT Google group. In it Letha offered solace and reassuring comfort, much needed balm to our wounded souls. She wrote,

> Like all of you dear sisters and brothers who have been sharing your thoughts on the three group e-mail threads now passing among us, I was shocked and stunned as the election results kept coming in last night. I stayed up until almost 3 a.m., turning off the TV just before Donald Trump was scheduled to speak. I couldn't believe what I was seeing and hearing. Was this really happening or was I having a nightmare?
>
> But so often at such times, when I'm about to sink into despondency, I find that a poem, hymn, or Bible verse pops into my mind from somewhere deep in my subconscious, and I feel God's comfort.

---

1. Originally the group was called the Evangelical Women's Caucus (EWC). Between 1980 and 1990 it was called the Evangelical Women's Caucus International (EWCI). Following 1990 the name was changed to the Evangelical and Ecumenical Women's Caucus (EEWC), and in 2009, to the Evangelical and Ecumenical Women's Caucus–Christian Feminism Today. Horner, "Trying to Be God in the World," 121.

> Here are three things that came to my mind in the middle of
> the night after I turned off the television. They enabled me to sleep
> peacefully in spite of what had just transpired.

She then went on to share with us a Bible passage and a couple of sets of hymn lyrics.[2]

Letha did not start out to create an organization or instigate a movement when she began writing about biblical feminism in the 1960s and '70s. Instead, she wrote to address the various ways women were oppressed by church leaders and theologians who made inaccurate assumptions about the Bible, and indeed about women. In fact, she and Nancy Hardesty stated in *All We're Meant to Be* that liberation for women is a "state of mind." "It is a realization," they claimed, "that men and women alike may be freed from sex role stereotypes and traditions which hinder development into the true humanness that God intended."[3] Their message, one that "enabled conservative Christians to claim biblical support for feminist positions," not only sent "shock waves" around the evangelical world, but it created a community that today looks to Letha as a founding mother.[4]

Indeed, no one has had more influence on EEWC-CFT than Letha. Her steady leadership and guidance as well as her longtime editorial work on the organization's newsletter (*EEWC Update*) and subsequent website shaped the mission and function of the organization. Additionally, the groundbreaking books she coauthored, *All We're Meant to Be* and *Is the Homosexual My Neighbor?*, transformed the lives of numerous people within the group. All of this is true despite the fact that Letha was not present at the earliest meeting when the seeds of the organization were first planted.

Letha's unfailing leadership within evangelical feminism is in part what is unique to Letha and her contribution to America's religious landscape. For most authors, writers, and speakers, their own growing body of work remains a gravitational center, driving them to new projects and opportunities. But for Letha, her vision, the organizing principle around which her life has focused, is the transformation of other people. She is a fierce supporter of other people's dreams, a true mentor to more people than we can include in this book. Her writing and speaking and leadership have never failed to be motivated by helping others understand and embrace their full potential, to be liberated in the fullest sense of the word.

2. EEWC-CFT Google group, November 9, 2016.

3. Scanzoni and Hardesty, *All We're Meant to Be* (1974), 11–12.

4. Dowland, *Family Values*, 130.

This outward direction reveals how Letha manages to be so singularly focused and sheds light on the distinctive position she holds within the broader feminist movement. It is easy to assume, for example, that since Letha began writing about equality in the late 1960s and early 1970s that she was largely a product of the burgeoning women's movement of the time, and that what she sought to do was make Christian faith acceptable to feminist sensibilities. Mark A. Smith, in *Secular Faith: How Culture Has Trumped Religion in American Politics*, seems to suggest this approach, where culture shapes religious trends perhaps more readily than religious commitments influence cultural trends. Writing about women's rights in the 1960s, Smith concludes that the battle lines between evangelical groups (Christians for Biblical Equality, Evangelical Women's Caucus, and the Council for Biblical Manhood and Womanhood) show the influence of culture within the broader evangelical movement. To buttress his case, he examines voting trends, looking for relationships between willingness to vote for a female president and perceptions of family dynamics related to work and family. Smith's overarching conclusion is that evangelicals, like other groups, were significantly affected by a changing culture that gave increasing awareness to the rights of women, and that even evangelical groups who sought to resist change nevertheless were deeply affected.[5]

Letha staunchly refutes this assessment, however. For example, in her 1978 address to EWC, she responded to Richard Quebedeaux,[6] who at the time claimed that evangelical feminism reflected the broader feminist movement. Letha commented, "I say it emphatically: Quebedeaux is wrong—dead wrong—in his assessment. We did not become feminists and then try to fit our Christianity into feminist ideology. We became feminists because we were Christians, and we knew that women and men were alike created in God's image and given gifts by the Holy Spirit." She continued:

> I was a Christian feminist as a teenager in the 1950s when a group of evangelical men attempted to throw cold water on my burning zeal to serve Christ . . . I was a Christian feminist as I sat in a class at Moody Bible Institute at age 19 and heard a professor tell us that 1 Timothy 2:11–15 meant that women were "unsafe repositories of doctrine"—that because God created woman last she was fragile like a delicate crystal goblet that could easily be broken as Eve was . . . And I was a Christian feminist when in the mid-60s I wrote

5. Smith, *Secular Faith*, 193–202.
6. She was referring to Quebedeaux's *The Worldly Evangelicals*.

an article for *Eternity* magazine called "Woman's Place: Silence or Service?" and pointed out how erroneous and foolish it was to deny women leadership roles in the church when God had given many women gifts for such roles . . . The Evangelical Women's Caucus is much more than a warmed-over, imitative, Christianized version of secular feminism, although of course we, as movements, share much in common.[7]

While it is true that Letha Dawson Scanzoni and Nancy Hardesty and others within the evangelical feminist movement were influenced by the wider culture, becoming familiar with Betty Friedan's *The Feminine Mystique*, this was not the precipitating force in their work. Dowland rightly points out that Letha and Nancy's book, *All We're Meant to Be*, enabled Christian women to find support for their feminist ethics within the biblical narrative, a statement that suggests influence extending in one direction.[8] However, it was the biblical hermeneutic employed by Letha and Nancy— that Christian theology "must treat women as full and equal persons," a belief that develops from the Genesis narrative of all people being made in the image of God—that drove their convictions and thus their activism.[9]

Pamela D. H. Cochran, too, examined the cultural context of EEWC-CFT, pointing appropriately not only to the publication of *The Feminine Mystique* in 1963, but also the founding of NOW (the National Organization for Women) in 1966, and *Ms.* magazine in 1972. These illustrations of a feminist milieu, Cochran notes, surely affected Letha and other women who saw within their faith communities ways women were subjugated to men. Still, she writes, "From the beginning, Scanzoni and other evangelical feminists paid more attention to historical argumentation and biblical exegesis than to arguments from secular culture." Indeed, Letha presciently mentioned in her early writings that she was especially hopeful to avoid criticism that she merely sought to add a feminist lens to Christian expression.[10]

Perhaps most important, though, evangelical feminism must be seen for how thoroughly committed it was to developing and sustaining a clear biblical exegetical methodology. Letha graduated from Indiana University in 1972 with a degree in religious studies while Nancy had a PhD in church

7. Scanzoni, "Marching On."
8. Dowland, *Family Values*, 130.
9. Ibid., 137.
10. Cochran, *Evangelical Feminism*, 23.

history from the University of Chicago. Part of their courses of study included biblical interpretation. They learned about critical methods of biblical study, approaches to the Bible that paid attention to cultural context, to analysis of original languages, to rigorous examination of the multiple voices making up the Bible, as well as to the role subsequent translators play in how readers understand the Bible. As students trained in the field of religious studies, Letha and Nancy became astutely aware of how people within the conservative Christian tradition had often not utilized all tools available to study the Bible and its multiple contexts. They could not, though, in good conscience refuse to use what they had learned, even if it meant re-visioning the Bible and what they understood it to say about women.

While it is appropriate to see a relationship between the feminist movement in America and evangelical feminists, for Letha and Nancy and other early members of EWC, including Virginia Ramey Mollenkott, employing scholarly methods of analysis to the biblical texts contributed more to their work than the larger feminist culture. For them, the Bible was the inspired Word of God and a source of authority within their lives. As more and more evangelical women attended colleges and seminaries, gaining exposure to contemporary hermeneutical methods, they accessed necessary tools to examine the Bible on their own, resulting in assessments that differed, in some cases radically, from what they had heard from their pastors *and* from leaders in the feminist movement.

Despite forging a new path that diverged from evangelical faith communities as well as from secular feminists, Letha was well acquainted with women from an earlier era: those whose activist work secured the vote for women and those who even earlier stepped outside their traditional places to work on behalf of abolition and prohibition. These early activists had also examined their Bibles, finding within the pages not only justification for their self-worth but also seeds for expanding their liberation work. Their model was one Letha embraced because it was grounded in faith rather than propelled by rejection of it. Her commitment to a Bible-centered feminism resulted in Letha's untiring nurture of a Christian feminist organization that recently celebrated more than forty years of advocacy and inspiration.

EWC: The Beginning[11]

EWC traces it history to 1973 when over Thanksgiving weekend a group of socially concerned evangelicals[12] gathered in Chicago, Illinois, to address several areas of challenge. Urban riots, antiwar protests, the behavior of President Nixon, among other concerns, all contributed to the ongoing social upheaval of the late 1960s, and while mainline Protestants had issued proclamations about their stances on a host of issues, evangelicals did not have the same organizing structure and so had yet to weigh in on what was occurring in their midst. Ron Sider along with several other key evangelical leaders responded by calling evangelicals together. Nancy Hardesty and Sharon Gallagher were among the women attending. When a decision was made to draft a statement that the group called the Chicago Declaration, Nancy and Sharon ensured it contained a statement about sexism. To that end, the Declaration included the following: "We acknowledge that we have encouraged men to prideful domination and women to irresponsible passivity. So we call both men and women to mutual submission and active discipleship."[13]

At a second (but greatly expanded) meeting of the concerned evangelicals group over Thanksgiving weekend in 1974, a women's caucus formed as one of six areas of reflection and action.[14] The women's caucus considered a number of issues ranging from the Equal Rights Amendment (ERA) to removing sexism from Sunday school and Christian education curricula. This was the beginning stage of EWC, which would meet for a conference in Washington, DC, one year later, no longer as part of Evangelicals for Social Action (ESA) but on its own. For those on the outside looking in, it might be difficult to assess the reasons the women's caucus removed itself from the larger ESA group. Some report that dissent over women's ordination created alienation and frustration leading to divergence. Letha, however, suggests there was a coalescing momentum. In any case, EWC emerged as

11. Some have written about how EWC began, including Cochran, *Evangelical Feminism*; and Horner, "Trying to Be God in the World."

12. Later called Evangelicals for Social Action (ESA).

13. Evangelicals for Social Action (ESA) "Chicago Declaration," para. 8.

14. Other areas included the Black Caucus and Task Forces on Economic Life Style, Consciousness-Raising (on evangelism and biblical social concerns), Education and Research, and Politics. Scanzoni, "Marching On."

a separate group as women awakened to a biblical foundation of women's full equality.[15]

While Letha had not been present at the initial ESA meeting in 1973, she provided early leadership within the embryonic movement through her two *Eternity* articles (mentioned in chapter 1), with "The Feminists and the Bible" article in *Christianity Today*, with the publication of *All We're Meant to Be,* and with her numerous speaking engagements.[16] She also was one of the participants in the 1974 Thanksgiving meeting when EWC was formally organized. Now desiring to keep on meeting as a separate group, and to plan the 1975 conference, EWC quickly went to work, looking for ways to implement a host of issues it had discussed at the 1974 workshop— among them pushing for inclusive language in churches and Bible translations, working for women's ordination, urging Christian colleges to initiate women's studies programs, promoting nondiscrimination for all people in the workplace, supporting egalitarian marriages and expanded definitions of family, recognizing singleness as a positive lifestyle, and forming networks for elderly persons.

Letha's early guidance to those seeking to bring together their evangelical faith with their nascent convictions about women's equality included encouraging people to evaluate all sorts of questions. Two articles published in 1976 provide a helpful lens through which to see the variety of topics she addressed. In June she wrote "How to Live With a Liberated Wife," in which she explored the potential fear men might feel as they learned to live with a spouse who was changing her view of her place in the world. "When you ask me what women want today," she wrote, "the answer is simple: we want to be free to live up to our *full human potential.*"[17] And yet, she recognized that the intricacies and challenges of daily living required deliberate attention. So, she examined the phrase of Ephesians 5 where husbands are told to love their wives as their own flesh. She suggested this meant having empathy, being willing to sacrifice time and energy, including contributing

15. Letha said of this early stage: "A sense that something that was just taken for granted and unquestioned as 'just the way things are,' suddenly begins being looked at differently. People were raising questions and objections to the way things were. Those who were similarly awakening began finding each other for support and action. It was time to work for change." Scanzoni, "It Just Keeps Rollin' Along."

16. Letha spoke primarily on Christian campuses around the U.S., including Calvin, Roberts Wesleyan, Dordt, Northwestern, Fuller, and Westmont. Scanzoni, "Door Reports," 19.

17. Scanzoni, "How to Live with a Liberated Wife," 6 (italics original).

equally to household chores of cooking and cleaning, and truly trusting that in their path toward liberation, women were not desiring anything less than the liberation men already experienced. Letha ended her intimately toned article with praise for her husband, John, noting, "I know how much my husband's support has meant in my own life." Rereading a letter he had written to her twenty years earlier, she remarked, "John looked for, encouraged, and 'stirred up' gifts in me that I didn't even know were there!"[18]

In October of the same year the *Reformed Journal* published an article excerpted from a convocation lecture Letha presented at Fuller Theological Seminary earlier in 1976. "The Great Chain of Being and The Chain of Command" rebutted a reactionary movement created in part by Elisabeth Elliot Leitch, who along with Bill Gothard and Larry Christenson had criticized the first national conference of EWC. In this piece, Letha drew upon her sociological background to identify the social stratification presented by the chain of command theory. Noting that slavery represented one of the most "despicable uses to which the chain idea" could be put, Letha resisted the notion that social change needed to be fearfully rejected in favor of the corresponding notion of order through hierarchy. Instead she argued that God is in the midst of change. The Spirit of God, she said, "frees from the confinement of chains! But it is not a selfish freedom simply 'to do one's own thing.' It is freedom to love and serve God creatively out of the fullness of one's own uniqueness."[19]

Beyond guiding EWC through her writing, Letha gave plenary addresses at their national meetings. Between 1974 and 1978 local chapters had formed throughout the United States, EWC had developed a mailing list of over fifteen-hundred people, and the organization used a newsletter (eventually called *Update*) to help foster their sense of active community.[20] Their first national conference was held in Washington, DC, in 1975, followed by a second one three years later, in 1978. In Washington Letha encouraged those gathered not to view social changes with fear but rather to embrace the upheaval with wonder and excitement. She exclaimed, "God's Spirit is at work today—just as on the Day of Pentecost!" And she explained that instead of feeling stifled and guilty for breaking gender norms, women could know that God was calling them to their full potential. "A whole new world is opening up for women," Letha asserted, a world where God was

---

18. Ibid., 9.

19. Scanzoni, "The Great Chain of Being," 18.

20. Cochran, *Evangelical Feminism*, 38.

"calling women to fulfill a potential they never knew they had before."[21] Three short years later, Letha urged the members in her 1978 "Marching On" plenary address to forge ahead. A call to action, her speech encouraged those gathered to see their work as guided not by their own initiatives but as an outpouring of the Spirit of God, which, she noted, empowers people to step out without fear. "It is clear that God is a God of action," she exclaimed. "'God's truth is marching on,' declares the song. And we, too, are marching on." She exhorted conferees to see God's motivating spirit at work as they more formally organized themselves as EWC.[22]

Drawing on her background in sociology,[23] Letha encouraged EWC members to take stock of their place in history. She explained how movements have an awakening stage characterized by individuals coming together over a shared vision, commitment, or both. EWC, she said, emerged when like-minded women, including herself and Nancy Hardesty and those who started the publication *Daughters of Sarah*, began locating each other and gaining sustenance and inspiration from learning that their journeys were no longer solitary ones. Their shared personal epiphanies had brought them together, and they had discovered they shared similar experiences of their values being violated. Letha went on to aver that out of these feelings of violation come possibilities of things being different, of a new vision for how things could be. Letha concluded that EWC had been in an awakening stage from its beginnings in 1973 until 1978. They collectively had awakened to the problem of sexism within evangelical Christianity, and they had, together, envisioned a new day, one characterized by equality and justice, where being made in the image of God was taken seriously.[24]

Letha counseled them, however, to realize that organizations cannot stay at an awakening stage, but they must mature, even as maturation causes instability and chaos. Letha contended that EWC was now at a building stage, which required clarification and reflection. Urging members to "carefully sort out" their goals, she asked, "We know we are not content with what has been, that we have a new vision of what could be; but what changes do we want?" And, "who are those who oppose us and what attitudes and strategies should we adopt toward them?" Also, she questioned, "who are those who are unaffiliated with us but yet sympathetic to our

21. Scanzoni, "God Is at Work in the Women's Movement," 8.
22. Scanzoni, "Marching On."
23. She drew specifically on the work of Baldridge, *Sociology*.
24. Scanzoni, "Marching On."

purposes and goals?" She encouraged them to think carefully about their goals; they were at a new point in their organization, and they needed to be clear about how to move forward. Surely with the work she and Nancy had done on her mind, she urged them to embrace their potential to bridge the secular feminist movement and Christians who were "fearful" or "misinformed" about gender equality. She reminded them that "we can show how our own studies of the Scripture have convinced us of the equality of the sexes." Rallying them on, she concluded that "we are ready to leave the 'loose network of EWC chapters' stage and move on to the status of a national formal organization."[25]

Such organizational work did, in fact, occur. At the business meeting, EWC passed a statement of faith, constitution, and bylaws for a national organization. The new constitution provided for both chapter development as well as individual memberships.[26] The bylaws indicated the caucus's purpose: "to honor and glorify the Lord Jesus Christ by engaging in religious, charitable, educational, and/or cultural activities in order to: a. Present God's teaching on male-female equality to the whole body of Christ's church. b. Call both women and men to mutual submission and active discipleship."[27]

EWC: Expanding the Circle of Justice

The reflective questions about their identity and mission that Letha put to the organization were critical, in part, because even as the group unified around the problem of sexism, another area of oppression was not far from the surface: homophobia. One has to wonder if both of these challenges were already in Letha's mind when she gave her 1978 "Marching On" speech and said:

> I believe that often the church is asleep on various social issues and has to be jolted awake by happenings in the world around us. Sometimes the world is more alert to human pain and human need than many Christians are. Evangelicals especially have been guilty of marching in the rear instead of being drum majors for justice.

25. Ibid.

26. Hardesty, "1978 EWC Conference Recap," para. 5. According to Horner, the first time the statement of faith was printed was in the September-November 1981 *Update*. Horner, "Trying to Be God in the World," 111.

27. Quoted in Cochran, *Evangelical Feminism*, 70.

After others have paved the way and it seems 'safe' to speak out on an issue, we evangelicals may do so—but even then, more often with timidity than with boldness. We need to learn that a prophet is not concerned about prevailing public opinion. A prophet cares about truth and justice and mercy. A prophet challenges the status quo. And that's what the evangelical feminist movement is doing. We're challenging the status quo—those structures and systems and traditions of church and society that keep women from being all that God intended us to be.[28]

When Letha and Virginia Ramey Mollenkott took an affirmative stance on LGBTQ relationships with the publication of *Is the Homosexual My Neighbor?* in 1978, Letha was aware that most likely her decision would have a detrimental effect on her place within American evangelicalism.[29] As we point out in chapter 1, this publication resulted in a reduction in speaking opportunities for Letha, a loss of prominence within evangelical circles for her, and untold personal pain from various people who rejected her because of her alliance with LGBTQ persons.

Similarly, as EWC was beginning to grapple with LGBTQ questions, its influence, too, would diminish as it moved toward an explicit and affirmative stance of LGBTQ persons. At the 1975 EWC conference, Nancy Hardesty and Virginia Ramey Mollenkott hosted the seminar "Woman to Woman Relationships," where anonymous questions were welcomed in a safe and friendly environment. At the conference in 1978—the same year *Is the Homosexual My Neighbor?* was published—there were alternative sessions on the topic, including one led by Letha and Virginia that provided an affirmative response, while one led by Don Williams held the opposite view. Conference planners had found themselves in a difficult situation. Letha and Virginia were both slated to have plenary addresses at the conference, and not only had they just published their positive stand on LGBTQ persons, but they had also already been attacked in the Christian media for being unbiblical. There was no way for EWC to avoid the issue because at the same time Anita Bryant and Jerry Falwell had mounted

28. Scanzoni, "Marching On."

29. This was not Letha's first foray into thinking about and writing on the subject. See Scanzoni, "On Friendship and Homosexuality" in which Letha addressed homophobia prevalent within Christian circles. She hoped to assuage fears over same-sex relationships, saying, not only that they do not have to entail sex, but that they can also be very fulfilling. She also wrote "Conservative Christians and Gay Civil Rights." In this article Letha suggests that certain complexities are often disregarded and that she saw "a continuum of views" emerging.

an anti-homosexual crusade, and Harvey Milk, the prominent gay rights advocate, was murdered that year. Within this milieu, the increased uneasiness that emerged during the 1978 conference is not surprising. Looking back, Letha commented, "Evangelicals were expected to take a traditional view condemning homosexuality as a sin and we had broken that mold and shocked the Christian world by asking what it really meant to love our neighbor as ourselves and to respect the worth, personhood, and dignity of every human being as created in God's image."[30] The 1980 conference in Saratoga Springs, New York, continued the conversation through a panel discussion. And in 1982, in Seattle, Washington, there was an unofficial "lesbian and friends" group.[31]

Two years later, at the conference in 1984 at Wellesley College several resolutions were considered during the business meeting, including one recognizing that LGBTQ persons are children of God and therefore ought to be supported by EWC. Letha had written her plenary address prior to the conference, but in light of the discussions emerging during the business meeting she added a few notes in the margins of her original speech titled "A Patch of Sky Isn't Enough: The Vision of *Yentl*."

Framing her remarks with *Yentl*'s image of a young Jewish girl facing limitations due to her society's prescriptions, Letha challenged EWC to refuse to be content with a portion of the sky, as if seeking only to get a fair share. Instead, she said they should imagine a sky with limitless potential, a fullness where no restrictions occur. Enumerating the various ways women had been restricted in the church and in society, Letha took her argument a step further, calling these restrictions a form of psychological abuse. Drawing on M. Scott Peck's definition of evil as something that kills the spirit, she argued that the church was guilty of this very thing: of killing the spirit of women.

Her original speech included this charge: "By that definition, many religious leaders are guilty of evil toward women." In the margin, however, she expanded her sentence in light of the business meeting held the previous day so that instead of "women," she said "women and toward certain other oppressed groups whose personhood is denied, some even cast out without any effort to understand, as in the case of that minority of persons whose involuntary orientation directs their love to same-sex partners." Too, she amended the expansiveness of compassion when she said, "How it

---

30. Scanzoni, "It Just Keeps Rollin' Along."
31. Cochran, *Evangelical Feminism*, 92–93.

must grieve the heart of Christ to see the way hurting persons are crushed again and again by being robbed of their human personhood—all in the name of Christ."[32] Her original speech had indicated "women," and she now changed it to "hurting persons." Emphatically, she claimed, "'Jesus included me.' Means *all* of us."[33]

Letha then shifted her attention from injustice to a call to action. She propelled EWC conference participants to take specific steps to extend the compassion and justice of Christ. First, she said, they should trust their perceptions. Even though women are often doubted, she noted, especially throughout the history of the church, there are biblical examples of women trusting what they knew. Second, she urged them to value their experiences. "No one else has lived your life," she exclaimed, "they cannot tell you what you're feeling or what you must do with your life." Third, she told them to affirm their strengths, noting that a common strategy of abusers is to get the abused to doubt themselves. Letha prompted them to esteem themselves highly by trusting in God.

Returning to what had transpired at the earlier business meeting, Letha reminded them that "by appreciating our own worth and dignity as persons in God's image, we can appreciate the worth and dignity of other persons and be able to speak out and act boldly for social justice from a position of inner strength and courage." Up to this point, Letha's edits to her speech would not have been known to her audience. Toward the end, however, she directly addressed their debate from the previous day in light of refusing to be afraid of taking a stand. She remarked, "That fear of risk and yearning for the safety of staying on the ground was apparent in yesterday's business meeting as we were faced with the challenge of expanding our social consciousness and concern in areas that many find scary." But God's message, Letha encouraged them, was to refuse to settle for a piece of the sky and instead to fly with unfettered wings.[34]

In addition to speaking at the 1984 conference at Wellesley College in June, Letha wrote an article that appeared in the tenth-anniversary edition of *Daughters of Sarah*, the publication that shared the vision of evangelical feminism and overlapped with EWC. In it, Letha reminded her readers that EWC had progressed from an awakening stage through a building stage, noting that between 1974 and 1978 the group had solidified itself, forming a

32. Scanzoni, "A Patch of Sky Isn't Enough."
33. Ibid. (italics original).
34. Ibid.

national organization with a statement of faith, bylaws, and elected officers. "Not only were we becoming organized," she wrote, "we were clarifying our ideology as well with growing numbers of us giving scholarly attention to biblical texts and theology, helping solidify the movement's belief system." Continuing, she also noted, "And while we were forming our own sense of ourselves as a movement of biblical feminists drawn initially from evangelicalism, we were coming to see ourselves increasingly as part of the broader Christian feminist movement within mainline Protestantism and Roman Catholicism as well. Our strong support of the Equal Rights Amendment also symbolized our bond with the *general* feminist movement."[35]

Letha then posed the question about whether the movement was still at the building stage, or whether it was moving toward the influence stage where a more pointed focus on grievances emerges along with demands for specific action. Letha intimated that people joining the wave of biblical feminism were likely in different places along their individual journeys, some just awakening and some at work in building and even some looking toward influencing structural changes within churches. She exhorted them to "sort out and agree upon some specific goals and then develop strategies for reaching them before we can say our movement *as a whole* is in the influence stage."[36]

Always the bridge builder, Letha acknowledged the perspectives of each. "Some movement members," she noted, "conscious that discrimination and oppression directed toward any group affects all of us, want to add other social justice concerns to the biblical feminist platform." Recognizing the other side, she wrote, "Still others see this as diluting the movement's purpose and scattering energies in too many directions."[37] In an effort to encourage them as a united group despite their various places within the spectrum of advocacy, she concluded, "'Let us not grow weary in well doing.' We're living in exciting times! . . . There's electricity in the air that tells me 'the whole creation is on tiptoe to see the wonderful sight of the *daughters* of God coming into their own.'"[38]

35. Scanzoni, "Biblical Feminism," 20 (italics original). She returned to Baldridge to frame the movement's identity. For more information about the beginnings of *Daughters of Sarah* as well as its relationship to EWC, see Cochran, *Evangelical Feminism*, 15–16.

36. Ibid.

37. Ibid.

38. Ibid. Sue Horner suggests that between 1979 and 1984 EWC functioned as a bridge builder, working across denominational divides, between secular and religious feminists, between evangelical and denominational histories, and between ideologies of personal and societal salvation (Horner, "Trying to Be God in the World," 110).

Despite Letha's consensus work, the 1984 Wellesley conference had highlighted their diverging positions. The membership had been assigned five task forces, each with varying positions to study the question of issues raised but not resolved during the Wellesley business meeting. Each task force polled the membership, but instead of providing greater clarity about the direction EWC would take, the results reflected a growing division within the group. According to Sue Horner, the range of variation included on the one hand concern over being seen as supportive of a gay lifestyle and on the other hand concern over not fully recognizing LGBTQ persons as members within the group.[39]

Because the divisions emerging from the 1984 Wellesley conference were not resolved, the 1986 Fresno conference was a watershed year for the group, the time when EWC could no longer contain its emerging differences over LGBTQ issues.

Reports on the specifics of the 1986 conference vary, though it is clear that this was an agonizing and perplexing business meeting with lingering reverberations continuing even until today. Sue Horner reports that even before the group considered resolutions tabled at the Wellesley conference, bad news emerged. A low turnout had resulted in a sizeable conference deficit, and the organization faced financial challenges. Two resolutions, one on racism and another on violence against women, passed. The third resolution was adopted despite clear opposition and abstentions. It read, "Whereas homosexual people are children of God, and because of the biblical mandate of Jesus Christ that we are all created equal in God's sight, and in recognition of the presence of the lesbian minority in the Evangelical Women's Caucus International, EWCI takes a firm stand in favor of civil rights protection for homosexual persons."[40] Following the meeting, the council met as was their usual practice, and their affirmation of the resolution appeared in the next *Update*, the organization's newsletter. The statement demonstrates an important aspect of who EWCI saw themselves to be.

> EWCI was reaffirmed as a vital organization . . . yet our faith remains central . . . EWCI remains committed to our sisters and brothers in conservative churches, yet we must also formally reach

39. Horner, "Trying to Be God in the World," 113.

40. Ibid., 115. See ch. 5 for more about this resolution. It was made by Anne Eggebroten. Since then Anne uses the last name Linstatter. See also Cochran, *Christian Feminism*, 97.

out to include our sisters of color, abused women and children, and Christians with a homosexual orientation. Such steps are frequently out of our "comfort zone" and may create much conflict within us. Yet we recognize that without change, or "turbulence," there is no movement.[41]

In hindsight it is impossible to know if things may have turned out differently had Letha attended this monumental conference. As it was, her mother was ill and dying, making it impossible for Letha to be there and to provide her usual bridge-building insight. True, she had earlier advocated for the organization to lead on without fear, to embrace the challenge of working for justice on behalf of all people, not just women. Too, she had urged them not to fold because of their fears but to embrace their potential of pointing the way forward for all. *Is the Homosexual My Neighbor?* provided the biblical justification for such a stance, and surely the exegesis put forward by Letha and Virginia had convinced many EWC members that the Bible supported equal rights for LGBTQ persons. Nevertheless, what about those who were not ready or willing to stand with confidence on behalf of LGBTQ persons? Those who could no longer see themselves supporting the organization but who wanted to continue working toward biblical feminism created what is now called Christians for Biblical Equality (CBE). Others stayed in EWC, although the group lost members and financial resources.

Four years later, Letha spoke to the pared down EWC gathering in her 1990 plenary address—"Back to the Future; Forward to the Dream"—where she once again encouraged the group to see itself within the scope of history, to remember that they started as a small segment within the ESA 1974 meeting when women found themselves left out and isolated. From that marginalizing event and the subsequent reality of locating a community of like-minded women, they drafted a statement that, in part, acknowledged that "the most revolutionary act is the building of community." Letha went on to say to those gathered sixteen years later, "From the beginning, we had a sense of being revolutionary—of marching to a different drummer rather than letting rigid tradition and gender stereotypes call the tunes. We would no longer fall into line. But in being revolutionary, our focus was not

---

41. Ibid., 117. Between 1980 and 1990, some people used the moniker EWCI to indicate Evangelical Women's Caucus International.

on tearing down but on building up—building up each other and building community."[42]

Letha's fondness for alliteration guided her as she pointed toward the original vision of EWC: equality, empathy, education, empowerment, and expansiveness. Letha reminded attenders that their convictions led them to stand in solidarity with women who had been ordained as Episcopal priests in defiance of official polity, just as they took a stance for the Equal Rights Amendment. She noted their courageous convictions on equality in marriage and on inclusive language put them in challenging places within their larger faith communities, but their commitments to empathy and equality required such stances. She recalled how freedom and openness had characterized EWC since its inception and had sustained them in the face of opposition. Turning her attention to LGBTQ persons, Letha acknowledged,

> we, like many other organizations and institutions in our increasingly pluralistic society, have come face-to-face with the fact that more and more marginalized groups are finding voices to speak out about their needs and aspirations . . . Today, even in women's organizations that are otherwise sensitive, caring, and progressive, the biggest anxiety appears to be over being affiliated with and identified with lesbians. We in EWC know this, because we too have experienced it.[43]

Regardless of the challenges, she exhorted them "to stand by all our sisters—our lesbian sisters, our bisexual sisters, and our heterosexual sisters and to tell the world, 'We're in this together.'" "The worry over an organization's public image if it appears 'too inclusive' is nothing new."[44]

Returning to the image of revolutionary community, Letha called them to "a new vision of community in which mutuality is the governing principle and where we all listen and learn from each other and give to and receive from each other, a community in which we seek for unifying themes in our diversity and yet at the same time respect and value our particularities and differences."[45]

Four years later, for the twentieth-anniversary issue of *Daughters of Sarah*, Letha revisited her sociological analysis of the movement and argued that, indeed, they had reached the influence stage evident in the

42. Scanzoni, "Back to the Future; Forward to the Dream."

43. Ibid.

44. Ibid.

45. Ibid.

changes that had occurred during the intervening years between 1984 and 1994. She noted, for example, how inclusive language was now taken seriously by many, that there was a growing openness to women as pastors, that women's experiences were more prominently evident, especially in feminist theologies and biblical studies. Calling attention to the backlash they were experiencing at the time, especially from other evangelical Christians such as Mary Kassian,[46] Letha urged her readers to forge ahead and yet also to be sensitive to those who as yet did not understand their movement. "Let's not give up on them," she cautioned. "Wherever each of us may be in our particular Christian feminist pilgrimage, we have reached that point over time. We need to be gentle and patient with the genuinely perplexed and not angrily dismiss them as incorrigible defenders of the status quo."[47] True to her bridge-building ethic, Letha asserted,

> I think it's crucial that we don't let our adversaries define what Christian feminism is. Some of us need to be translators to the sincere, earnest people of faith who are genuinely puzzled by what they're hearing. Not all people who express dismay over the alleged heresy of Christian feminism are inquisitors ready to haul us before a tribunal. Some Christians simply want to know what is going on.[48]

EEWC-CFT: Evaluating the Past, Looking toward the Future

From 1994 through 2013 Letha continued her steady guidance of EEWC-CFT as editor of *Update*, the quarterly print magazine, and then of the online version called *Christian Feminism Today*. In addition to serving as the editor of EEWC-CFT publications, from 1998 through 2013 Letha managed the online content of the EEWC-CFT website. For almost twenty years, Letha poured her energy into guiding the organization that reflected her spiritual and intellectual convictions. She did this with minimal remuneration, supplementing her income with editorial and freelance writing work. Her penchant for assimilating information from a wide range of disciplines can be seen in her "Link of the Day" feature, where she pointed to something new that caught her eye while she took advantage of the research available

---

46. Kassian, *The Feminist Gospel*.
47. Scanzoni, "Reflections on Two Decades of Christian Feminism," 10.
48. Ibid.

through the Internet. Too, her vision to work across boundaries can be seen in the two blogs she created and maintained. *FemFaith* and *72–27* were both initiated by Letha with specific goals of creating cross-generational conversation. She included interviews with authors and artists in the publications, seeking to go beyond what people had written or developed. She intentionally sought to highlight personal stories, to show how people are connected to each other through our shared humanity. Her dedication to EEWC-CFT, to be its guiding force, demonstrates how important community, friendship, and advocacy are to Letha's vision of liberation.

In 2014 Letha delivered once again a plenary address intended to rally the group to keep moving forward. Far from the heady days of its origins when hundreds of people poured into such gatherings, more recently the public numbers appear to be miniscule. In 2014 those attending numbered approximately one hundred—including many who have stayed with the organization since its inception, and some new members unaware of the past challenges that have occurred and that have resulted in the group's diminished size. It would be easy if one were in Letha's shoes to feel a sense of despair or concern that what once seemed so promising forty years ago today seems paltry by comparison. But such an estimate would not be true to Letha's view of change or community. In her address, she referred to the image of a river composed of several smaller streams. EEWC-CFT is one of those streams, Letha claimed, and it has been and continues to be an important agent of justice.[49]

Letha remarked that she was the most unlikely person to speak out about biblical feminism when she first published an article in *Eternity* as a response to what she saw as a sexist rant by Charles Ryrie.[50] From the outside, she said, "most people thought of me as a homemaker—a stay-at-home mom. I had even written an article for a national Christian publication called, 'Homemaking—Prison or Privilege?'[51] around that same time. I seemed anything but a rabble-rouser!"[52]

Drawing from her life of faith and open-mindedness, Letha demonstrated how she came to understand the intersection of justice issues, that feminism grounded in a commitment to the Bible could not be embraced

49. Scanzoni, "It Just Keeps Rollin' Along."

50. Scanzoni, "Woman's Place: Silence or Service?"

51. Scanzoni, "Homemaking—Prison or Privilege?"

52. Scanzoni, "It Just Keeps Rollin' Along."

in a vacuum. It was but one expression of liberation, and there are other people who likewise need to be freed from oppression.

As she had in her earlier plenary addresses and guiding articles, Letha used the opportunity in 2014 to provide a sense of history and to urge EEWC-CFT members to move forward. "There is no lack of challenges calling for our voices and actions as Christian feminists today," she remarked. At the same time she noted:

> Likeminded Christian feminists are finding each other and reaching across both geographical boundaries and ideological lines that once kept us apart from other women of faith. Feminist scholars have made us more aware of intersectionality and the importance of seeing all biases, discrimination, and oppressions linked together, whether on the basis of class, race, ethnicity, gender, sexual orientation, gender identity, age, disability, or anything else . . .We need to work individually and together to see that gender justice keeps rolling along.[53]

Despite no longer serving as the editor or webpage manager, Letha still is at work continuing to nurture pockets of gender justice, reaching across lines and finding ways of building bridges and making connections. Recently, Letha contributed to a volume entitled *New Feminist Christianity*, a collection of essays exploring the intersections between Christianity and feminism. In her essay "Why We Need Evangelical Feminists," Letha analyzed EEWC-CFT, returning to the theoretical framework of sociologist J. Victor Baldridge. She recalled how he identifies social movements as they progress through a three-phase cycle: awakening, building, and influence. Letha expanded his framework to five stages: awakening, building, catalyzing change, backlash, and awakening with a new set of participants. Additionally, instead of setting EEWC-CFT and CBE[54] at odds, Letha investigated how together they make up different aspects of evangelical feminism.

In the awakening phase, evangelical women realized the injustice of gender-based ideologies as they began sharing their experiences. In the building phase, they did the work of creating an organization: they instituted chapters, held conferences, and published a newsletter. In 1986 when several resolutions were put forward for consideration, some decided to

---

53. Ibid.

54. CBE (Christians for Biblical Equality) is the group that broke away from EWC after the 1986 conference. Scanzoni, "Why We Need Evangelical Feminists," 69.

break away from the group as a way to disassociate themselves from what they saw as "an unbiblical endorsement of homosexuality."[55]

The third phase, catalyzing change, witnessed each group engaging in advocacy both inside and outside of their churches. Letha explained their respective contributions:

> The two groups, while not abandoning their evangelical roots, overlap in some respects but also differ in their respective audiences, with CBE's outreach concentrated more directly on the moderate evangelical community (taking great care to remain within certain theological and socially conservative boundaries), whereas EEWC has a more expansive outreach, offering a safe and welcoming place to those who have felt emotionally and spiritually abused by conservative churches (both Protestant and Catholic), or have been marginalized because of their gender identity or sexual orientation, or have been ready to give up on Christianity because of its teachings on women, or whose general doubts and theological questioning have not been welcome elsewhere.[56]

The change that evangelical feminism has fostered is considerable, ranging from calling for inclusive language in Bible translations and churches to influencing how theology is constructed to creating a ministry climate welcoming to women. This change, Letha asserted, has put other evangelical groups on the defensive and has led to the fourth phase, backlash.

Letha cited several examples of backlash in popular books, conferences, websites, and denominations—including America's largest Protestant denomination, the Southern Baptists. Despite the plethora of material pointing to the prevalence of this backlash, Letha suggested that evangelical feminism is also witnessing a new awakening in which "young people are asking the same questions today that we were asking as the biblical feminist movement emerged in the second half of the twentieth century."[57]

It is this sense of an ever-widening circle of justice that punctuates Letha's view of where EEWC-CFT has been and where it will continue to go. While some may look at the many name changes associated with this evangelical feminist group—EWC, EWCI, EEWC, EEWC-CFT—as evidence of an identity problem, Letha would adamantly disagree. She is steadfast in her belief in the expansive grace of God and therefore in the corresponding

55. Ibid., 70.
56. Ibid., 70–71.
57. Ibid., 75.

expansiveness of faithful communities. Writing in 2003, Letha offered an image of EEWC that reflects this conviction:

> The *firm foundation* metaphor sees EEWC as a construction project. It is not abandoning its strong foundation, as shown in our statement of faith, or even its foundation in evangelicalism (in the best sense of that word). But it has not stopped with the foundation. EEWC has been *building upon that foundation* with new understandings of our experiences with God and with each other as persons created in God's image, new insights through an openness to the Spirit, new callings as we see God at work in the world, and a fresh look at Scripture, seeking answers to new questions. As these new "rooms" are added to the structure, we find, like any truly loving family, that we have lots of space for the diversity of interests and viewpoints among our members.[58]

This dynamic understanding of faithful living is held creatively by EEWC-CFT in part because that is Letha's legacy, a vision she has successfully conveyed. In her most recent communication to an EEWC-CFT conference audience, Letha reinforced this call to be an expansive community. In a "Welcome Letter" to the group in which she utilized her penchant for alliteration while echoing an earlier speech, she reflected how EEWC-CFT has a long history of being evangelical (promoting good news for all people) as well as ecumenical (reflecting a rich diversity, including LGBTQ persons, even when this wasn't as accepted as it is now). Too, she noted the group's commitment to equality for all people, believing that God's gifts are given not through roles but through individual gifts to be developed and celebrated. She remarked on the sense of empathy, EEWC-CFT's ability to create an atmosphere of acceptance and love. Education as an ongoing process is demonstrated in how the group celebrates a multiplicity of images and names for God, including revisions to accommodate gender fluidity. Letha also pointed to EEWC-CFT's ability to empower. Instead of falling into victimization, the group uses their collective energy and inspiration to work for justice. Finally, Letha acknowledged that prophetic circles are not always very large numerically. But that smallness suggests being part of the "broadening vision of the Holy One and the work She has entrusted to us."[59]

The path Letha has cultivated has not been an easy one in large part because she has been so misunderstood by her adversaries, those who have

---

58. Scanzoni, "Editorial: Where We've Been," para. 14.

59. Scanzoni, "Welcome Letter," para. 12.

not been willing to take Letha's dynamic faith seriously. Evangelicals who are comfortable staying within ideological lines dismiss her as a transgressor, as someone who couldn't possibly be evangelical. Yet, those who know Letha and who trust her faith convictions are genuine realize that she is committed to following Jesus, she is a well-informed student of the Bible, and she is willing to sacrifice her life for others, perhaps the most important ethic Jesus taught.

Additionally, Letha has clearly guided EEWC-CFT to chart a similar course. Just as Letha has paid a price for her convictions, EEWC-CFT has owned the cost of its decisions. Of the two feminist Christian groups—Christians for Biblical Equality (CBE) is the other—EEWC-CFT is smaller and has fewer financial resources. EEWC-CFT's determination to be faithful to its foundation and expansive in its application has resulted in substantial, continuing challenges.

Nevertheless, neither Letha nor EEWC-CFT finds these obstacles to be detrimental. Instead, focusing on the process of transformation, no matter how small, always brings a buoyant hopefulness. This is evident in Letha's optimistic view and can be seen in how people within EEWC-CFT reflect on their life perspectives as well.

In this first part of our book we have explored the contours of Letha's life and work. We now turn our attention to those who have been affected by Letha's presence and guidance. One of the aspects of Letha that sets her apart is her unwavering focus on others. It is only fitting that some of the people whose lives have been transformed by Letha's midwifery work be part of telling this story. The narrative began with Letha, but just like her life, it doesn't end there but instead continues through the numerous people whose own faith journeys have taken on new and exciting contours precisely because of Letha.

What better legacy could there be?

Resources for Church Groups

In this chapter we explore how Letha has provided guidance to EEWC-CFT over time, in part because of her dedication to transformation of others. She has demonstrated a willingness to forgo personal advantage in order to do the diligent work of seeking justice for all people, even when this comes at a cost.

> » Begin by talking about experiences group members have had of giving up something in order to achieve a higher purpose.

Letha's work with EEWC-CFT speaks to the power of community. In this chapter we see both the power of community and its challenges, especially as a group grows and stretches with an expanding vision.

> » Have members write about (or draw) their personal experiences of being part of a community. What have been some of their positive gains, and where have they witnessed challenge or conflict?

> » What observations do people have about how to successfully negotiate conflict within groups?

> » What insights come to you in the way Letha responded to conflict?

Bible Reading: John 3:1–10

Jesus converses with Nicodemus about being born from above.

> » Ask people to share their conversion stories. Include in the conversation people who do not have a conversion story.

> » Identify key contextual elements in the narrative: who were the Pharisees, for example? Why might Nicodemus approach Jesus at night? What does the title rabbi mean?

> » The primary image in this narrative is of birth. Ask participants to reflect on what is involved in the birthing process. Don't overlook items as seemingly mundane as water, womb, darkness, pain, and anguish.

> » Consider why Jesus accepted the image of birth as a viable one for what it means to follow him.

> » Explore reasons why the church has generally disregarded the feminine image here of birthing (a process reserved for women or female species). Why do you think this has been the case?

Implementing New Ideas

» Sing Jann's hymn "O Holy Darkness, Loving Womb" (https://www.youtube.com/watch?v=HTdZyBcg9iw), and discuss your response to the lyrics and to singing this hymn together.

» Consider how you could foster greater attentiveness in your community to the transformative process of birth. What elements—for example, water or darkness—could you use in worship?

PART 2

Expanding the Vision

This section of the book illustrates the ongoing influence of Letha Dawson Scanzoni's work, drawing from interviews with people whose lives have been changed by her writing, her mentoring, and her cofounding of the Evangelical & Ecumenical Women's Caucus–Christian Feminism Today. In keeping with her feminist ideals of collaboration, we connect Letha's story with the stories of many other people. These stories illustrate ways she continues building bridges to fulfill her prophetic call to spread the good news of liberation.

4

Claiming the Divine Image

"**W**omen have just as much right as men to think of themselves in God's image and of God as similar to them. Men have no more right than women to think of themselves as God's image bearers, God's representatives."[1] Letha Dawson Scanzoni and Nancy A. Hardesty write these statements near the beginning of *All We're Meant to Be: A Biblical Approach to Women's Liberation* (1974). In this chapter, titled "Understanding the Bible," they provide the theological foundation for the book. Scanzoni and Hardesty follow established principles for interpreting Scripture to arrive at their main theme: the equality of women and men based on the divine image including female and male (Gen 1:27).

Females Created Equally in the Divine Image

Learning that we can be all we're created to be in the divine image, women have claimed our gifts and our callings. Biblical support for gender equality continues to be good news indeed for countless women and men. First published in 1974, *All We're Meant to Be* "became an instant hit" and "flew off the shelves of Christian bookstores."[2] In 1975, based on a survey of 150 evangelical leaders, *All We're Meant to Be* received *Eternity* magazine's Book of the Year award. Historian Pamela D. H. Cochran calls it "the most

---

1. Scanzoni and Hardesty, *All We're Meant to Be* (1974), 21.
2. Lee, *Rescuing Jesus*, 53.

influential work in helping launch the evangelical feminist movement."[3] Religion professor Seth Dowland praises it as the "most important text in the nascent evangelical feminist movement," differing from most second wave feminist works in that it enlists the support of the Bible.[4] Asbury University history professor David R. Swartz commends the book for marshaling "cutting-edge psychological, biological, and exegetical research."[5] *All We're Meant to Be* spread through evangelical Christianity and beyond, going through seven printings by 1978. A second edition came out in 1986, and a third edition, "revised and expanded for the nineties," came out in 1992. *All We're Meant to Be* continues to free people from prescribed gender roles to flourish according to our gifts.

This liberating message of gender equality is needed today just as it has been since the first edition of *All We're Meant to Be* came out in 1974. Although some people believe that we live in a postsexist world where feminism is no longer needed, patriarchy is still all too prevalent, and indoctrination in gender inequality continues on a wide scale. Distorted biblical interpretations on gender that come from evangelical culture remain a pervasive force in our society.[6]

Letha Dawson Scanzoni and Nancy A. Hardesty begin their third edition of *All We're Meant to Be* with readers' responses: "'Your book changed my life!' Over the past two decades, hundreds of women and men across the country from Seattle to Savannah, Los Angeles to Boston, have walked up to us and uttered those words. Each time we have felt a bit overwhelmed and humbly grateful to God for the impact this book has had on so many people's lives."[7]

Letha continues to change lives not only through her writing but also through her mentoring and friendship, and through EEWC-CFT, an organization she cofounded. Letha challenges people to become all we're created to be in the divine image. She inspires the flourishing of authors, ministers, teachers, counselors, activists, organizers, and artists.

---

3. Cochran, *Evangelical Feminism*, 25.

4. Dowland, *Family Values*, 129.

5. Swartz, *Moral Minority*, 199.

6. Weddle and Mock, *If Eve Only Knew*. This book deconstructs evangelical popular culture's messages that girls and women, as descendants of Eve, are weak and inferior, and with thorough biblical support constructs positive messages that empower us to be all we're created to be in the divine image.

7. Scanzoni and Hardesty, *All We're Meant to Be* (1992), viii.

Editor and writer Linda Bieze celebrates the changes she has experienced. She calls *All We're Meant to Be* a "revolutionary" book that changed her "thinking about what the Bible says about women's callings."[8] She says that since she read this book, she has been seeking her callings: "*All We're Meant to Be* opened my eyes to the possibility that I could be someone other than a teacher (or nurse, or pastor's wife—the three holy callings for women in the church I grew up in)."[9] The book helped Linda see that women could be ordained leaders in churches, and she has served as an elder in the Christian Reformed Church, and more recently as a deacon in the Presbyterian Church (U.S.A.). The book also encouraged her to complete a certificate of study from the Women's Leadership Institute at Hartford Seminary, directed by another of her strong feminist role models, Sister Miriam Therese Winter.

In addition to Letha's writing, her supportive friendship and mentoring have inspired Linda to reach beyond what she has seen as personal limitations. For many years Letha and Linda have been colleagues in EEWC-CFT. "Letha has encouraged me to do things that I didn't dare do at first: launch a freelance career, attend the Women's Leadership Institute at Hartford Seminary, continue to seek God's next calling," Linda says. "I probably would not have become as involved as I have been in EEWC-CFT if it were not for Letha." Linda has served several terms as a representative on the Executive Council and as council coordinator a couple of times. Letha's example—first as editor of the newsletter *EEWC Update* (later called *Christian Feminism Today*) and then as the prime content provider for the EEWC website—prompted Linda to continue to volunteer for EEWC-CFT. Letha has also encouraged Linda to write for the magazine and the website.

Letha's influence spans generations, as illustrated in the membership of EEWC-CFT and in a Bible study that she and Linda began more than fifteen years ago and invited Alena Ruggerio to join a year later. Letha, Linda, and Alena meet every Friday night for Bible study through a three-hour conference call across three states. In an article titled "Friends for All Seasons," published in *Christian Feminism Today*, Linda writes about the deepening of their friendship through this Bible study: "Sometimes we call ourselves the Transcontinental Trigenerational Telephone Trio." Linda describes their Bible study as a "friendship church" and a "feminist church."

8. Linda Bieze, letter to Letha, dated June 2014.

9. Linda Bieze, e-mail interview with coauthor Jann Aldredge-Clanton on December 7, 2015. Unless otherwise noted, all subsequent quotes from Linda Bieze are from this interview.

In their meetings a large portion of time is devoted to sharing personal joys and concerns so that they can pray for one another throughout the coming week. They use resources by Reta Halteman Finger and other feminist authors, and their "own Spirit-guided understanding of God's Word," Linda writes. True to feminist egalitarian ideals, they have no designated leader but simply share their thoughts on the passage of the week and talk about what each person has gleaned from it. Linda calls this Bible study group a "multigenerational community of sisterhood." She celebrates EEWC-CFT also as a caring, diverse community: "We are multigenerational people, women and men, befriending each other in all seasons."[10]

Anne Linstatter,[11] an English professor and founding member of EWC,[12] read *All We're Meant to Be* shortly after it was published in 1974. A graduate student at Berkeley at the time, Anne found the book transformative. "Letha first entered my consciousness when I noticed a four-inch, one-third column advertisement on a random page in *Christianity Today* magazine in August 1974," Anne recalls.[13] "The ad announced a forthcoming book, *All We're Meant to Be: A Biblical Approach to Women's Liberation*. I wondered if this could be the book I had been looking for since 1971— one that would approve of a born-again Christian also being a feminist and having equality in her marriage. Or would the 'biblical approach' be yet another condemnation of feminism, saying 'the husband is the head of his wife'? I'd never heard of the authors, Letha Scanzoni and Nancy Hardesty. Exactly what did they think we were meant to be?"

The pastor of her Presbyterian church had advised Anne that 1 Cor 11:3 and Eph 5:22 meant that wives should be subject to husbands. But Anne still believed that God approved of her "equality-based marriage." *All We're Meant to Be* gave her the biblical support she needed. "That consultation with the pastor had occurred a year before I held the book in my hands," Anne says. "It was September when the book arrived, and I went to pick it up, quickly scanning the table of contents, especially Chapter 8, titled 'Love, Honor, and _____?' The opening words of the chapter looked

10. Bieze and Ruggerio, "Friends for All Seasons," 2.

11. formerly Anne Eggebroten.

12. In 1990, the name of the organization was changed to Evangelical & Ecumenical Women's Caucus, and in 2009, to Evangelical & Ecumenical Women's Caucus–Christian Feminism Today.

13. Anne Linstatter, e-mail interview with coauthor Jann Aldredge-Clanton on January 11 and 13, 2016. Unless otherwise noted, all subsequent quotes from Anne Linstatter are from this interview.

like the answer I had so long wanted to find. I rushed off to my study carrel in the English department and sat down in quiet to scrutinize the chapter, along with Chapter 9, 'Living in Partnership.' I read with trepidation, expecting each moment to come across the proviso that the husband should theoretically rule over the wife, however equal their relationship worked out in practice. But no, I found only sentence after sentence of realistic advice and sensible ways of handling the biblical texts. Then on page 106 I came across the words 'each for the other and both for the Lord,' which the authors called 'an old marriage motto.' Interesting that no one had ever quoted that to me." At that moment Anne felt a great burden lifted off her shoulders. She began crying, both from anger and anxiety over the past few years and from relief and joy at "being reconciled to God again, a God who loved me and whom I could love with my whole heart." Anne believed God had this book written for her and had guided her to find the ad in *Christianity Today.*

Anne then wrote letters to Letha and Nancy, thanking them for writing *All We're Meant to Be.* Anne was amazed by their quick response: "These authors were real people who had taken time to read a letter from an unknown college student—and furthermore, they invited me to a conference in Chicago they would be attending in late November." As a "not-quite-starving graduate student," Anne didn't think she could afford the trip, but her husband encouraged her to go to this meeting of Evangelicals for Social Action (ESA). "Soon after entering the conference hall, I met my heroines, Letha and Nancy," Anne recalls. "'Sit by me,' Letha said, gesturing to the chair next to her, and soon I was in baby-feminist heaven."

Letha also invited Anne to join a caucus of women at this ESA conference. About twenty enthusiastic women gathered in a small room to write a list of goals and to plan ways to implement them. Letha, Nancy, and Lucille Sider Dayton sat behind a long table with Anne and the others gathered around. They had a full agenda: working for women's ordination in evangelical churches, expanding the numbers of women in seminaries, working for equality in church leadership, teaching mutual submission in marriage and the home, reaching out to other evangelical women. It became clear that they needed to found their own organization in order to reach all these goals. ESA had a wider spectrum of concerns, and the major denominations each had a task force on women. But evangelical churches needed a push on women's issues. By the end of that day, Anne realized she would be taking her place in the long line of women and men who would continue the work inspired by *All We're Meant to Be.* She determined to devote the rest of her life to sharing biblical equality with other women and working for change in the church.

Anne joined the committee of five women planning the first conference of EWC, held in November 1975 in Washington, DC. With some of her friends she started a chapter of EWC in the San Francisco Bay Area. Anne is glad she "stuck with EWC through thin times financially and difficult decisions organizationally" over the next forty years as it became the Evangelical & Ecumenical Women's Caucus (EEWC) and then the Evangelical & Ecumenical Women's Caucus–Christian Feminism Today (EEWC-CFT); now it is often known simply as Christian Feminism Today (CFT).

For more than forty years Letha has been a role model and mentor to Anne, setting a high standard of research and writing. "Because she has done so much, I know 'Yes, it can be done' when I set my own goals," Anne says. "I marveled at Letha's energy and fierce determination to write while also raising two children, accepting speaking engagements, teaching Sunday school, and working to complete her college degree." Even before her groundbreaking book *All We're Meant to Be*, Letha had published two books, *Youth Looks at Love* and *Why Am I Here? Where Am I Going? Youth Looks at Life*, as well as articles in *Eternity*: "Woman's Place: Silence or Service?" and "Elevate Marriage to Partnership." When Anne feels overwhelmed by family and writing commitments, Letha encourages her to keep writing. Letha has also been a mentor through editing everything Anne has written for the newsletter *Christian Feminism Today* and for the website. Anne expresses gratitude: "With her encyclopedic knowledge of biblical and evangelical history, Letha catches mistakes ranging from factual errors to incorrect biblical citations to misspelling, improving my usage, clarity, and style and making me look like a better writer than I am."

Another founding member of EWC, Jeanne Hanson, takes her place in the long line of people inspired by Letha's work. "Letha and the whole family of EEWC-CFT have changed my life and brought me closer to understanding what is going on between my Creator and me," she says.[14] For many years Jeanne has been exploring God's call in her life and taking risks to fulfill this call. "In 1946, when I felt that God wanted me to be a missionary, I got on a Greyhound bus one rainy day, with fifty dollars in my pocket that my mom gave to me, and I went off to Bible school, all on my own, to

14. Jeanne Hanson, e-mail interview with coauthor Jann Aldredge-Clanton on December 10, 2015. Unless otherwise noted, all subsequent quotes from Jeanne Hanson are from this interview.

prepare for the mission field," she writes. "And on a late night in November 1959, I took another courageous step when I went on board as the only passenger on a slow freighter headed for Inchon, Korea, to work at a missionary radio station."[15] Jeanne attended conservative Christian schools Multnomah School of the Bible[16] and Bible Institute of Los Angeles,[17] and then served as a missionary in Korea with the large conservative interdenominational mission board TEAM (The Evangelical Alliance Mission). While on the mission field, Jeanne began to question the gender inequities she observed and experienced: "I was mulling over in my mind as a field administrator how inequitably wives and single women were treated as compared to men."

When Jeanne returned from the mission field in 1972, she enrolled at Seattle Pacific College[18] and majored in education and psychology with the intention of returning to the field better prepared to address inequities she had seen. At Seattle Pacific Jeanne received an education she did not expect. "I had missed all the '60s in the U.S. and for the first time met face-to-face with a changed U.S. culture," she recalls. "I met Christian women who were calling themselves feminists. Of course, this raised huge question marks in my conservative mindset and challenged me, but I was intrigued and wanted to know more."

In 1977, in a Christian feminist class at a large Presbyterian church, Jeanne learned more. The presenter of the class, Fuller Seminary professor Phyllis Hart, introduced several Christian feminist books available at that time. One of these was *All We're Meant to Be,* by Letha Scanzoni and Nancy Hardesty. "Like manna from heaven, this book was meant for me," Jeanne says. "It was solidly based in Scripture and validated my spiritual journey toward knowing and understanding our feminine Godde.[19] Here was someone clearly declaring the importance of ministries of women—in Scripture and in church history. Legitimacy for women to respond to their call from the Holy Spirit to ministry—whatever it be—was clearly centered

15. Hanson, "Taking Leaps of Faith," 1–2.

16. In 1993 Multnomah School of the Bible became Multnomah Bible College and Seminary. In 2008 it became Multnomah University.

17. Bible Institute of Los Angeles became Biola University in 1981.

18. Seattle Pacific College became Seattle Pacific University in 1977.

19. Some Christian feminists use the word "Godde" as a combination of "God" and "Goddess." They choose to use "Godde" because of the long history of association of the word "God" with an exclusively masculine image of the Divine and because "Goddess" is a word that Christians have not traditionally embraced.

in the Scriptures." Jeanne has read *All We're Meant to Be* many times and lost count of the number of copies of the book she has given to others.

Inspired by *All We're Meant to Be* to continue claiming her gifts and calling, Jeanne earned her MA degree in psychology from the University of Washington and served as a school psychologist and then as a high school principal. Even after she retired, Jeanne ventured into new challenges with Letha's encouragement. When Jeanne reached age seventy-five, she talked with Letha about what it means to be getting older. Letha encouraged Jeanne to write her feelings about growing older and her experience of aging for the EEWC newsletter.[20] "On my 80th birthday I went skydiving, and Letha wanted me to write about that absolutely wonderful experience for the newsletter,"[21] Jeanne says. "I hadn't considered myself a writer, but I did the best I could, and she made what I wrote into something marvelous and professional. She helped make me a 'writer.'"

Jeanne also appreciates Letha as an encouraging friend and collaborator in EEWC-CFT. When Jeanne served as office manager of the organization, Letha was always available for consultation. "Actually my phone seemed tied to Letha's phone because whenever I needed to ask a question or get some ideas or directions, I would give Letha a call," Jeanne says. "Usually we would talk for ten or fifteen minutes about the issues, but we were also just being friends."

Another founder of the Christian feminist movement, Reta Halteman Finger, recounts her discovery of *All We're Meant to Be* soon after the book came out.

> It was the fall of 1974. My sons were turning three and one. Our family was living in Harrisonburg, Virginia, so one weekend that fall I tucked them into their car seats and drove to my parents' home in eastern Pennsylvania. While there, I visited a college friend, Helen Longenecker Lapp, one of the "kindred spirits" in my life.
>
> "I have a new women's book to share with you!" she announced.
>
> "I don't like women's books," I replied, thinking of books like *The Total Woman.*
>
> "This is not what you're thinking of," Helen said. "It's called *All We're Meant to Be* and it's written by two Christian feminist women, Letha Scanzoni and Nancy Hardesty."

20. Hanson, "Climbing the Mountain of Age," 2.

21. Hanson, "Taking Leaps of Faith," 1–2.

> Though I had never heard of either author, I doubt that any-
> one was more ready for this book than I was. The secular feminist
> movement was in the news; *The Other Side* magazine had printed
> an article on women in the Gospels; and I had recently found
> an article about women's equality in the main publication of the
> Mennonite Church (followed by a strenuous backlash from both
> women and men). I had even started doing a bit of research and
> writing myself. And here was a book that put it all together![22]

Reta recalls her excitement also about attending the first national EWC conference in Washington, DC, the following summer of 1975. There she heard Letha Dawson Scanzoni, Nancy A. Hardesty, and Virginia Ramey Mollenkott, all pillars of the fledgling Christian feminist movement, along with Lucille Sider Dayton, editor of a newly born journal called *Daughters of Sarah*. This conference, titled "Women in Transition: A Biblical Approach to Feminism," attracted more than 360 women from thirty-six U.S. states and from Canada.

Soon after the conference Reta moved to Chicago, where she joined the group of women creating *Daughters of Sarah*. She served as editor of this groundbreaking journal for fifteen years. At the beginning of each edition of the journal is this statement of identity and purpose: "We are Christians. We are also feminists. Some say we cannot be both, but for us Christianity and feminism are inseparable."

Reta and Letha soon became colleagues in the growing Christian feminist movement. Letha wrote articles for *Daughters of Sarah*, and Reta wrote for *EEWC Update*. For many years Reta taught Bible classes from a feminist perspective at Messiah College, and she currently writes a Bible study blog, "Reta's Reflections," for the *Christian Feminism Today* website. Always encouraging, Letha has pushed Reta to do more writing for EEWC-CFT than she ever would have done on her own, Reta says. "My Bible study blog on our website was her idea a few years ago; it would have never oc-curred to me. In addition, and even after she 'retired' from editing, she edits every lesson I write. I have never had an editor like Letha. Her ability to understand awkwardly-stated ideas and to rewrite them in smooth and in-viting ways is a gift I have never received with such care from anyone else."

Writer and editor Juanita Wright Potter, also active in *Daughters of Sarah* and EWC in their formative years, comments on her discovery of

---

22. Reta Halteman Finger, e-mail interview with coauthor Jann Aldredge-Clanton on December 7, 2015. Unless otherwise noted, all subsequent quotes from Reta Halteman Finger are from this interview.

Christian feminism through Letha's writing. Juanita's awakening came in 1966 through Letha's article "Woman's Place: Silence or Service?" in *Eternity*. "I read her words over and over when I was sixteen years old, living on a farm about fifty miles from St. Louis in one direction and fifty miles from Springfield, Illinois, in another," Juanita recalls.[23] "I felt about a million miles from anyone else asking the same questions that I was starting to ask. I had already noticed that a woman's name, Nancy Hardesty, was appearing in the masthead of the magazine as 'assistant editor.' This, along with Letha's work, gave me hope that eventually there would be a place for women who were thinkers, readers, and writers to have a part in the conversation within Christian tradition."

Fifteen years later Juanita met Letha, Nancy, and "a host of other questioning women" at the 1981 EWC Conference in Saratoga Springs, New York. By this time Juanita had graduated from a Bible college and Wheaton College Graduate School, and had worked as an editor and writer for a missionary organization in Missouri and a publisher of Sunday school materials in Wheaton. When she noticed an ad in *Ms. Magazine* for the EWC Conference and recognized the names of Letha and Nancy in the list of participants, Juanita decided to attend. At the conference she picked up a copy of *All We're Meant to Be*, heard Virginia Ramey Mollenkott speak, and learned about *Daughters of Sarah*. Juanita says that even more important for her than working on the magazine was the monthly potluck and discussion the group hosted: "This was a place where I learned to listen carefully to other voices and to speak up with my own."

Juanita served on the editorial committee and the administrative board of *Daughters of Sarah*, and helped form a Chicago chapter of EWC in 1985. Currently, she writes book and movie reviews for EEWC-CFT, with Letha's encouragement. Juanita comments: "I deeply admire Letha's courage to speak up early and often and clearly on issues that desperately need to be addressed with a new, compassionate, inclusive voice within the evangelical church. A courage that is straight from her heart. I and thousands of other women and men have benefited from her open-hearted friendship, encouraging us to follow our hearts and keep our eyes and minds wide open."

Letha's writing contributed to the Christian feminist awakening of Sharon Bowes, EEWC-CFT office manager for many years, and to her

23. Juanita Wright Potter, e-mail interview with coauthor Jann Aldredge-Clanton on December 7, 2015. All subsequent quotes from Juanita Wright Potter are from this interview.

strong commitment to the organization. As a young adult Sharon began to question the "fundamental" Christian teachings of the "God-designed" roles for women that she had learned. "As a female I was expected to accept limited responsibilities in the church, limited advanced education, and not continuing my career when becoming a mother," she says.[24] "After the birth of my daughter, I began reading and agreeing with writings of the feminists of the 1970s concerning equality for women in the home, work, and society. I was a supporter of the Equal Rights Amendment. This was a very difficult period in my life as I struggled with the question of how I could be a Christian woman and a feminist." During this time Sharon learned of biblical feminism through *All We're Meant To Be*. As she read this book, she gained peace and confidence that she could be both a Christian and a woman who used her God-given abilities in her life. This "enlightening" book, she says, changed her understanding of biblical passages that "seemed so negative to women" by putting them into historical context and correcting misinterpretations and faulty translations. "Trust and belief were created in me that my little girl and I were made in our loving God's image and valued equally. I learned that I could be a Christian Feminist!"

As she filled the position of EEWC-CFT office manager, Sharon recounts that Letha became an "awesome mentor" and supportive friend. Letha and Sharon were the two staff members contracted to run the organization—Letha as the creator of the website and the quarterly newsletter, and Sharon as the office manager. Sharon recalls that when she needed guidance on the office process, she called Letha. But when they both felt that phone conversations were not enough, Letha flew to Sharon's home where they spent several days at the computer working on the procedures involved in running the office and in conversations about the organization of EEWC-CFT. "From her unbelievable knowledge and memory, Letha so willingly shared the history of EEWC, its leaders, and its experiences through the years."

Sharon's husband died several months after she became the office manager. "The sensitivity and understanding that Letha showed me were such an amazing support, encouraging me with both the EEWC role and adjusting to my personal loss," Sharon says. "During my years as EEWC-CFT office manager my belief in and commitment to the organization and

---

24. Sharon Bowes, e-mail interview with coauthor Jann Aldredge-Clanton on November 15, 2015. All subsequent quotes from Sharon Bowes are from this interview.

its mission grew very strong. Letha's guidance and friendship played a large role in that."

Letha has had considerable influence on the vocation of Ann Steiner Lantz, a United Methodist minister. When Ann was in high school, she met Letha at a weekend retreat at First United Methodist Church in Anderson, Indiana, where Ann's father served as an associate pastor. The first edition of *All We're Meant to Be* had just come out, and Letha was the featured speaker at the retreat. Ann attended the Saturday session with her mother and was intrigued by Letha's discussion of *All We're Meant to Be*. "I was transfixed by what Letha was saying," Ann recalls. "I had never heard such 'freeing talk.' Letha spoke of such an exciting understanding of the Bible that was so very different from the patriarchal understanding I had been taught."[25]

Following the session, Ann stood in line waiting with her mother to have Letha sign her copy of *All We're Meant to Be*. "I cherished that book," Ann says. "I devoured every word; it opened an entire new world to me. It opened my eyes and my understanding that as a young woman I had a place in the church. I was enthralled by the idea that a woman could be in ministry. I was stunned! This was a concept that I had never heard of or considered other than being a missionary—usually as the missionary's wife." Hearing Letha speak and then reading the book gave Ann a fresh look at God and what she could do with her life. Her church and culture had been giving Ann messages that she was a second-class citizen simply because of her gender. She's not sure where her life would have gone if she hadn't met Letha, heard her speak, and read *All We're Meant to Be*.

Years later, Ann wrote Letha to express appreciation. Ann had come across a website that had Letha's e-mail address and had written to her, sharing the story of meeting her but never expecting to hear from her. "I wrote Letha about how much her book and life example had influenced my life and career," Ann says. "Much to my surprise, I received a beautiful note back from Letha. In that note she asked if I still had the book. I explained that it had been destroyed in a house fire in 1991. Letha promptly signed another book and sent it to me! It was a great surprise."

When Ann was in the process of discerning whether or not to change from her position as a United Methodist minister serving as the director of chaplains for a large health care system, Letha served as a mentor, advocate,

25. Ann Steiner Lantz, e-mail interview with coauthor Jann Aldredge-Clanton on December 24, 2015. All subsequent quotes from Ann Steiner Lantz are from this interview.

and friend. "What I love most about Letha is that she didn't tell me what to do," Ann says. "Instead, she listened, reflected, listened, and reflected some more. Through her listening, I was able to work through the period of discernment and come to understand how God was calling me in a different direction." Ann was unsure if she had the skill set needed to pursue an executive director position with a not-for-profit. Through a process of thoughtful questions, Letha helped her gain the confidence to apply for and get the position of executive director of a large social service organization that serves the economically disadvantaged and those experiencing homelessness.

Letha has inspired Ann to become involved in EEWC-CFT. "Letha is the sole reason I am involved in EEWC," Ann says. "Her commitment to this organization is contagious to anyone who is around her."

About the time of the first publication of *All We're Meant to Be* and the forming of EWC, Mark Olson became editor of *The Other Side*, a progressive Christian magazine founded initially to deal with race and gradually expanded to cover a variety of other issues, including economic justice, militarism and U.S. imperialism, feminism, and LGBTQ concerns. Mark had heard about Letha's insightful research on gender equality and invited her to write for *The Other Side*. He was delighted that she contributed many important articles and also coauthored with John Scanzoni, her husband at the time, a regular column for the magazine on family and gender issues.

Earlier, Mark had learned that his friend Nancy Hardesty was working on a book with Letha. At that time, Mark had not met Letha or read any of her articles. But he gained a positive impression of her through Nancy's animated reports of conversations they were having, discoveries they were making, and research they were undertaking. "I couldn't help thinking that here was a perfect match," Mark says.[26] "Nancy and Letha seemed like ideal coauthors. They each brought great energy and passion to the task, and they were each clearly supportive of each other, not competing with each other. You couldn't ask for a better situation." Mark was already sympathetic to the perspectives Letha and Nancy were advancing. He was "deeply pleased" they were providing the kind of "sociological, theological, and biblical evidence that could change minds and move hearts." Mark believed the book on which they were working would result not only in richer individual lives and personal relationships but also in better congregational and ecclesiastical experiences for many people. Letha recently reminded Mark

26. Mark Olson, e-mail interview with coauthor Jann Aldredge-Clanton on November 28, 2015. All subsequent quotes from Mark Olson are from this interview.

that shortly before the publication, he had suggested a change in the title of the book from *All That We're Meant to Be* to *All We're Meant to Be*, and she expressed gratitude to him for this more compelling title.

About the time that *All We're Meant to Be* first appeared in print, Mark met Letha in person at a party Nancy hosted for some of their Christian feminist friends. "I couldn't help but be in awe of Letha's remarkable memory for facts, details, people, sociological data, and biblical interpretations," Mark recalls. "Hearing her talk, I knew she not only had a great 'filing system' in her wide-ranging intellect but also, most likely, had a great tangible filing system as well. Her attention to detail has made her not only a fine researcher, writer, and editor but also an incredible listener to others' personal stories—and thus a great friend of many."

One of Letha's many friends, Nadine Grass, recalls that Letha went beyond traditional female roles when they were in church together in Lookingglass, Oregon. Nadine was a young middle school student when Letha and her husband, John, were just starting out in home missions work under an organization called Village Missions. They were called to serve the small rural church Nadine's family attended in Lookingglass. John served as pastor, and Letha served as youth leader, music director, and Sunday school teacher. Nadine says she admired Letha for playing the trombone in church because at that time "the trombone was not typically defined as an instrument for women."[27] Letha's nontraditional choice helped Nadine when she had the opportunity to participate in the band at school. At first Nadine chose the trumpet, but then decided on the baritone. Her parents were not "thrilled" with her choice to play this instrument they thought was for boys. But she loved the way the baritone sounded, and delighted in playing it in the band and playing duets with Letha in church. "I was terrified to play with Letha because she was so accomplished, but she was so encouraging that I made it through," Nadine recalls. "Lookingglass was a very conservative community where the roles of women and men were clearly defined, especially in the church. There was something special about Letha that I picked up on even at that early age. She stood out for me because she redefined the role that women should have in the church. She was strong, she expressed her opinion, she was eloquent and well read. Letha led a group called 'Jet Cadets' in Bible lessons, singing, and games designed to train us to become future leaders in the church. I remember thinking I wanted to be as strong as her, especially in my spiritual life."

27. Nadine Grass, e-mail interview with coauthor Jann Aldredge-Clanton on November 30, 2015. All subsequent quotes from Nadine Grass are from this interview.

When Letha moved from Lookingglass, Nadine lost track of her. Not until almost fifty years later did they reconnect. "I found myself needing some spiritual guidance," Nadine says. "I was reading my Bible, but not getting what I needed. I tried reading a few books about spirituality and faith and was not connecting with any of it. I felt stagnant in my faith, knew that I wanted and needed more. I was unable to find a church and unable to find friends who could help." One night as Nadine was searching on the Internet, she thought about Letha and Googled her name. Nadine was delighted to find everything she wanted to know about Letha on Wikipedia. Nadine found Letha's website that had her contact information and decided to give her a call. Nadine was surprised when Letha asked her why she had thought of her: "How could she not know that she was a hero to me and had such an influence on my life?"

Nadine asked Letha for help with her spiritual search, and Letha agreed to mentor her. "I felt guilty when I realized how busy Letha was, but she reassured me that she could take some time," Nadine says. When they talked, Nadine could feel herself making progress. Letha recommended much reading material. But listening to Letha helped Nadine the most. "I am constantly amazed by the depth of her knowledge. No matter what topic I threw to her, she nailed it." Letha also encouraged Nadine to look at the EEWC website and to attend EEWC conferences. "I will forever be grateful that she came into my life when I was a child, and then later, an adult."

Letha's friendship and mentoring have also been invaluable for Alena Ruggerio, a professor of communication at Southern Oregon University. Letha stepped in as a mentor and encourager to help Alena finish her PhD dissertation. When Alena was hired at Southern Oregon University while still a graduate student, she struggled to finish her dissertation while also working a full-time job. "Bless Letha forever for her forbearance," Alena says.[28] "It must have felt quite odd for her to shepherd my dissertation through the writing process when an entire chapter was dedicated to my rhetorical analysis of *All We're Meant to Be*, yet I didn't have approval from the university's human subjects review board to go beyond the text to interview her directly about the book. Her masterful skills as a dissertation coach and editor made it possible for me to finish my PhD and keep the job I loved in Oregon."

---

28. Alena Ruggerio e-mail interview with coauthor Jann Aldredge-Clanton on October 28, 2015. Unless otherwise noted, all subsequent quotes from Alena Ruggerio are from this interview.

Alena grew up in a mainline denomination but says she's "always been attracted to evangelical culture for the way their everyday choices are grounded in religious faith." She describes herself as a "Gen-Xer who benefited from the (albeit complex and incomplete) victories of second wave American feminism." In a graduate course on the rhetoric of religion Alena read Mary Stewart Van Leeuwen's *After Eden: Facing the Challenge of Gender Reconciliation*, and discovered the connection between evangelical Christianity and progressive feminism. She began reading other Christian feminist books, including *All We're Meant to Be*. As her academic and personal interest in Christian feminism continued to grow, Alena chose to write her PhD dissertation on the intersection of rhetoric and feminist hermeneutics and to include *All We're Meant to Be*.

On a Christian feminist LISTSERV she requested suggestions on getting a copy of the out-of-print third edition of *All We're Meant to Be* for her research. One of the people on the LISTSERV was in e-mail contact with Letha, and forwarded Alena's query to her. Letha contacted Alena, offering to send her a copy of the edition she was looking for, and asking about her personal story and studies. "At that time, I was researching third wave feminism, and Letha invited me to write an article about it for what was then called *EEWC Update*," Alena says. "I have a distinct memory of hanging up the telephone and zooming around the room, crowing to my husband, 'You're never going to guess who just called me, and she wants me to write for her magazine!' Of course, scores of other people have the same story—of Letha reaching out, demonstrating interest in our stories instead of calling attention to her own achievements, and drawing us into participation in Christian feminism with an invitation to write, to speak, and to lead. My efforts to find a copy of *All We're Meant to Be* introduced me to one of the dearest friends of my life, who has personally shaped my Christianity and my feminism."

Letha's influence has contributed to Alena's active involvement in EEWC-CFT for sixteen years. Alena has served on the Executive Council as coordinator, secretary, and regional representative; spoken at many of the conferences; and served as the assistant to the editor and guest editor of four issues of *Christian Feminism Today* magazine. Letha invited her to attend her first conference in 2000 and to stand for election to the council, Alena says; but the main role Letha has played in her involvement in EEWC-CFT has been to create an atmosphere in which all Christian feminists are welcome to contribute. "At the time I joined EEWC, secular American feminism was ripping itself apart with generational drama. Because of her commitment to the radical inclusivity and expansive love of God, Letha led EEWC in embracing young women's voices instead of discounting or feeling threatened by them. People of all ages, races, sexual orientations, abilities, genders, faith traditions, and social classes are treasured in the organization Letha co-founded."

Alena also delights in the inclusiveness of a weekly Bible study with Letha and Linda Bieze. "Somehow, the fact that we're from three different Christian traditions and three different generations only enhances the richness of our personal conversations and interpretations of the Bible," Alena says. "These Friday night conference calls are convenings of my family of choice." In a *Christian Feminism Today* article Alena writes, "Even though we are scattered across the country, the regular appointment we keep with each other for weekly Bible study and personal sharing makes Letha and Linda feel unwaveringly present in my life . . . Our friendship transcends the boundaries of age, location, and life circumstances because God is at the center of our circle."[29]

The Divine Image Including Female

Like EEWC-CFT, subsequent editions of *All We're Meant to Be* became more inclusive. Coauthors Letha Dawson Scanzoni and Nancy A. Hardesty grew in their understanding of the connection between gender equality and gender-inclusive language for humanity and divinity. The second edition of *All We're Meant to Be*, published in 1986, and the third edition, published in 1992, expand the discussion of inclusive language, raised in the first edition. Even more important is the change to inclusive language for humanity and divinity throughout the second and third editions, applying the foundational theology of female and male created equally in the divine image. In chapter 1 Letha and Nancy explain why they make this change. "Many people think that the language issue is trivial; we did at one time. But the passion which the issue generates belies that conclusion (witness the furor raised by the *Inclusive Language Lectionary*, on which Virginia Mollenkott worked with a committee of the National Council of Churches). Indeed, since our thoughts and our theology are expressed in language, changing our language affects every bit of our thinking to the core."[30]

---

29. Bieze and Ruggerio, "Friends for All Seasons," 3.

30. Scanzoni and Hardesty, *All We're Meant to Be* (1986), 32–33; Scanzoni and Hardesty, *All We're Meant to Be* (1992), 17.

Before the publication of the second edition of *All We're Meant to Be* in 1986, Virginia Ramey Mollenkott had addressed the issue of inclusive language. Her book *The Divine Feminine: The Biblical Imagery of God as Female* first came out in 1983. In 1987, just a year after the publication of the second edition of *All We're Meant to Be*, which applies inclusive language, Nancy A. Hardesty published a book-length work on the subject: *Inclusive Language in the Church*. True to their beliefs in mutual relationships, Letha, Virginia, and Nancy have had reciprocal influence on one another.

Although Letha and Nancy raise the importance of language for humanity and divinity in the first edition of *All We're Meant to Be*, they use "generic" male pronouns in reference to "a person whose sex is unknown" and male references to God to indicate "generic personhood."[31] They do, however, quote some Bible verses that include female images of Deity; for example, "In Isaiah 42:14 God says, 'I will cry out like a woman in travail, I will gasp and pant,'" and "In Isaiah 66:13 God promises, 'As one whom his mother comforts, so I will comfort you.'"[32] In their second and third editions, they include all the biblical female divine images from the first edition while adding some of the images that Virginia elucidates in her book *The Divine Feminine*: bakerwoman, mother hen, homemaker, Dame Wisdom, midwife, female pelican, and she-bear. The second and third editions of *All We're Meant to Be* also emphasize, as Nancy does in her book *Inclusive Language in the Church*, that since Divine Mystery exceeds all human words, all our language about Deity is metaphorical and analogical.

In *The Divine Feminine* Virginia demonstrates the importance of including female images of God so that women and girls can become all we're meant to be. "If God can be compared to a woman as well as to a man, then no real-flesh human being should be categorically subordinated to another on the basis of her sex," Virginia writes. "We cannot fully implement human sexual equality as a basis for every other kind of equality until we have first renewed our minds by thinking and speaking only in terms that affirm that equality . . . Our almost exclusive focus on male God-imagery has resulted in an idolatry of the male . . . The best way to heal ourselves of the idolatry we have fallen into is to utilize the full range of biblical imagery for God."[33] *The Divine Feminine* provides a wide variety of biblical female images of God—images that continue to be excluded from worship in most churches,

31. Scanzoni and Hardesty, *All We're Meant to Be* (1974), 21.

32. Ibid., 20. The biblical translations quoted here are from the Amplified Bible, Classic Edition (AMPC).

33. Mollenkott, *The Divine Feminine*, 112–14, 116.

images such as nursing mother, midwife, *Shekinah*, female pelican, mother bear, female homemaker, female beloved, *ezer*, bakerwoman, mother eagle, mother hen, and Dame Wisdom. In addition, Virginia recommends using material and nonmaterial images such as rock, water, and light. The second and third editions of *All We're Meant to Be* show the influence of Virginia's writing about inclusive language.

Nancy's book *Inclusive Language in the Church* also underscores the connection between including female references in our worship language and gender equality. Nancy, like Virginia, calls out the idolatry of exclusively male images of the Divine that still predominate in most churches: "As theologian Mary Daly declares in *Beyond God the Father*, 'If God is male, then the male is God' . . . We persist in speaking of God in male terms despite the second commandment's prohibition of making images and likenesses of the Deity."[34] Nancy advocates inclusive language also because it expands our experience of God and contributes to social justice. "The more ways in which we learn to understand God and to speak of God, the more deeply we will know God," she writes. "On a human level, an effort to use more inclusive language makes us aware not only of our sexism, but also of our racism, elitism, nationalism, classism, ageism, homophobia, and all our other prejudices . . . Thus, using inclusive language is not merely a matter of taste or literary sophistication but a matter of faithfulness to God and to our moral responsibility for our neighbors."[35] Nancy emphasizes that God is beyond human ability to describe, and that all our language for Deity is metaphorical. For the fullest experience of divine revelation, she encourages the use of many metaphors found in Scripture and church history, including female divine images such as *Shaddai*, mother, midwife, sister, and *Shekinah*; animal images such as eagle and lion; and inanimate images such as rock and fire. Nancy also recommends avoiding masculine pronouns for Deity or balancing them with feminine pronouns. In the second and third editions of *All We're Meant to Be* Letha and Nancy include biblical female and nonhuman images of Deity, show that "one can speak of God without using masculine pronouns," and that "one can include women in one's language without being ungrammatical or convoluted."[36]

Around the time of the publication of the second edition of *All We're Meant to Be*, Reta Halteman Finger was also writing about the importance of

34. Hardesty, *Inclusive Language in the Church*, 10.

35. Ibid., 14–15.

36. Scanzoni and Hardesty, *All We're Meant to Be* (1986), 34; Scanzoni and Hardesty, *All We're Meant to Be* (1992), 20.

expanding images of Deity. A 1988 issue of *Daughters of Sarah*, a Christian feminist journal Reta edited, featured an article by Susan Cady and Hal Taussig connecting Jesus and Sophia,[37] along with a graphic illustration by Kari Sandhaas of Sophia creating the world. Years later in *Christian Feminism Today* Reta included this illustration with one of her Bible study blog posts titled "Gender Remixed: Sophia and Word." In this post on the Prologue to John's Gospel she writes:

> To a Greek-speaking Jewish reader, *Logos* would have been inter-
> changeable with *Sophia*. Thus it is appropriate and meaningful for
> both women and men today to insert "Sophia" into the Prologue
> of this Gospel. "In the beginning was Sophia, and Sophia was with
> God, and God was Sophia . . . Logos/Sophia became flesh and lived
> among us." Here we find, first, the mystery of incarnation. Divin-
> ity clothes herself in human skin. No Gnostic thinking here! This
> theme of descent in order to embrace the Below will permeate the
> first half of this Gospel. Second, we are also confronted with the
> mystery of gender. The descent of Word/Sophia implies that the
> human, fleshly Jesus, though male, will also reflect the feminine
> characteristics of a personified Sophia. Watch for these motherly
> tendencies in the lessons to come![38]

In one of these subsequent lessons, "A Fish Story: Mother Jesus Serves Breakfast—John 21:1–14," Reta highlights the image of Jesus as Mother: "By the time everyone arrives, Jesus is making breakfast, just as he did in John 6 when he fed 5000 people. Like an ordinary housewife, he fries flat-bread and cooks some of the fish they had just caught. I can see the disciples standing around awkwardly, unused to helping with women's work . . . Just as in the past, Mother Jesus 'takes the bread and gives it to them, and does the same with the fish.' Yes, it is the same Jesus as before—like a mother serving and eating breakfast with her children."[39]

Another biblical divine image important to Reta is "Rock," and she connects this image to Letha. "There are about 25 references in the Psalms where God is called a Rock," Reta says. "The point is that God is not an inanimate object, but that She is a solid foundation to whom we can cling through the storms of life." Reta associates the image of "Rock" with Letha

---

37. Cady and Taussig, "Jesus and Sophia," 7–11.

38. Finger, "Gender Remixed," para. 11, 13–14.

39. Finger, "A Fish Story," para. 9–10.

for similar reasons. For many years, Letha has been the solid foundation upon which EEWC-CFT rests. She has been a Rock for Reta as well.

Letha has also inspired Melanie Springer Mock, author and professor of English at George Fox University, to become active in EEWC-CFT and to write on gender equality. After Melanie had written a few articles for *Christian Feminism Today*, Letha asked if she wanted to be on the EEWC-CFT board. Melanie felt deeply honored and accepted this invitation. She describes herself as "a relatively new convert to Christian feminism, having just claimed that identity in the last decade or so, and having little to no familiarity about Christian feminism as a movement, with its foremothers, until even more recently."[40]

In 2011 Melanie met Letha for the first time at an EEWC-CFT Council meeting and then read *All We're Meant to Be*. This book inspired Melanie and her friend Kendra Weddle in their writing of *If Eve Only Knew: Freeing Yourself from Biblical Womanhood and Becoming All God Means for You to Be*, which they dedicated to Letha. The idea that has resonated with Melanie most fully is the claim central to Letha's book and to *If Eve Only Knew*: that we are created to be all God means for us to be, and that we need to live fully into God's calling, despite the many barriers placed in our way. Melanie says she has taken on this language, not only in the book, but also in her discussions with students, colleagues, and friends. "It's a pretty compelling argument to make, that God longs for us to be all God created us to be: who is willing to argue against that? And yet, as Letha's writing has shown us, there have been plenty of barriers that keep women from being all they were meant to be. I imagine Letha's lifework has been knocking down those barriers, then moving aside for women to reach their potential. I also wonder and often think about how this same principle applies in other ways. What are the barriers that keep those with disabilities from becoming all God wants them to be? Or those with a mental health diagnosis? Or those who are marginalized because they are a racial or religious minority? These questions challenge me to consider the barriers I put up myself—how I stand in the way of helping people become who God wants them to be. I appreciate that challenge, and imagine it will stay with me for the rest of my life."

Even before they met, Letha encouraged Melanie in her writing and served as a mentor to her. Melanie had queried Letha about writing a book

40. Melanie Springer Mock, e-mail interview with coauthor Jann Aldredge-Clanton on November 10, 2015. Unless otherwise noted, all subsequent quotes from Melanie Springer Mock are from this interview.

review for *Christian Feminism Today*. Letha accepted Melanie's offer and guided her through the writing process, providing valuable feedback and the autonomy she needed as a writer. Melanie also recalls Letha's invitation to write an article on her experience as a mother of adopted children. "I was walking down to the school to get my boys when she called to ask whether I wanted to write about my experience as a mother for a Mother's Day edition of *Christian Feminism Today*. She had secured another mother to write a piece about her experiences with motherhood and feminism, and specifically with giving birth to her children. Letha wondered if I might also like to write a piece, given that my children were both adopted. I remember the conversation so well because few other people had considered the unique situation I was in as a mother of adopted boys, and no one had ever really allowed me to tell my story in the way Letha was requesting."

In this article titled "God's Gift of Motherhood Comes in Different Ways," Melanie writes about the joys and challenges of adopting her two sons, Benjamin Quan from Vietnam and Samuel Saurabh from India. Through this experience Melanie discovered more fully the power of female images of Deity. "I have been given the gift of motherhood, and this, in turn, has allowed me to comprehend God's nature in profound ways. I experience biblical metaphors describing God's love for her children more powerfully now. My children do not bear my genetic code, but this matters not at all: I love Ben and Sam as God loves me, fiercely, overwhelmingly, unconditionally. As God is to me, so I am to my boys; I am as the she-bear in Hosea, the mother hen about whom Jesus speaks, the comforter in Isaiah, and so know God more fully in those terms as well."[41] Melanie says that this article remains one of her favorites because of what she was able to articulate about mothering her sons and understanding the Divine Mother through that experience. "More than anything else I've written in my life, I felt God's creative presence working through me, and I remain grateful to Letha for giving me that opportunity."

Melanie also expresses gratitude for the opportunity to take part in a blog with Letha and Kendra, published on the EEWC-CFT website. On this blog, called *FemFaith: An Intergenerational Conversation*, they address theological and practical concerns of connecting their feminism with their Christian faith. In one post Melanie writes that Letha, Kendra, and EEWC-CFT have influenced her to include female language for Deity: "Kendra, Letha, and others in EEWC have helped attune my ears especially to the ways religious language has shaped our reality and created hegemony

41. Mock, "God's Gift of Motherhood," para. 7.

within the church. I appreciate how they teach me, by example and by gentle instruction. Because people have been central to my own journey toward accepting Sophia in my life—and because I am still learning this acceptance—I try to tread as gently with others who are also on a pathway similar to my own, and who are just now beginning to embrace Her." Melanie expresses the difficulty of accepting Her when deeply entrenched sexist messages in our culture affect her self-image. "But embracing Her is also crucial to my own wholeness, my own sense of well-being."[42]

Presbyterian pastor Rebecca L. (Becky) Kiser has claimed her gifts and expanded her images of God because of Letha's writing and her encouragement. When she was a student at Wheaton College, Becky first read *All We're Meant to Be*. Becky describes the book as a "lightning strike in her fundamentalist/evangelical life." At that time she was amazed that the book was written by women, using the same level of biblical exegesis as male evangelical writers, and "advocating, shockingly, a biblical argument for feminism."[43]

More than twenty years later, Becky first met Letha. After hearing Becky talk about names for God, a friend said to her, "I bet you'd like my friend Letha!" Becky immediately asked, "Letha Dawson Scanzoni?" There aren't too many Lethas around, so Becky jumped to the name she had remembered since she had read *All We're Meant to Be*. She had been so impressed by the book that she had memorized the two authors' names to look for more from them. She was "absolutely floored" by the prospect of meeting Letha in person.

Letha invited Becky to attend the 1996 EEWC conference in Norfolk, Virginia, where they both lived at the time. At one of the conference sessions Becky met Virginia Ramey Mollenkott, another author she was reading, as well as Nancy Hardesty, coauthor with Letha of *All We're Meant to Be*. Becky thought, "Wow, what a group!" Letha loaded Becky up with past issues of the *EEWC Update* newsletter so she could see the kind of topics the organization discussed.

For many years, Becky says, Letha has been a special mentor and supportive friend, encouraging her to write for the *Update* and for other publications. "She accompanied me to a church where I was preaching, listened to my life raising children and my stories of being dissed as a clergywoman,

42. Mock, "Even Wikipedia Has a Messaging Problem," para. 7, 9.

43. Rebecca L. Kiser, e-mail interview with coauthor Jann Aldredge-Clanton on December 13, 2015. Unless otherwise noted, all subsequent quotes from Rebecca L. Kiser are from this interview.

and was a support as my marriage dissolved." Letha and Becky went out to eat at various places with others from Letha's large circle of friends. There was always so much to talk about—and often an invitation to write another *Update* article.

Becky has watched Letha's loving care of many others and of the EEWC-CFT organization. Letha stayed up late to make sure the editing and layout were immaculate on the articles she commissioned for the *Update*. Because Letha didn't have a car, Becky often drove her to take those "precious disks" containing editions of the *Update* to the printer and drove her to many speaking engagements. "I was always impressed by the depth of Letha's thought and eloquent expression," Becky says. "Letha has always impressed me as a 'glass half full' person. Despite a difficult divorce, being shunned by her former evangelical audience after her book with Virginia about homosexuality, limited income, and physical challenges of hip, knee, and shoulder replacements, she keeps her drive and her upbeat perspective. She continues to be tireless for the good of EEWC. She seems inexhaustible in curiosity, energy and love."

One of the articles Letha encouraged Becky to write for the *EEWC Update* is titled "God of the Casserole." In this article Becky relates the transformation that took place for her in imaging the divine after the death of her six-week-old daughter, Emma. "As I began sorting out and dealing with my anger and grief, images of God in the feminine arose in my prayer and became agents of healing and restoration. This was surprising to me because, at the time, I was not comfortable using feminine pronouns or imaging God in the feminine." Becky describes one of these images as similar to the picture of Jesus standing and knocking at the heart's door, but now in the form of a woman carrying a covered casserole like so many women who had brought dinners to show their love and care. Becky pours out her grief, raging at this "God of the Casserole" for not doing more to save her daughter, and then comes to a deeper understanding of God.

> She is who she has always been: compassionate, strong, present, passionate, truth, connected from the womb, unafraid, encompassing, mysterious . . . . Encountering God this way made me reevaluate the notion of God as beyond gender and see God as encompassing both genders—gender-*full* rather than genderless. I look on the growth of spirit and creativity I have experienced as gifts from my daughter Emma and think it is somehow appropriate

that it was she who, through her brief time on earth, introduced me to the Great Mother in God.[44]

The transformational work of Letha and other cofounders of EEWC-CFT has guided this organization to become one of the most inclusive Christian groups, expanding "metaphors for God to include biblical female images," such as the Great Mother, and welcoming *"members of any gender, gender identity, race, ethnicity, color, creed, marital status, sexual orientation, religious affiliation, age, political party, parental status, economic class, or disability."*[45] EEWC-CFT is one of the few Christian organizations including female divine names and images. Even many progressive Christian groups who are inclusive in all other ways still exclude female images of the Divine.

Susan Cottrell founded FreedHearts, a progressive Christian organization that advocates for LGBTQ people, supports their families, and provides resources to help churches be fully inclusive and affirming of them. But until she discovered EEWC-CFT, Susan named and imaged God as exclusively male. "EEWC came during a whirlwind change for me and changed the course of my spiritual life," Susan says.[46] "Through it I discovered the Divine Feminine, wiped out my male pronouns for God—hooray!—and found the spiritual foundation for gender equality. I speak, live, and believe as a feminist more deeply and profoundly than ever before. I am currently in seminary with a beautiful road ahead of LGBTQ advocacy and pastoring that Letha's tireless lifelong work has made possible. Letha changed the course of evangelicalism and thus Christianity in the U.S. For that I am deeply grateful."

In an article in *Christian Feminism Today* titled "Is There Healing for the Church's 'Mother Wound'?" Susan also underscores the power of the Divine Feminine. Susan laments the church's focus on task rather than relationship. The "patriarchal, task-based church" rejects the relational "feminine Holy Spirit" and views LGBTQ persons and other marginalized people as problems to be overcome. "A task-based approach shoves LGBTQ people aside and offers answers like 'reorientation' therapy or celibacy," Susan writes. "This is where the Mother Wound comes in because *task-focus* is the exact opposite of the life and calling of Jesus; it is the opposite

44. Kiser-Lowrance, "God of the Casserole," 2–3.

45. *Christian Feminism Today*, "About Christian Feminism Today," para. 8. (italics original).

46. Susan Cottrell, e-mail interview with coauthor Jann Aldredge-Clanton on December 1, 2015. Unless otherwise noted, all subsequent quotes from Susan Cottrell are from this interview.

of the Holy Spirit, the feminine helper Jesus sent to lead us in all truth and provide the nurturance we long for."[47]

EEWC-CFT's Director of Public Information, Lē Weaver, also affirms the healing power of the Female Divine. Lē writes a blog called *Where She Is* as part of the *Christian Feminism Today* website. Lē refers to the Divine Presence using feminine pronouns, explaining that "She" moves beyond the traditional, exclusively male Deity to deepen spiritual experience and bring healing. "The more I talked about Her, the more present She became in my life, the more intimate my experience of the Divine became. I started to understand that my lingering feelings of brokenness were being healed by this new tender and loving Deity who felt like soft folds of skin and moved through me like grace."[48]

Lē celebrates the groundbreaking work of Letha that brought healing by challenging patriarchy, advocating gender equality, and beginning a revolution in the late sixties and early seventies. Letha was one of the first evangelical Christian writers who saw not only how the big problem of sexism was weakening the church and was counter to the liberating message of Jesus, but also the ways it was hurting all people, not just women. "Letha could coauthor a book like *All We're Meant to Be* and make it resonate so deeply with the individual people reading it, making it so important, so reasonable, that it was hard to notice the thesis of the book was basically inciting a revolution, that of tearing down one of the main pillars of institutional Christianity, namely, patriarchy and the subordination of women," Lē says.[49] "The impact of *All We're Meant to Be* has been profound. It was a perfectly timed book, written in the perfect way to have the greatest impact on the evangelical Christian community it was written for."

Letha has also been an invaluable mentor for Lē, making her a better writer and social justice advocate. Lē says it's impossible for Letha to just edit a piece and send it back "fixed." Lē often gets an e-mail response in which Letha explains what she corrected and why, often including links to more information. As important, Letha increases Lē's confidence to frame and illuminate subjects. Letha always finds something to compliment, and Lē often thinks, "If Letha Dawson Scanzoni believes I can write, then

47. Cottrell, "Is There Healing," para. 14.

48. Herder, "The Power of an Unexpected Pronoun," para. 15. The author of this article now uses the name Lē Weaver.

49. Lē Weaver, e-mail interview with coauthor Jann Aldredge-Clanton on November 29, 2015. Unless otherwise noted, all subsequent quotes from Lē Weaver are from this interview.

maybe I can! I guess it wouldn't be too far-fetched to say it's because of her I am now able to think of myself *as* a writer." But there's something more important that Letha has been teaching Lē. "I think what matters most to Letha is to help me learn how to be the best social justice advocate I can be. The writing is just the surface of that. What matters most to her, and what she spends time trying to help me to understand, is the importance of what lies underneath and is intertwined with my words."

Because Letha knows the importance of words and of what lies underneath words, her writing and social justice activism continue to be life-changing. She understands the power of naming females in the image of the Divine and naming the Divine as female. Acknowledging her transforming work, *Christianity Today* ranked *All We're Meant to Be* number 23 on the list of the top fifty books that have shaped evangelicals.[50] In this chapter we have brought to light representative stories of the countless lives Letha has shaped through her writing, mentoring, supportive friendships, and leadership of EEWC-CFT. Through her egalitarian, collaborative ways of relating and working, she builds bridges for people to become all we're meant to be in the divine image.

Resources for Church Groups

This chapter includes narratives of people who experienced transformation through Letha's writing. Reflect on transformational experiences in your life.

» What influenced you to make a change in your life? Did a book or books contribute to this change? Did a person or persons influence you? Identify other influences.

» Think about the process you went through in making this change.

» Write or share with the group your story of transformation.

In her books Letha demonstrates that the Bible teaches the equality of females and males based on the divine image including female and male (Gen 1:27). She gives biblical support for gender equality in church, home, and society.

» What messages have you received about females and males?

50. *Christianity Today*, "The Top 50 Books," 51.

» Use online or print Bible reference sources to find passages that illustrate Jesus's teachings on gender equality.

» Use reference sources to find other biblical passages that teach gender equality.

Bible Reading: Prov 1:20–23, 3:13–18, 4:5–9

This passage names God "Wisdom" and refers to Her as female.

» Use reference sources to make a list of other female and nongendered names of God in the Bible (e.g. *Shaddai*, Mother Eagle, Rock, Light)

» Study together *The Divine Feminine, Inclusive Language in the Church*, or both.

» How did you picture God when you were a child? What influenced this picture?

» How do you picture God now? What influences this picture?

» Many of the narratives in this chapter reveal the transforming power of including female names and images of God. Think about how you name and picture God and about how these names and pictures relate to your experience with God.

Implementing New Ideas

» Try expanding your language for God in your personal prayers, small groups, and church worship services.

» What difference does this make in your experience with God? What difference does this make in the church?

5

Welcoming All

"The question that makes up the title of this book shouldn't be necessary,"[1] Letha Dawson Scanzoni and Virginia Ramey Mollenkott write at the beginning of *Is the Homosexual My Neighbor?* Sadly, this question is still necessary today. In the second edition, revised and updated, they elaborate.

> The question shouldn't be necessary because Jesus made it clear that every person is our neighbor. And the Bible likewise makes clear our responsibility to our neighbor: "You shall love your neighbor as yourself." Yet, all too often, the Bible is brandished as a weapon to clobber gay and lesbian people. Claiming to be doing the will and work of God, some Christians are hurting their neighbors, bearing false witness against them, and assaulting their dignity and sense of self-worth.[2]

The authors state that their purpose in writing both editions of *Is the Homosexual My Neighbor?* is to alleviate "such hurtfulness (which harms us all)."[3]

Is the Homosexual My Neighbor? not only has alleviated pain but also has saved lives. This book with its biblical, scientific, and psychological research has been a balm for LGBTQ people, who have been stigmatized, ostracized, excluded, and persecuted by Christian communities. Many

1. Scanzoni and Mollenkott, *Is the Homosexual My Neighbor?* (1978), ix.
2. Ibid., iv.
3. Ibid.

LGBTQ people have been victims of hate crimes, and many have committed suicide when their agony became unbearable. An Episcopal priest remarked, "This book quite literally saved my life."

Letha and Virginia had the courage and compassion to write one of the first books by Christians that takes a positive stand on homosexuality. The book sparked controversy in their evangelical community, as well as among Catholics and in mainline Protestant denominations. It also brought awareness of the damage done by misinterpretation and misuse of biblical passages to condemn homosexuality, and proved healing for people longing for loving acceptance by church and society. Richard Woods, OP, in a review in *Library Journal* praised the book. "Working from a solid basis in Christian ethics, scripture, and recent psychosocial research, Scanzoni and Mollenkott present a compassionate, persuasive case for a fundamental shift in Christian attitudes and practice."[4]

Through *Is the Homosexual My Neighbor?* as well as her other writing and advocacy, Letha continues to build bridges between LGBTQ and heterosexual people, between evangelicals and other Christians. Her ministry of welcoming all continues to bring good news indeed to countless people.

A Liberating Collaboration

In the preface to the second edition of *Is the Homosexual My Neighbor?* Letha and Virginia tell the story behind the book. For many years they had appreciated each other's work and sensed a kinship. After meeting in 1973 at Denver Theological Seminary where they both spoke at a symposium on women and the church, they began to discuss collaborating on an ethics book. They agreed that Letha would write the chapter on homosexuality because she had already written a book on sex education and a college sociology textbook, and because she lived near the Kinsey Institute at Indiana University, where she had access to the latest human sexuality research. It wasn't until August 1975, well after they were at work on their project that Virginia traveled to Letha's home. There Virginia shared with Letha that "she herself was a lesbian Christian and had been aware of her homosexual orientation since her earliest memories."[5] In the preface the authors also discuss their respective reactions to this disclosure, and they include correspondence showing how they worked through their mixed feelings and

4. Woods, "Is the Homosexual My Neighbor? (book review)," 985.

5. Scanzoni and Mollenkott, *Is the Homosexual My Neighbor?* (1994), vii.

learned from each other. As Letha moved ahead with her chapter, it grew so long that Virginia called her to say, "You don't have a chapter here; we have a book!"[6] So they put aside the general ethics book project to write *Is the Homosexual My Neighbor?*

Recently Virginia commented on why they included in the preface this exchange. "It was Letha's idea to include the whole backstory of my visit to her home to tell her that she would be publishing a book with a lesbian. I had told her because I felt it was not fair to Letha if I should leave her thinking I was, like herself, simply arguing for justice, rather than standing up for my own sexual orientation and those who shared it. We had worked our way through the whole long correspondence over her going pale and what it meant to each of us."[7] Years later, when they heard that Harper wanted a new edition, Letha was sure people would be interested in every detail of that correspondence, but Virginia wasn't so sure. Virginia now acknowledges that Letha was right. "We got more positive commentary on that section than on anything else in the entire revision!" When Virginia reread it recently, she was surprised to be reminded of her own feelings at the time. "Years of public activism have made me secure about my identity, but it was important to be reminded that many Christian LGBT people are still at the relatively insecure stage I was in back in 1978." Virginia also credits Letha for the title *Is the Homosexual My Neighbor?* "Letha had come up with the title that made many antigay Christians angry because it tweaked their guilt over their judgmentalism."

Even before they met and collaborated on *Is the Homosexual My Neighbor?*, Virginia and Letha had formed a supportive friendship. Through correspondence they had been encouraging each other's feminist work. Virginia recalls their first meeting at the Denver Theological Seminary conference on women and the church. "At that conference, where the more conservative women attacked my presentations in ways that reflected their disapproval of my gender presentation—they even objected to my wearing floor-length skirts and would have blown up had I dared to wear the pants I would have preferred—Letha was always right there with comforting and encouraging words."

---

6. Ibid., xiii.

7. Virginia Ramey Mollenkott, e-mail interview with coauthor Jann Aldredge-Clanton on October 26 and November 1, 2015. Unless otherwise noted, all subsequent quotes from Virginia Ramey Mollenkott are from this interview.

At the 1975 EWC national conference during a packed workshop on homosexuality that Virginia led with Nancy Hardesty, Letha again gave Virginia much-needed support. During the time for Q&A, some tried to force Virginia to admit her lesbian orientation, but Letha ran interference for her and thus made it possible for her to keep her sexuality private until she got the "inner go ahead" that it was time to take a public stance. "I had not yet fully understood that as a Christian lesbian I was living in occupied territory and therefore had to engage in subversion," Virginia says, "so I needed the confidence that Letha's support inspired in me."

Virginia also appreciates Letha's affirmation of her work. "At a time when my work had become too radical for *Christianity Today* and was becoming too radical even for *Christian Century*—when I was effectively silenced by simply ignoring (not reviewing) my work—Letha Scanzoni amazed and encouraged me by writing an article about my life and work for the encyclopedia *American Women Writers: A Critical Reference Guide from Colonial Times to the Present.*" In this article Letha commends Virginia as "an important literary scholar, an articulate Christian humanist, and an influential evangelical feminist."[8] Letha describes Virginia's writings on English literature, religion, education, feminism, and social justice:

> All of her writings may be subsumed under the theme of oneness
> ... The emphasis is on seeing God in all things and serving God
> in all activities, integration of the human personality around a
> unifying center, and awareness of humanity's interdependence ...
> Equality, compassion, social justice, oneness—all are viewed by
> Mollenkott as grounded in redemptive grace.[9]

Letha inspired Virginia to preserve her work for history. Letha's praise for Virginia's vision came at just the right time to encourage her to collect her papers for the archives at the Pacific School of Religion. Virginia had long believed the principle that history is the record of those who made the effort to preserve their documents, but Letha's example made this principle come alive for Virginia and pushed her into action. "In fact, her example helped me to overcome my feeling that my work was probably not significant enough to deserve preservation. Anyone who has seen Letha's humongous boxes of EEWC-related documents will realize that she has always been determined to supply historians with the resources necessary to get our story right. Moreover, Letha is able to find the documents she

8. Scanzoni, "Virginia Ramey Mollenkott," 204.

9. Ibid.

has saved, and can write about them in a clear and accessible style. For that reason, Letha Dawson Scanzoni is the lifeblood of EEWC's reputation."

In EEWC-CFT Virginia has found her "greatest ongoing experience of community." In *Transforming the Faiths of Our Fathers*, she writes:

> Through the sisterhood of these great women and men and various transgenderists, all of whom are warmly welcomed, I have come into myself by joining with others in a way that could not have occurred without such a nurturing context . . . From the beginning, EWC affirmed my gifts. But after Letha Dawson Scanzoni and I coauthored *Is the Homosexual My Neighbor?* and began to lead workshops on the topic, some members of EWC made a point of shunning me, or tried to undermine my authority by asking intrusive questions about my sexuality before I was ready to emerge from the closet. Eleven years into the life of the organization, I was wondering whether I should withdraw my time and energy from a group that would not defend my civil and human rights. Finally, at the Fresno conference in 1986, the Evangelical Women's Caucus passed a resolution in support of those rights. At that time we lost at least half of our membership, who then proceeded to found an organization for heterosexual feminists only.[10]

Responding to Pamela Cochran's account of EWC's loss of members and the forming of Christians for Biblical Equality (CBE) in *Evangelical Feminism: A History*, Virginia sets the record straight. She objects to Pamela's characterization of CBE as the "more traditionalist evangelical feminists" who held true to biblical inerrancy while EWC shifted emphasis to biblical interpretation. "When Pamela Cochran speaks of a 'shift from inerrancy to hermeneutics,' she is writing nonsense. Whether or not one believes in inerrancy, and whether or not one acknowledges any particular hermeneutic strategy, *everybody* interprets what they read." Virginia continues her challenge. "Although Cochran claims that I have 'switched' to liberationist hermeneutics, I see my progression as based on a gradually deepening grasp of what the Bible is all about." Virginia calls out the "doublespeak" in Cochran's discussion of religious authority. Cochran's "major contrast between EEWC and CBE is based on EEWC's 'pluralism' and CBE's greater adherence to 'exclusive truth claims' and 'transcendent authority' . . . The only solid distinction Cochran makes is that EEWC welcomes lesbian, gay, bisexual, and transgender people, whereas CBE does not."[11]

10. Mollenkott, *Transforming the Faiths*, 69–70.

11. Mollenkott, "Cochran's Evangelical Feminism," 3–4.

In Virginia's presentation at the 2002 national EEWC conference when she mentioned that she considered herself a "transgender lesbian," she got a "feminist and genuinely human and loving" response. Conferees wanted to understand more about what it means to be transgender, and after the presentation they lined up to buy copies of her book *Omnigender*. Virginia describes this experience as "the most joyous" she has ever had of "unconditional love" apart from the love of her partner, Suzannah Tilton, and "God Herself."[12]

Life-giving Love

Among the people who have experienced unconditional love and life-giving power through the work of Virginia and Letha is Jim Lucas, currently an ordained minister who serves as a chaplain for Gays in Faith Together (GIFT), Spectrum Health, and First United Methodist Church in Grand Rapids, Michigan. In 1978, soon after the publication of the first edition of *Is the Homosexual My Neighbor?*, Jim learned about the book. At that time he was a senior in the preseminary program at Calvin College in Grand Rapids. A sincere Christian, Jim was also an *A* student preparing for ordained ministry. From all outward appearances he was considered to be a "model Christian young man."[13]

During this time, however, Jim was experiencing a deep inner struggle. Soon after beginning at Calvin College, he had become honest with himself about his sexual identity. At the time, he believed being gay was the worst thing he could be because that is the message he had learned from his culture. "I thought that there was only one way to look at being gay—that the feelings of same-sex attraction were sick and disgusting, a kind of disability or mental illness, and that any same-sex relationships would be sinful. I had never heard any other approach, and the thought never occurred to me that there could be another Christian approach." Jim's life was dominated by feelings of shame, anxiety, and depression. Then he saw posters around campus for a lecture by Virginia Ramey Mollenkott titled "Homosexuality, Homophobia, and Healing." Jim seized this opportunity to hear Virginia talk about the book that she and Letha had just coauthored.

12. Mollenkott, *Transforming the Faiths*, 71.

13. Jim Lucas, e-mail interview with author Jann Aldredge-Clanton on November 4, 2015. All subsequent quotes from Jim Lucas are from this interview.

Shortly after Virginia's lecture, Jim read *Is the Homosexual My Neighbor?* It was the first time that he had heard or read anything remotely compassionate about LGBTQ people. He learned that homosexuality had been taken off the DSM's list of mental disorders five years earlier, and for the first time learned of the many famous LGBTQ people in history. And most significant, for the first time he learned about devout Christian scholars who believed that the Christian community had misinterpreted the Bible on homosexuality. Too, there were even Christian scholars who believed that the church should bless faithful, loving, committed same-sex life partnerships. At the time few if any were imagining same-sex marriage. Jim remembers feeling "thunderstruck." He began thinking, "Maybe I don't have to hate myself. Maybe God loves me the way I am." Jim says because he is a "cautious person," he did not fully accept this message right away. "But as I studied the book, I found its message was profoundly life-giving. It gave me hope. So I was powerfully drawn to it."

Jim goes on to relate his journey of the next few years as he became fully convinced of the message of *Is the Homosexual My Neighbor?* and came to peace with himself. Since then Jim has read most of the other books by Christian scholars encouraging the Christian community to fully affirm LGBTQ people. But he celebrates the special part *Is the Homosexual My Neighbor?* has played in his life and vocation. "It was the very first book I read that articulated a new approach, one that brought me emotional and spiritual healing." That emotional and spiritual healing made it possible for Jim to complete a bachelor's degree at Calvin College and a Master of Divinity degree from Calvin Seminary. Jim also acknowledges that the healing he experienced through this book made it possible for him to become an ordained minister and serve a congregation at the start of his professional career, and later to begin with many others a new ministry in the early 1990s. Through that ministry, which is now Gays In Faith Together (GIFT), he has been providing pastoral care and advocacy for lesbian, gay, bisexual, and transgender people for more than twenty years. "Thanks to the healing message of *Is the Homosexual My Neighbor?* and the many books that followed it, I have been able to offer a message of hope to hundreds of LGBT Christians—a message that yes, you can be gay and Christian."

Although Jim has never met Letha, two books she coauthored have had a "profound impact" on his life, Jim says. Those books are *Is the Homosexual My Neighbor?* and *What God Has Joined Together: A Christian Case for Gay Marriage.* Now in his various ministries Jim provides resources in answer to questions raised by LGBTQ Christians. Currently many of these questions center on same-sex marriage, and he most often recommends the book that Letha coauthored with David G. Myers, *What God Has Joined Together.* "The book addresses the key questions that people most frequently ask on the subject," Jim says. "And it does so in a way that employs careful, responsible scholarship in a very readable style. There simply isn't another book that does such a good job addressing the psychological, social, biblical, and theological questions related to marriage for gay couples. I deeply appreciate the writings of Letha Dawson Scanzoni on being gay and Christian. I know that she has helped to bring life and healing to many people, including me!"

Letha's writing has also brought life and healing to Elizabeth Kaeton, an Episcopal priest who has served as a three-time elected deputy to the Episcopal Church General Convention and currently serves as a hospice chaplain, pastoral counselor, and assistant priest at her local parish in Rehoboth Bay, Delaware. She tells the story of how *Is the Homosexual My Neighbor?* "quite literally saved [her] life."[14] In 1976, two years before the publication of the first edition of this book, Elizabeth came out when she fell in love with her best friend, Barbara, now her spouse. "It was so different then than it is now. I still can't believe that we have marriage equality because in 1976 the only lesbians I knew were in medical texts. And they were described as deviants and psychologically ill. I saw them in my nursing texts with 'cures' like prefrontal lobotomies, electric shock therapy, and cold therapy (wrapping them in ice to 'cure' them). Pictures of women dressed as men illustrated what a lesbian was. I didn't know personally any woman who was a lesbian."

Elizabeth grew up in the Roman Catholic Church, where she learned that homosexuality was evil. She went to daily mass with her grandmother, and the Roman Catholic Church became an integral part of her identity. "It was devastating to have part of my identity tell me that I was evil. This is why I say that *Is the Homosexual My Neighbor?* saved my life."

Growing up in a "very sheltered" Portuguese immigrant community in Fall River, Massachusetts, Elizabeth recalls the negative messages she received, including when the nuns taught her that "sex is disgusting; save it for someone you love." Her mother talked about sex as a woman's duty to her husband. Her grandmother married when she was sixteen and had

14. Elizabeth Kaeton, phone interview with coauthor Jann Aldredge-Clanton on February 9, 2016. All subsequent quotes from Elizabeth Kaeton are from this interview.

twenty-two children, fifteen of whom lived to be adults. She told Elizabeth that it took her the first two or three pregnancies to "figure out the connection between what her husband 'did' to her and the fact that she got pregnant." Elizabeth says that all these messages made it even more difficult for her to realize her lesbian identity. "This was just beyond anything that I could have imagined being possible. Any feeling that I had for women was quickly squashed down because I surely didn't want to be a deviant. And so I had all of these feelings and dread. Coming to understand myself as what was called 'homosexual' in that day, and then later 'lesbian,' was just fraught with all sorts of bad, really bad things."

When Elizabeth realized she was in love with Barbara, she began to question the teachings of her church and family. "This love for Barbara was good and wonderful and healthy and me," Elizabeth says. "When I looked into her eyes and saw a reflection of myself that I knew was in there but I didn't dare dream was that good, I knew that all of that other stuff was really wrong; it was just wrong. I looked around for anything, a life rope that I could hold onto."

The lifeline came to Elizabeth through three books: *Is the Homosexual My Neighbor?*, John J. McNeill's *The Church and the Homosexual*, and John E. Fortunato's *Embracing the Exile*. She had been "horribly distraught" over the conflict between her feelings for Barbara and the church's teachings on homosexuality. She experienced her relationship with Barbara as wonderful, but the church and culture were telling her that "it was forbidden and evil" and that she "was going to go to hell."

The first book Elizabeth read was *Is the Homosexual My Neighbor?* It was hard for her to believe that the book came from Letha, whom she knew to be evangelical and heterosexual. "Holy moly! How could that be?" Later Elizabeth learned that Letha's coauthor, Virginia Ramey Mollenkott, was lesbian. "Virginia was saying in front of God and everybody that she was a lesbian. Holy moly! She sure sounded healthy to me." Elizabeth recalls that she couldn't get through more than four or five pages without putting the book down and sobbing for joy and relief, and saying, "I'm going to be okay; I'm going to be okay. This is good; this is not evil." Elizabeth says her world "turned right side up" as she read *Is the Homosexual My Neighbor?* "It did change my worldview. It did change my perspective. I appreciated Letha's honest questioning. Her voice was one that carried some of the honest, intelligent questioning of a heterosexual without being pejorative or put down or judgmental. This book was a gift, just a gift. It saved my life."

When Elizabeth came out, her entire family abandoned her and remained alienated for the next ten years. Although she reached a "sort of reconciliation" with her parents before they died, she is still estranged from her siblings and her cousins. "I was literally dead to people in my family, worse than dead because nobody talked about me," Elizabeth says. "That was devastating. I was completely cut off."

Adding to her struggle at the time she came out, Elizabeth lost custody of her two children. She was in and out of court for five years before she got them back from her former husband. During this time her friends Clair Barden and Lois Johnson, who founded the Daughters of Bilitis[15] in Boston, had given her a copy of *Is the Homosexual My Neighbor?* and said, "You have to read this." Elizabeth notes that the Daughters of Bilitis had a newsletter, and *Lesbian Nation* had just come out. "All of that was just fine. But there was nothing that spoke to my spirit and my religion until I read *Is the Homosexual My Neighbor?*" Then she read John McNeill's book, and thought, "Are you kidding me? A Jesuit?" She explains how "huge" it was to her that leaders in organized religion were taking a "positive stand on the children of God who were gay and lesbian."[16] That changed her whole perspective on life and world and possibility. "This was a gift of hope! I would not be alive. I don't know how else I could have gotten through coming out as lesbian and being the first open lesbian custody case in Bristol County, Massachusetts."

Elizabeth celebrates the progress LGBTQ people have made. Throughout her thirty years of ministry hers has been among the prophetic voices for change. Her activism began with advocating for people with AIDS and continued as she served on the board of Integrity USA[17] and the New Commandment Task Force,[18] became a founding member of

---

15. The Daughters of Bilitis (DOB) was the first lesbian civil and political rights organization in the United States.

16. Elizabeth further comments that all they "identified at the time were gays and lesbians and later expanded to LGBTQ."

17. For more than four decades Integrity USA has been working for the full equality of LGBTQ persons in every part of the Episcopal Church.

18. Formed in 2000, the New Commandment Task Force has focused on promoting reconciliation within the Episcopal Church over disagreements related to LGBTQ issues.

Claiming the Blessing,[19] served for six years as the national convener of the Episcopal Women's Caucus,[20] and advocated for marriage equality.

Straight allies have made progress possible for the LGBTQ community, Elizabeth believes. "While there are many lesbian, gay, bisexual, and transgender saints in the church, I grow more and more convinced that this would not have happened if it were not for straight people like Letha who took a stand, took a risk and stood in solidarity with us and said to the church, 'This woman is my neighbor, and Jesus said love your neighbor and that's what I'm doing.'" Elizabeth hopes that people who read about Letha will understand what a huge risk she took without counting the cost, and as we move forward and continue to work on discrimination at all levels, "that allies, meaning straight people for LGBTQ people, meaning white people for people of color, meaning cisgender[21] people for trans people, will take risks because when that happens, then the revolution begins." Elizabeth explains that the revolution would not have happened without people like Letha taking risks for her faith, living out her faith, taking a stand. "It would still just be LGBTQ people saying, 'What about Jesus and what about us and what about the Bible.' But someone like Letha saying this made all the difference. I hope that this kind of work continues because that's what the church is supposed to be about."

Courageous Justice Advocates

Like Letha, Peggy Campolo is a heterosexual ally who has taken strong stands for LGBTQ people. *Is the Homosexual My Neighbor?* inspired Peggy and gave her courage to become one of the most powerful LGBTQ advocates, even for many years in opposition to her husband, Tony, a well-known evangelical author and sociology professor. "The book that Letha wrote with Virginia was one of the things that gave me courage to speak

19. Claiming the Blessing is an intentional collaborative of organizations and individuals within the Episcopal Church advocating for full inclusion of all the baptized in all sacraments of the church—including the blessing of same-sex relationships and equal access to all orders of ministry by qualified gay, lesbian, bisexual, and transgender candidates.

20. The Episcopal Women's Caucus is a justice organization dedicated to the gospel values of equality and liberation, and committed to the incarnation of God's unconditional love.

21. *Cisgender* is a term used for people whose gender identity corresponds with the sex they were identified as having at birth.

out against the grave injustices being done by the church to homosexual people," Peggy says.[22] "I am not the only one to be inspired by Letha's brave stand as a heterosexual advocate. Letha caught my attention when she seemed to risk everything and lost much to take a stand for those children of God who happen not to be straight."

God had also put "gay brothers and lesbian sisters" on her heart, Peggy says, but not until she read *Is the Homosexual My Neighbor?* did she take action. Peggy became a frequent pro-LGBTQ speaker to church and campus groups around the country, often serving on panels with her husband, who took an opposing view. In addition, she played a part in founding the welcoming and affirming Open Door Community Church in Little Rock, Arkansas. People in this church refer to Peggy as the patron saint, because she was "the inspiring force behind the creation of Open Door Community Church."[23] As a writer and editor, she has also advocated for the LGBTQ community, contributing to books such as *Homosexuality and Christian Faith: Questions of Conscience for the Churches*, edited by Walter Wink, and *Reasoning Together: A Conversation on Homosexuality*, by Ted Grimsrud and Mark Thiessen Nation.

Peggy worked as an advocate "for those children of God who do not happen to be straight" for twenty-five years before she met Letha. "Letha had been one of my heroes ever since she and Virginia Mollenkott wrote the groundbreaking book, *Is the Homosexual My Neighbor?*," Peggy recalls. "I knew that Letha, a notable sociologist, had used her discipline and her communication gifts to be a leader in the evangelical feminist movement, blazing a trail that many others followed. However, I was never part of the early feminist movement." The passion Peggy and Letha have shared is justice for the LGBTQ community, especially in the church.

In 2011 Peggy presented an award to Letha for her lifetime support of the LGBTQ community. This was the first time they met. Peggy felt "deeply honored" to present Letha with the Peggy Campolo Carrier Pigeon Award, given annually by Open Door Community Church "to a straight supporter of the LGBTQ community in the church of Jesus Christ." This award is named for Peggy to honor her highly visible advocacy work for LGBTQ people and to honor the work of someone every year who exemplifies her ideals of inclusiveness and equality. Peggy further explains the title of the

22. Peggy Campolo e-mail interview with coauthor Jann Aldredge-Clanton on December 17, 2015. All subsequent quotes from Peggy Campolo are from this interview.

23. "Peggy Campolo Carrier Pigeon Award Recipients 2007–Present," para. 1.

award: "It bears that rather strange name because of a statement I made years ago about being privileged to be a 'carrier pigeon with a message from the misunderstood to the misinformed." Letha, like Peggy, has been for many years carrying the liberating message of loving acceptance and inclusion. Peggy loved seeing how many members of the congregation and guests were "absolutely thrilled" to meet Letha, "a legend to them as well as to many others." The church's website includes recipients of the Peggy Campolo Carrier Pigeon Award; under Letha's picture is a paragraph citing some of her many contributions, including coauthoring *Is the Homosexual My Neighbor?* and *What God Has Joined Together.*[24]

Is the Homosexual My Neighbor? transformed the life of Jeff Lutes, a licensed professional counselor. Jeff is the former executive director of Soulforce[25] and the founder of the annual Contemporary Relationships Conference.[26] Jeff begins his story: "Letha Dawson Scanzoni made me break one of the Ten Commandments. To be honest, she didn't even know me. Yet, I was compelled by her work to commit a crime that altered the trajectory of my life for the better."[27]

Jeff grew up in a prominent Southern Baptist church in central Kentucky. With his family he attended worship services twice on Sunday and every Wednesday night. His mother was a Sunday school teacher, and his father a deacon. Jeff gave his testimony every Youth Sunday, actively participated in a missions organization for boys called Royal Ambassadors, and sang in a traveling music group called the Jesus Kids.

In his conservative religious and social circle, Jeff never heard the words "gay" or "homosexual." Yet he says he knew "the love that dare not speak its name" was considered "too evil and sinful" to mention. So like many gay Christian young people, Jeff kept his sexual orientation hidden as it began to emerge in his teens. By the time he began undergraduate studies in psychology at the University of Kentucky, he was "struggling terribly" to reconcile his faith and sexuality.

In the early 1980s, when Jeff was completing his psychology practicum requirement by working at a small community mental health center, he saw

24. Ibid., para. 17.

25. Soulforce is an activist organization for ending the political and religious oppression of LGBTQ people.

26. This conference brings together people from around the country to explore dating, relationships, and parenting within the LGBTQ community.

27. Jeff Lutes e-mail interview with coauthor Jann Aldredge-Clanton on May 17, 2016. All subsequent quotes from Jeff Lutes are from this interview.

Is the Homosexual My Neighbor? in his supervisor's office. "At one of our meetings my supervisor got called away to handle a crisis and asked that I wait for him," Jeff recalls. "As I sat in silence, my eyes caught a little green book poking out among hundreds on the shelves behind his desk. I began to ponder how I might ask to borrow *Is The Homosexual My Neighbor?* I grew anxious, fearing that such a request would out me as a gay man when I was not yet ready to be honest with others." Impulsively, Jeff decided to snatch the book, read it cover to cover that night, and replace it the following day before anyone discovered it missing. But he was never able to find or create a circumstance that would allow him to return the book unnoticed.

Now Jeff treasures his stolen copy of the first edition of *Is the Homosexual My Neighbor?* More than thirty years later, that same worn and tattered book sits on the shelf in his office in Austin, Texas, where he practices as a licensed professional counselor. "I protect it like Indiana Jones might guard the ark of the covenant," Jeff quips. "It's a treasure with scholarly and pastoral words that helped heal a young man decades ago." Now it helps heal his LGBTQ clients. They borrow it often, with full permission.

Jeff gives Letha credit for her contribution to the rewarding life he now enjoys. "In no small part because of Letha Dawson Scanzoni, I've been able to express my sexuality in ways that are loving and life-affirming. I met my husband in 1997 and we have three adopted children. Life is good and I know that God loves me without reservation. There will be no hurdle for me at the pearly gates. Assuming that is, that I can atone for that one act of unrepentant larceny!"

A year after the first edition of *Is the Homosexual My Neighbor?* came out, Letha spoke at a convocation at Perkins School of Theology on the topic of homosexuality. Schubert M. Ogden, at that time a theology professor at Perkins, had recommended Letha as featured speaker for this convocation, held on the morning of November 28, 1979. That evening Letha joined several other Perkins professors on a panel to discuss the topic.

After the evening meeting Schubert stayed to talk with Letha about her presentations, telling her that he and others liked her scholarly approach and the way she answered questions from the audience. The spirit of her approach, he said, "disarmed those who came to oppose her position."[28] Schubert summarized and affirmed Letha's main points: "Recognizing that

28. Schubert M. Ogden e-mail interview with author Jann Aldredge-Clanton on February 23 and 24, 2016. Unless otherwise noted, all subsequent quotes from Schubert M. Ogden are from this interview.

although we don't understand everything about homosexuality, homosexual persons are in the image of God no less than anyone else, and it is
this ethic of neighbor love upon which the church must act responsibly
toward homosexual persons." Every time someone in the audience opened
the door for Letha to in some way move away from this emphasis on homosexual personhood, Letha slammed it shut immediately, Schubert said.
"Letha's approach was just the right one for laying groundwork for the
church to deal creatively with this issue. This was a historic day for Perkins
that opened a new day of dialogue and dealing with a subject previously
feared."

A few months later, in February of 1980, Schubert published an article
titled "The Church and Homosexual Persons: The Issue of Ordination" in
the *Perkins Newsletter*. He gives Letha credit for contributing to his prophetic stand on this issue. "Letha did me the service of confirming my own
attempts at understanding by hers and encouraging me to proceed accord-
ingly in something like the way in which I tried to confirm her attempts and
encourage her." In the *Perkins Newsletter* article he raises strong objections
to a "compromise solution" that people in the church at that time put forth:
"to allow that homosexuals can indeed be members of the church, even
while refusing to allow that homosexuals can ever be eligible for ordination
as its representative ministers." He denounces this position.

> In effect, even if not in intention, it allows for two classes of
> Christians: first-class Christians who live up to moral demands
> and, therefore, are qualified to be the church's representative
> ministers and second-class Christians who, failing to live up
> to moral demands, are disqualified from thus representing the
> church, even though they are still qualified to be its members. But
> from the standpoint of the Christian witness of faith, any such
> class division between Christians is intolerable.[29]

After the publication of this article, Schubert continued to speak out
on what he calls the "theologically intolerable contradiction between the
United Methodist Church's crypto-Catholic position on the whole issue
of homosexuality in denying the possibility of ordination to homosexual
persons while conceding their qualification for church attendance and even
church membership."

Mary E. Hunt, cofounder and codirector of Women's Alliance for
Theology, Ethics, and Ritual (WATER), also confirms the profound impact

29. Ogden, "The Church and Homosexual Persons," 7.

of *Is the Homosexual My Neighbor?* "Letha and Virginia's collaboration on *Is the Homosexual My Neighbor?* remains one of the happiest joint projects in the history of theology. Yes, it was gay, but it was also happy in that so many people found so much insight, solace, and motivation in their study that the work had world-shaping impact. It is impossible to imagine the relatively rapid change in consciousness in Christian churches (much more needs to happen, of course) without this volume. When the revised and updated version came out in 1994, and the story of this special collaboration was told, the book only became more important and cherished."[30]

In 1978, shortly after the original edition of *Is the Homosexual My Neighbor?* came out, Mary read the book. At the time she was a doctoral student at the Graduate Theological Union in Berkeley. "How fortunate I was to have this resource, though I admit I did not know the full extent of its power on first reading," she recalls. "I remember looking at the pictures of the authors on the dust jacket and noting how lovely they looked. Little did I know that I would come to know them both and that knowing them would reinforce exponentially my initial sense of their goodness."

As a progressive Catholic, Mary was not well versed in the literature and theopolitical struggles of evangelicals, she says. "We lived in separate worlds then, though we feminists have come to recognize our kinship and parallel struggles in the meantime." Mary notes the publication of *Is the Homosexual My Neighbor?* at around the same time as the publication of *The Church and the Homosexual*, by John McNeill, a Jesuit priest. "The kyriarchal[31] Catholic Church received John McNeill's *The Church and the Homosexual* with about the same enthusiasm that most evangelical leaders mustered for *Is the Homosexual My Neighbor?* Letha and Virginia cited John's pioneering work in the bibliography of their equally prophetic book, linking the projects that have proved so foundational for change. Today, those two books look so tame, so clear and obvious in their arguments, so crystalline in their theoethical commitment to inclusion. But when they debuted, both books were roundly rejected by people who called into

30. Mary E. Hunt e-mail interview with coauthor Jann Aldredge-Clanton on December 10, 2015. Unless otherwise noted, all subsequent quotes from Mary E. Hunt are from this interview.

31. The word "kyriarchal," coined by Elisabeth Schüssler Fiorenza, is derived from the Greek words for "lord" or "master" (*kyrios*) and "to rule or dominate" (*archein*); she uses the word "kyriarchy" to redefine the category of patriarchy in terms of multiple "intersecting structures of domination and subordination, of ruling and oppression" (*Wisdom Ways*, 211).

question the Christian *bona fides* of the authors. It is great that all three authors have lived to see their work accepted, embraced, celebrated for what it was: smart, ahead of the curve, courageous, pastoral, life-saving."

Acknowledging continued resistance to acceptance and inclusion of LGBTQ people, Mary celebrates the changes that have come because of *Is the Homosexual My Neighbor?* "Some people, especially some Christians, persist in their ignorance when it comes to things queer. But much has changed because of *Is the Homosexual My Neighbor?* and the subsequent movements for LGBTIQ equality in society and in religions. Today the words 'evangelical' and 'gay'; 'Christian' and 'lesbian'; 'bi' and 'religious'; 'trans' and 'holy' are no longer mutually exclusive. To the contrary, we have come to be and know our neighbors, and it is good." *Is the Homosexual My Neighbor?* gave Mary a sense of what Letha and Virginia were up against in evangelical circles. Since Catholics did not put so much emphasis on the Bible, Mary had not worried too much about biblical injunctions and clobber texts. She was more familiar with mainline Protestant work through seminary studies both at Harvard and the interdenominational Graduate Theological Union in Berkeley. They tended toward the same conclusions as their evangelical counterparts, but with the "genteel sherry sipping and Germanic footnotes that masked some of the more soul-chilling conclusions."

Thus despite differences in approaches to theology, Mary has felt an affinity with Letha and Virginia. "No wonder I felt a kinship with these evangelical sisters. Our experiences as women in men's churches, indeed as lesbians and allies among closeted colleagues, were enough to bring us together." Mary realized that feminism was about as welcome among evangelicals as it was in her Catholic world. LGBTIQ issues were simply verboten in both circles. "We who insist on both are double trouble. It is a good thing we work hard and are undeterred by challenges!"

In the summer of 1982, Mary met Letha at the Women's Spirit Bonding Conference at Grailville, a retreat center in Loveland, Ohio. That gathering brought together a diverse group: evangelical, liberationist, and pagan feminists of many religious traditions, races, and sexual orientations. At this conference Mary heard Letha speak on "The Great Chain of Being and the Chain of Command." Mary admits that she had been naive about evangelicals and was surprised and amazed by Letha's analysis. "I began to see the larger contours of Letha's project—her feminist vision rooted in Christian faith, her keen look at dominance and submission ideology, her use of women's music and poetry to express best what we meant by the new experiences we were having as we lived into equality, her analysis of the power chains that bind. She concluded, 'The dance goes on. And we can all be part of it, moving with joy and grace and beauty as those who have been unbound.'[32] We have been dancing ever since."

Letha's social justice activism has also inspired Lē Weaver.[33] Oblivious to Letha's work for many years, Lē wishes she had known about it sooner. She believes that *Is the Homosexual My Neighbor?* especially would have made a big difference. Growing up, Lē was very active in a Presbyterian church. Her grandmother, who played piano for Sunday school, and her mother, who worked with the children's choirs, groomed Lē to be a church musician. Lē sang in the choirs and worked with younger children. She says that when she was young, the church was the only place she felt she belonged. Then in her teens, she came out as lesbian to a minister in her church. He told her that he would no longer allow her to work with the children. Slowly Lē realized that her life with the church was over. "When I came out as a lesbian and lost my church in 1979, I lost Christianity, and I lost the entire sense of myself as a spiritual person. How interesting it is to consider what might have been if I had access to a copy of *Is the Homosexual My Neighbor?*, published in 1978. At the time, all I knew was that you couldn't be gay and Christian. Just couldn't. The terms were mutually exclusive. To have held a book in my hands that made the point you could be both, could have been a game-changer."

But at that time it would have been difficult to access *Is the Homosexual My Neighbor?* or any book that would have been helpful, Lē explains. "Things weren't like they are now. I couldn't have gone looking for this book. I wouldn't have known there was anything to look for. It wasn't like you could type 'gay Christian' in a search engine and have millions of references come up. I would have had to go ask a librarian, who might not have even known about the book. At that time, walking in somewhere and basically telling someone else you were gay was still a pretty dangerous thing to do."

Although in 1968 Troy Perry had founded the Metropolitan Community Church, a Christian denomination affirming LGBTQ people, few other Christians took this affirming position in 1978 when Letha and Virginia published *Is the Homosexual My Neighbor?* Lē wonders why Letha and Virginia took risks to write a book advocating such an unpopular

32. Scanzoni, "Great Chain of Being," 55.
33. See ch. 4, p. 110.

position. "What would have made someone think to write a scriptural argument for this position that almost everyone considered deviant and heretical? What allowed them to find the courage to do it, even though they must have known most people would certainly not react favorably? It makes you stop and ask, why? Why do it? Why serve *these* people, why make it their problem, why ask the questions? I figure, though I'm not sure of the timing, that Virginia must have been starting to understand this work was about her own life. But why would Letha do it? That, I think, sheds light on who Letha is."

Letha became a Christian social justice advocate, Lē says, because of her "very compassionate personality" and "lifelong certainty about the truth of Jesus." But Letha has paid a price for her advocacy for LGBTQ people. *Is the Homosexual My Neighbor?* changed Letha's life in "pretty disastrous ways." She went from being seen as the "interesting champion of evangelical women's equality to being the heretic cast out by the celebrities of evangelical culture for endorsing the 'sin' of homosexuality." Letha has never regretted writing *Is the Homosexual My Neighbor?,* even though in many ways it has limited her access to her primary audience, evangelical Christians. "How could this deeply compassionate woman regret writing a book that has literally saved lives?" Lē asks. "While almost all Christians were driving LGBTQ people away from Jesus, away from the message of the gospel, the book that Letha and Virginia wrote was a healing balm for some very tortured Christian souls. For Letha, this is what serving God is all about. Speaking the truth in love, as illuminated by the life and ministry of Jesus Christ. Using the gifts God has given you, whether it's playing the trombone, writing paradigm-changing books, or mentoring the next generations of Christian feminist social justice advocates."

Because *Is the Homosexual My Neighbor?* was so far ahead of its time, it appears to have had less impact on evangelical Christianity than did *All We're Meant to Be,* Lē believes. "Even now, as some people are being lauded for writing basically the same arguments that Virginia and Letha put forth forty years earlier, their prescient work remains almost lost in time. I think, for Letha, it doesn't matter if you are known or forgotten, as long as the work has been done well. She has spent her life creating as Jesus would have it done, with compassionate intent, in service to the Spirit, with loving kindness for all."

Lē has learned from Letha about responding to conservative Christians who hurt her by demonizing LGBTQ people or working hard to keep the gates closed to exclude them. "Keeping us out means we cannot be experienced as people, no better or no worse than other Christians," Lē says. "If we are not visible, if we are kept at a distance, we are seen only in the terms of the 'issue of homosexuality.'" Lē admits that it's easy for her "to demonize and rail against" those who try to keep LGBTQ people invisible. "To see the harm they are causing. To see them causing people like me to turn away from Jesus and God. The wounds inflicted on their children and others in their faith communities in the name of Jesus are unconscionable. It's so easy for me to stop seeing them as people with their own very valid fears, people who are extremely confused about all these jarring societal changes. In my own anger and pain I start lumping them all together, and they stop being people and become the 'issue of Christian homophobia.'"

Lē appreciates Letha's help to become a better social justice advocate by treating even bigoted people as individuals. "When we start lumping other people together, seeing them as 'an issue,' we stop seeing them as human beings. It happens on all sides when we can only see the forest, not the individual trees. Letha is teaching me, kindly, patiently, gently, that the only way you can change a forest is by changing the trees."

In social justice work we cannot start by working on the forest, Lē continues. The forest is just a concept, but the individual trees exist. So we have to start with the trees. Christian homophobia exists only as a concept, but there are real people who are very afraid and confused by LGBTQ people. "It's almost like Letha was born knowing this. She didn't attack Christian patriarchy as others did, because it didn't really exist objectively. It was a subjective construction. So she approached and educated the real people who acted in ways that perpetuated the patriarchal subjugation of women. And in changing the people, she changed the impression most people have of Christian patriarchy. Change the trees and the forest changes with it. This is the great lesson Letha is helping me to understand. And for a social justice advocate, there may be no more important lesson."

Is the Homosexual My Neighbor? led Anne Linstatter[34] to become an advocate for LGBTQ people. When she first read this book in 1978, it answered many questions she had about her close Christian friend and college roommate who had come out as lesbian. "I needed to know if the Bible was as opposed to same-sex unions as it appeared to be," Anne recalls. "I thought that as a Christian lesbian, my friend needed to be celibate, and

34. Formerly Anne Eggebroten; see ch. 4, p. 88.

I had written this to her in a letter. Was I wrong? Could I support her if she found a female life partner?"

Because Letha and Virginia had proved themselves with previous books, Anne says that she trusted them to answer her questions. She had complete trust in Letha and Virginia to do thorough research and present reliable conclusions. Because of the church's misinterpretation of biblical texts related to gender roles, Anne was prepared to consider that, once again, what the Bible actually said and what the church taught might be two different things. Anne cites the chapter headings of *Is the Homosexual My Neighbor?* as revealing the care with which Letha and Virginia approached their topic, as well as Letha's background in sociology: "Who Is My Neighbor?"; "The Risks and Challenges of Moral Growth"; "The Homosexual as Samaritan"; "Stigma and Stereotyping"; "What Does the Bible Say?"; "What Does Science Say?"; "From Homophobia to Understanding"; "The Debate in American Christendom"; "Proposing a Homosexual Christian Ethic." In 1994 the authors issued a revised and updated edition with an added chapter, "The Continuing Challenge," reflecting the many social and church changes since the publication of the first edition.

As Anne read *Is the Homosexual My Neighbor?*, she discovered that the church had indeed misinterpreted biblical texts and misused them to condemn homosexuality. She found the book to be "reasonable, biblical, and compelling." Anne learned since the Bible does not mention a lifelong homosexual orientation, all Christians need to consider science and theology and rethink views on faithful, long-term, same-sex unions. The final chapter of the book, following evangelical theologians Lewis Smedes and Helmut Thielicke, proposes cautious accommodation, rethinking, avoiding placing a stigma on homosexual persons, and being willing to pay the high price of caring for these neighbors as much as we care for ourselves. Anne comments that this chapter seems mild from a contemporary point of view, but that "it caused a firestorm in 1978."

The firestorm spread to EWC, which Letha helped found in 1974. Anne explains the cultural mindset in 1978 and before. At the time some of her friends in EWC "were rumored to be lesbian." Others of her friends were reconsidering their involvement with EWC because of their concern that there might be lesbian members and leaders in the organization. They were asking if EWC could "effectively reach out to evangelical churches with our message of biblical feminism if we were 'tainted,'" and whether or not it was "true as our opponents claimed that 'women's libbers' were mostly lesbians." Letha also acknowledges this charge of opponents.[35] Anne admires Letha for having the courage and compassion to challenge religious and cultural norms by writing a book on homosexuality in light of history, science, and the Bible. "As soon as Letha understood how her lesbian friends and others suffered, she began research for *Is the Homosexual My Neighbor?* People who have less empathy may be more inclined to stick with whatever has been handed down to them as the authoritative church teaching."

Is the Homosexual My Neighbor? transformed Anne's beliefs and actions, beginning with helping to support her friends. "The book enabled me to understand my lesbian college friend better and to support her as she bravely worked out a new life for herself," Anne says. "It also caused me to feel more supportive of the lesbians in EWC, most of them still closeted." At the 1984 EWC conference in Wellesley, Massachusetts, when she heard the announcement of an optional 10:00 p.m. meeting for lesbians and friends, Anne attended and learned how unwelcome many of these members felt. At the next EWC conference in Fresno, California, in 1986, she again attended the lesbians and friends meeting. Because of reading *Is the Homosexual My Neighbor?*, Anne now agreed with them that the organization should allow a vote on a resolution supporting the civil rights of lesbians and gays.[36]

EWC members had voted to table consideration of this resolution at the 1984 conference, and after a poll of the membership the Executive Council had decided to end further resolutions on any political issue except support of the equal rights amendment. "Not content with the Council's decision, however, my lesbian friends wanted to introduce some resolutions at the 1986 conference business meeting," Anne recalls. Wanting to support them in any way she could, Anne introduced the resolution on civil rights for homosexual people, while sitting next to a friend who had read *Is the Homosexual My Neighbor?* and who had not been persuaded to rethink her views. The unexpected motion on this resolution and its passing with a hand count and then standing count "caused much pain" among the 120 members present—all the "divisiveness, discord, and polarization" that the council had tried to avoid. It had been eight years since Anne had first read *Is the Homosexual My Neighbor?* and suddenly some of her friendships were broken, and her "beloved organization was deeply wounded." On the other hand, she became more committed to her lesbian friends, to those

35. Scanzoni, "Back to the Future."

36. See ch. 5, n. 16 (p. 122).

remaining in EWC after many members left, and to the ideals Letha and Virginia articulated in their book.

Like Virginia, Anne takes issue with Pamela Cochran's account in *Evangelical Feminism* of the "disagreement on homosexual issues among biblical feminists" that led to the formation of Christians for Biblical Equality (CBE) in opposition to the progressive stand EWC took in 1986. Anne counters Pamela's assertion that the disagreement stemmed from differing views of scriptural authority and her questioning whether or not EEWC can claim to be within evangelicalism because of the organization's more "flexible" interpretations, mainly on homosexuality.

> If my careful analysis of the Bible leads me to the conclusion that gay and lesbian faithful partnerships are not forbidden, then suddenly I am outside the fence. My commitment to biblical authority, my hermeneutics, and my behavioral norms are suddenly not good enough. It's like becoming a leper overnight. If on top of that I conclude that God is not male and that the use of male language for God is idolatry, my ostracism from the evangelical community is cemented. Never mind that I still love and serve Jesus Christ in the kind of personal relationship typical of the early evangelical and revivalist movement.[37]

In the summer of 1987 Anne spoke at a conference of Evangelicals Concerned, a national network of gay and lesbian evangelical Christians and friends. She brought her six-week-old daughter, wearing a political button with the word "Dykette" to this conference, held on the University of California, Santa Cruz campus. Anne continues to be an open, strong LGBTQ ally. "Recently I discovered that a shy high school friend from the church in which I had been born again had been living with a female partner for twenty years, and I made sure they knew of my support for LGBTQ issues," Anne says. She raised her three daughters to be accepting of LGBTQ people, and they were surprised when they found out that their preacher's-kid cousins were being taught opposite views. Later Anne learned that her sister was a leader in a denomination of conservative Presbyterians, formed after the Presbyterian Church (U.S.A.) in 2011 lifted its ban on noncelibate LGBTQ clergy. Their relationship has been difficult, "navigable" only if they avoid political topics. Anne affirms the profound impact *Is the Homosexual My Neighbor?* has had on her views and choices over the last thirty years. "Some of those choices have resulted in the fulfillment of Jesus's prediction:

---

37. Linstatter (née Eggebroten), "A Personal Reaction," 10.

'Do not think that I have come to bring peace to earth . . . one's foes will be members of one's own household' (Matt 10:34–36)."

Joan Olson, a sociology professor, likewise values the gifts of Letha's writing and actions. Joan expresses gratitude for Letha's willingness to take unpopular public stands for social justice. "Letha, along with Nancy and Virginia, has labored diligently to systematize scholarly evidence support- ing biblical feminism and biblical pro-gay perspectives." Joan believes the Spirit has led her to feel all along what the Christian perspective *ought* to be about these issues, and she has relied on Letha and Nancy and Virginia to do the hard work of researching and publishing the supporting arguments in a scholarly and systematic fashion. "Thus, Letha's incredible dedication and disciplined work ethic have made *my* life so much easier!" Joan has also appreciated being able to refer others to Letha for support. Another gift has been Letha's willingness to be "on the front line, absorbing the criticism and the vicious attacks, and having to face the loneliness of public rejection." Yet, Letha has remained "Christ-like, practicing forgiveness and showing compassionate grace to those same foes." Joan celebrates Letha's influence for good in the world, reaching "far beyond what most of us ever imagine."

Letha has also been a valued personal friend to Joan, who taught so- ciology at Trinity College in Deerfield, Illinois, where Nancy A. Hardesty taught English. Joan's relationship with Letha began through their com- mon friendship with Nancy. Joan and Nancy became friends, sensing their shared outlooks. They both graduated from Wheaton College, Nancy five years before Joan. But they both knew they weren't the "typical" Wheaton graduates, Joan recalls. They were "committed Christians to be sure," but they were also "feminists, had gay friends, and didn't see any problem with that combination of identities."

When Joan left Trinity College to pursue a PhD in sociology at Northwestern University and Nancy left to pursue a PhD in history at the University of Chicago, they remained good friends. "Our friendship continued, since it was based in broader commitments, and not just as co- workers at Trinity," Joan says. "Partly because of our shared interests, but also because of my work in sociology, Nancy thought it would be great if my husband, Mark, and I could meet her friend Letha, along with Letha's husband at the time, John, who was a sociologist at Indiana University." Because Nancy's apartment on the South Side of Chicago was small, and because Mark and Joan were renting a "lovely Chicago-style two-flats," Nancy proposed their home as the perfect place for her to host a party in which Letha and John would be the featured guests. Nancy invited various other people whom she saw as kindred spirits. Joan was excited to meet Letha for the first time at this party.

Later, after moving away from Chicago, Joan and Mark continued their friendship with Letha and formed a professional relationship with her. "Letha wrote important articles for *The Other Side* magazine, where Mark served as editor, when it was progressively addressing the issue of homosexuality," Joan says. "As each of Letha's books and articles were published, we were of course thrilled." Joan and Mark joined EWC shortly after it was formed, and attended a national EWC conference in Saratoga Springs, New York. In the years when Letha served as editor of *EEWC Update*, later called *Christian Feminism Today*, she contacted Joan to contribute to projects that had a "sociological slant."

The first edition of *Is the Homosexual My Neighbor?* came out in 1978, the same year that *The Other Side* devoted a full issue of the magazine to the topic of homosexuality. The magazine's editor, Mark Olson,[38] found out about this book through his correspondence with Letha. "I learned more about the important and influential work that Letha and Virginia Ramey Mollenkott were doing together on Christian responses to those richly gifted individuals to whom God had given a different identity and role." The staff of *The Other Side* had been exploring and debating the subject for about a year. Mark says it was a "tremendous encouragement" to him that Letha and Virginia were also hard at work, "making their own important and unique contribution, one that has brought encouragement and hope and an inclusive, Christ-like embrace to so many individuals and families over the years." Letha and her writing partners "have been courageous, groundbreaking channels through which God's Spirit has done marvelous things."

For her brave work Letha has paid a price in the form of hate mail, personal rejection, wall building, and scornful dismissals from the circles in which she formerly moved, Mark says. "Of course, when a person is as courageous as Letha, as willing as Letha to break new ground, as willing as Letha to speak hope and live hope in a world that prefers to practice self-serving arrogance and cruel exclusion, that person almost always pays a price."

Mark notes that Letha, Nancy, and Virginia grew up in churches and religious institutions that called themselves evangelical or fundamentalist. In those contexts they learned the transforming power of Scripture, the

38. See ch. 4, p. 97.

power of divine love, and the power of remaining true to their convictions even in the face of human rejection. Virginia confirms that her conservative background provided valuable gifts. "Although many right-wing Christians despise what I have done with the keys they put into my hands, the fact is that the same Bible that deeply oppressed me has also been the most vital element in setting me free. It is not an overstatement to claim that I have been radicalized by the Bible."[39]

In time, Letha, Virginia, and Nancy found themselves pushed out from the churches and communities who had nurtured them. "But it was their encounters with God's own self in those churches and communities that initially set them on the path to a liberating faith that wouldn't take chains for an answer," Mark says. He compares their experience to that of enslaved people in the early years of our country, who were transformed by their encounters with the God of their owners. Because the slaves experienced the "true heart of their owners' faith, a heart that the owners themselves no longer understood, these enslaved people of color were set on a liberating path that alarmed and disturbed" those who had first taught them the gospel.

"Something similar happened for people like Letha. How sad for those well-meaning individuals who, unlike Letha, have chosen to keep their faith as tiny as a mustard seed! With eyes closed and hearts shut, they stubbornly insist on being 'left behind' as God's Spirit swoops and soars over deep waters, snapping chains and opening doors, bringing together as a new creation the scattered and beleaguered children of God." Mark expresses gratitude for Letha, "who has not only chosen to grow and flower but also chosen to skillfully mother others in the same growth, in the same flowering, in the same liberating response to God's enduring call."

The preface to the second edition of Is the Homosexual My Neighbor? concludes: "We send forth this edition of Is the Homosexual My Neighbor? as we sent forth the earlier edition, with the prayer that hearts and minds will be open to new ways of seeing, understanding, and caring in a world that is all to often characterized by neighbor-against-neighbor instead of loving our neighbor as ourselves."[40] Letha and Virginia have experienced the reward of witnessing answers to this prayer. At considerable personal and professional cost, they wrote this book because their love of all neighbors

39. Mollenkott, *Transforming the Faiths*, 55.

40. Scanzoni and Mollenkott, *Is the Homosexual My Neighbor?* (1994), xiv.

compelled them to do so. As we have seen, *Is the Homosexual My Neighbor?* has had transforming power in the lives of LGBTQ and heterosexual people.

Letha has continued to expand her prophetic work for LGBTQ inclusiveness by coauthoring with David G. Myers a book supporting marriage equality, *What God Has Joined Together: The Christian Case for Gay Marriage*, and by writing articles and speaking on LGBTQ justice. Although the Supreme Court ruled in favor of marriage equality in 2015, violence and discrimination against LGBTQ people persists, often fueled by conservative Christians. Letha's work is still needed, now as much as ever. Letha continues to call people to live the liberating words of Jesus, "You shall love your neighbor as yourself" (Matt 22:39).

Resources for Church Groups

This chapter includes narratives of people who express appreciation that Letha stood for justice for LGBTQ people, in spite of personal and professional costs. Reflect on times in your life when you've taken unpopular stands for what you believe is right.

» Why did you take this unpopular stand? Did you count the costs before you took this stand?

» Think about the process you went through in deciding to take this stand.

» What consequences of taking this unpopular stand did you experience?

» How did taking this stand make you feel?

» Write and/or share with the group your story of taking this stand.

In this chapter people recount life-changing and life-saving experiences through discovering that biblical texts had been misinterpreted and misused to condemn homosexuality and through learning more accurate interpretations.

» Reflect on a life-changing experience you've had through new discoveries about the Bible.

» Who and what contributed to these biblical discoveries?

» Write about and/or share with the group your life-changing experience.

Bible Reading: Acts 10

Is the Homosexual My Neighbor? includes this biblical passage to illustrate God's welcome and inclusion of marginalized groups and all people.

» Use online or print biblical reference sources to explore the cultural context of Acts 10. How did Jews view Gentiles? How did Peter change his views?

» Dramatize this passage with people in your group, rotating the character parts. Describe how you felt as these biblical characters.

Implementing New Ideas

» Encourage your congregation to study biblical passages that show God's inclusive love, and to study *Is the Homosexual My Neighbor?*

» Work with your group and your whole congregation to become more inclusive.

6

Increasing Connections

"I had been amazed at how relevant *All We're Meant to Be* was to my 20-something generation—despite having been written before I was born—and I remember thinking that Letha must have certainly faced even more opposition back then than I was feeling now."[1] Kimberly B. George writes these words in the first post on the *72–27* blog on the *Christian Feminism Today* website. This blog, a cross-generational dialogue between two Christian feminists, Letha and Kimberly, takes its name from their ages. As they launched the blog in the summer of 2008, Letha and Kimberly noted that the digits of their respective ages were exactly reversed. Letha was 72 and Kimberly was 27, so they titled the blog *72–27*. The blog began after Kimberly wrote Letha expressing the discouragement and loneliness she felt as a Christian feminist. "'The reason I am writing you is because I find myself needy of conversations with older women who have walked something of this road. Honestly, I daily face discouragement with these issues. Can the church really change? Does my voice on this matter? Can I hope? Can I believe in what I have to offer?'"[2] Letha responded immediately, and they began their conversations that became this intergenerational *72–27* blog.

Several years later Letha joined Kendra Weddle and Melanie Springer Mock in another intergenerational blog, called *FemFaith*. The name of this blog comes from the authors' desire to be "feminists, faithfully" and to

---

1. George, "How It All Began," para. 3.
2. Ibid., para. 4.

show how their Christian faith and their feminism, "connect, draw upon, and foster growth in both areas."[3]

For many years Letha has increased her connections not only with people of many generations but also with people of diverse races, sexual orientations, and religious affiliations. Even before third wave feminists began emphasizing the intersectionality of justice issues, Letha understood the connection and worked to make EEWC-CFT more diverse. As we have seen, the organization took a stand for LGBTQ justice at the 1986 conference, losing many members but growing as a prophetic voice in the world. Following the 1986 conference, the EWC Council reaffirmed commitment to "include our sisters of color, abused women and children, and Christians with a homosexual orientation."[4] Earlier, in her report on the 1978 conference Nancy Hardesty, one of the cofounders of EWC, raised the need for greater inclusivity of race and class. "To those sensitized to oppression of class and race as well as sex, the absence of poor and minority women was obvious . . . As the Spirit continues to bring liberation, future conferences hopefully will include a greater spectrum of the world's women."[5] This organization, which Letha also cofounded, continues to live into this inclusive vision with "*members of any gender, gender identity, race, ethnicity, color, creed, marital status, sexual orientation, religious affiliation, age, political party, parental status, economic class, or disability.*"[6]

Prophets in Every Generation

Along with Letha's cross-generational blogs, the 2016 Christian Feminism Today Gathering highlighted the generational diversity of the organization. The theme of the Gathering was "Prophets in Every Generation," drawn from this Scripture passage referring to Divine Wisdom: "Although she is but one, she can do all things, and while remaining in herself, she renews all things; in every generation she passes into holy souls and makes them friends of God, and prophets." (Wisdom of Solomon 7:27). Holy Wisdom continues to pass from the prophetic work of Letha and other founders of EEWC-CFT into succeeding generations.

---

3. Weddle, "About the FemFaith Blog," para. 1.

4. Bailey, "Summer Council Meeting," 7.

5. Hardesty, "1978 EWC Conference Recap," para. 10–11.

6. "About Christian Feminism Today," para. 8 (italics original).

One of these young prophets is Kimberly George, mentioned above as coauthor with Letha of the *72–27 Christian Feminism Today* blog. Kimberly is a creative feminist writer, scholar, teacher, and activist whose work focuses on bringing greater public education to urgent and intersecting issues of our time—such as gender-based violence, racism, homophobia, and economic and environmental injustices connected to Western colonialism and genocide.

One night in the spring of 2008, when she was working on a book about faith and third wave feminism, Kimberly felt disheartened. "The task was starting to feel daunting and very, very isolating," she writes. "Looking out at my city, I was aware that the pastor of Seattle's fastest-growing church (one of the most rapidly growing churches in the country, actually) was boldly promoting a message on femininity that once again threatened to strip women of their whole selves and force them into a very tight prescription of 'Biblical Christian womanhood.'" Just when she thought feminists had made progress, Kimberly saw a "cultural backlash laced with its own neofundamentalism." She laments the prevalence of this backlash, especially in churches. Despite all the advances nineteenth- and twentieth-century feminists made for gender justice, she believes there is so much more work to be done in the twenty-first century. "It's crucial that we continue casting new visions for equality. But that night, I found myself exhausted with casting visions. I wasn't sure that I could even hold on to my own hope, let alone be a voice to encourage anyone else. Writing itself is lonely work, but the problem was more than just the isolation of a computer screen. I needed connection with others who had walked this road and found endurance for the journey."[7] Earlier that afternoon she had been reading *All We're Meant to Be* and decided to write Letha.

At a social justice conference Kimberly had met a woman who lent her a copy of *All We're Meant to Be*. This book changed her life, Kimberly says. "I saw mirrored back to me—really, for the first time—that feminist ideas actually work really, really well with faith and spirituality. I couldn't believe that this revolutionary book had been written decades ago. I felt as though women in my generation were trying to reinvent the wheel, because we didn't realize our elders had gone before us and already done this brave writing."[8] So late that night in the spring of 2008, Kimberly dashed off an

7. George, "How It All Began," para. 2–3.

8. Kimberly B. George e-mail interview with coauthor Jann Aldredge-Clanton on January 12, 2016. Unless otherwise noted, all subsequent quotes from Kimberly B. George are from this interview.

e-mail to express her gratitude to Letha and was amazed that Letha wrote back right away.

Soon Letha and Kimberly became friends and began cowriting the *72–27* blog on the *Christian Feminism Today* website. "What began that night of first 'meeting' was a series of e-mails, letters, and phone calls, in which Letha and I have become friends and learned from one another as we discuss life, faith, and feminism," Kimberly writes. "I am so grateful for her, and I am excited by how much fun intergenerational conversations can be."[9]

Kimberly expresses gratitude for Letha also as mentor and editor. Letha was one of Kimberly's first mentors who saw how important writing was to her and who encouraged her dreams to become a writer. Kimberly says that Letha is also the "kindest, most skilled editor" she could have asked for. Letha taught her some foundational ideas that transformed her writing and her teaching of writing. For example, Letha acknowledged that after spending a lot of time on something, writers may realize it's not what they most need to write. At that point, they need to have the courage to start over and write what they actually want to write. Now, Kimberly always asks herself before finishing writing an essay, chapter, or article, "Is this *really* what I want to say?" This question orients her in "pretty profound ways as a writer," because it helps her "check in" with her "authentic, honest self."

Wisdom from Letha about the publishing industry also helped Kimberly grow as a writer. Letha encouraged Kimberly to stay grounded in knowing herself and her own voice so that she can negotiate feedback from publishers and stay true to herself. Kimberly remembers precisely where she was when Letha gave her these words of encouragement: "walking along the beach at Golden Gardens in Seattle, Washington, having an existential writer-girl crisis in my late twenties and talking to Letha on the phone." Kimberly says she was so eager to be published, but it was becoming clear to her that she first needed many more years of practice to develop her voice. "In a culture where we forget that writing takes decades to develop, I appreciated Letha's wisdom and permission to be patient with myself."

Letha has modeled for Kimberly nontraditional ways of being a scholar and writer. While supporting Kimberly's work toward her PhD, Letha has exemplified other ways to be an intellectual. "Letha writes textbooks but chose not to get her PhD," Kimberly says. "Instead, she continually stays curious and hungry for knowledge and is self-taught—and is one of the most

9. George, "How It All Began," para. 5.

educated people I know!" Kimberly respects Letha's intellectual passion, her drive, and her great courage to keep publishing work that contributes to so many people's well-being. Kimberly believes that much of the power of Letha's writing comes from her positioning herself "strategically outside the hegemonic university system" and instead building other alliances to distribute feminist ideas. "This is perhaps a more radical and freeing way to be an intellectual. Letha understands writers and scholars who want to work outside the traditional system of teaching and publishing. She understands that revolutions happen in ways that often defy status quo arrangements."

By coauthoring her major works and cofounding the Christian feminist movement, Letha has also shown Kimberly the value of collaboration. "I am a PhD student in Ethnic Studies, and I really enjoy and appreciate my work within the university," Kimberly says. "However, I am equally committed to collaborating with activists, thinkers, and writers outside the university." Letha has taught Kimberly that "we overcome personal limitations by stepping outside of individualism and collaborating with people in creative, innovative ways." Trained as an academic, Kimberly is also "committed to rethinking the status quo system of education," an attitude she credits to Letha's mentoring. "Both of us appreciate and love the resources that traditional education has to offer, but we also both recognize that our work as writers must be beyond that system because the real work as writers is to connect to social movements. I am supremely grateful for how Letha modeled and taught this value to me."

Katie Deaver, a recipient of the Nancy A. Hardesty Memorial Scholarship, also aspires to combine academic and activist work. EEWC-CFT established this scholarship to honor Nancy, coauthor with Letha of *All We're Meant to Be*, and advocate for women's equality and LGBTQ justice. Katie plans to teach theology at a college, university, or seminary while at the same time making scholarship "understandable, liberative, and life-giving for women who have questions and doubts." While Katie considers herself a scholar and desires to excel in the academic field of Christian feminism, her faith inspires her to write for people in the pews on Sunday mornings. She wants to help make theology "a life-giving and enriching aspect of the daily lives of all people of faith."[10]

All We're Meant to Be had a profound influence on Katie's developing theology. When she was a sophomore at Luther College in Decorah, Iowa, Katie discovered the field of feminist theology. "Feelings of enchantment

---

10. Deaver, "The 2015 Nancy A. Hardesty Memorial Scholarship Recipient," para. 6–7.

and gratification washed over me as Dr. Wanda Deifelt gave me words to articulate the things I had always believed," Katie recalls.[11] "Shortly after that experience I began searching out feminist voices in theology to read in my spare time." Letha Dawson Scanzoni and Nancy Hardesty were two of the first feminists Katie found, and *All We're Meant to Be* was one of the first additions to her feminist library. Reading this book for the first time set the foundation for Katie's continued work in feminist theology. She remembers smiling and nodding as she read each chapter, delighted to have finally found a legitimate scholarly source that was addressing topics she was passionate about. "The book addressed so many of the questions and critiques that I personally had concerning the Bible in a way that was actually applicable to me as a woman of faith who was beginning to feel called to serious theological study."

As a PhD candidate in feminist theology and ethics at Lutheran School of Theology at Chicago, Katie continues to find *All We're Meant to Be* helpful in her academic work and in her personal life. "There are so many connections between this book and my current dissertation research," she says. "So much so in fact that I just added it to my upcoming examination bibliography so that I can focus on it even more fully." Katie found the chapters on "The Single Woman" and "Living in Equal Partnership" to be especially personal as she reread the book. "It is sometimes difficult to be an outspoken advocate and self-proclaimed feminist and be able to navigate the dating, sexual, and gendered 'norms' of our current cultural reality, and it is refreshing to read a text that deals with these issues. We have come so far in so many ways and yet so much of what Letha and Nancy were writing about then is still occurring 40+ years after the original edition of this book."

Although she does not know Letha personally, Katie values her as a mentor. "Letha's writings and work have functioned as a kind of mentoring of me as part of the next generation of Christian feminist scholars," Katie says. She expresses gratitude for women like Letha and Nancy, who not only have set the groundwork but also have provided guidance and inspiration for emerging feminist scholars who continue their work. "There are certainly times when the road of feminist theology seems all uphill and we must continually fight the same battles, but it is during those difficult times that I personally turn to the works of these great women and remember

---

11. Katie Deaver e-mail interview with coauthor Jann Aldredge-Clanton on January 6, 2016. Unless otherwise noted, all subsequent quotes from Katie Deaver are from this interview.

how important it is to continue working for real change in the here and now."

In her writings Katie follows the example of Letha and Nancy in working for change. In an online magazine *Café*, Katie writes about overcoming sexism and all forms of oppression. "I believe we first need to acknowledge that sexism is rooted within the socially constructed gender roles that our society imposes upon us from the moment we are born." Katie critiques these imposed gender roles as hurting all people, not just women. Assigning genders to characteristics that are merely human characteristics limits the flourishing of all individuals. Katie challenges us to call out gender discrimination and abuse whenever we see it. "Not being the one who is telling the sexist joke is not enough. Rather, standing up and saying 'Hey, that isn't funny' is an everyday way to call out oppression and sexism. In addition, we must accept that when it comes to oppression, inaction is a form of action. Even if we are not directly victimizing someone else or the one being victimized, we are bystanders within the larger narrative of society and have a responsibility to stand in solidarity against all forms of oppression." To strengthen her points Katie draws on the Pauline metaphor of the body of Christ, made up of many members: when one member suffers, all suffer, but when all members are able to flourish, the whole body flourishes (1 Corinthians 12).[12]

Receiving the Nancy A. Hardesty Memorial Scholarship has affirmed Katie's call to Christian feminism and engaged her with the EEWC-CFT community. "It has been such an honor to be connected with a scholar as enlightened and important as Nancy Hardesty as well as a dynamic group like EEWC," Katie says. "Being one of the only feminist scholars at my current academic institution has at times been extremely alienating and discouraging, but being connected to a community like EEWC has been absolutely life-giving." EEWC-CFT and Christian feminists like Letha and Nancy show Katie how to critique documents and practices of faith while still proclaiming her faith. Their groundbreaking work and guidance empower new generations of feminists "to continue moving forward toward the goal of a truly holistic and equality based life for all people of faith."

Another Nancy A. Hardesty Memorial Scholarship recipient, Jennifer Newman, credits *All We're Meant to Be* as setting her on the path to Christian feminism. "I first came across *All We're Meant to Be* on the bookshelf at the evangelical university where I completed my undergraduate

12. Deaver, "Elsa and the New Roles of Gender Equality," para. 7–10.

degree," Jennifer says.[13] "It was 2013, and I was searching for something that would put the pieces together of a feminist biblical hermeneutic that spoke to the harmful biblical interpretations that I had grown up with in the church." She believes that her "stumbling across" *All We're Meant to Be* was a divine act. The message of this book was exactly what she needed to hear: "affirming the people we are meant to be, eschewing language about God's design for people based on our genders, and focusing on messages of empowerment and hope."

Growing up in an evangelical, nondenomination church in California from the late 1990s through the early 2000s, Jennifer received messages about how to be a "godly, biblical" woman. Her church followed Focus on the Family[14] in guiding young people. When she started "becoming a woman" at puberty, she was also "steeped in what is now called the Purity Movement," which emphasizes virginity as important for her relationship with God, Jennifer recalls. The first book used to teach her about sex was *And the Bride Wore White*, by Dannah Gresh, which argues that because a woman's hymen, in most cases, is broken and spills blood the first time she has sex, her sexual union with her husband is a blood covenant between her, her husband, and God.[15] In addition, Jennifer learned that modesty was her duty to her brothers in Christ, to keep them from lusting after her body. One of the books presented in her "teen girl Bible studies" was John and Stasi Eldredge's *Captivating*, which gave her the message that it is sinful to be a "dominating woman" who "needs no one," who is "in charge," and who "knows how to get what she wants," because she is not living out her God-ordained "femininity" that is "merciful, tender, and vulnerable."[16] Jennifer spent her teenage years confused and worried that she was "sinning" in the ways she was living as a young Christian woman.

Wanting to understand what being a Christian woman meant for her, Jennifer chose to go to an evangelical university. At George Fox University she encountered female professors who did not fit the definition of biblical femininity that her church had taught. These professors became role

13. Jennifer Newman e-mail interview with coauthor Jann Aldredge-Clanton on February 15, 2016. Unless otherwise noted, all subsequent quotes from Jennifer Newman are from this interview.

14. Focus on the Family, founded in 1977 by James Dobson, is an evangelical parachurch organization that promotes socially conservative views such as traditional gender roles, abstinence-only sex education, and opposition to abortion and same-sex marriage.

15. Gresh, *And the Bride Wore White*, 131.

16. Eldredge and Eldredge, *Captivating*, 52.

models as Jennifer began to awaken to the knowledge that what she had been taught all her life as "truth" was instead interpretation that she could reject. She began reading Rachel Held Evans's blog and then her book *A Year of Biblical Womanhood*. "Although Held Evans wittily describes inconsistencies with the Biblical Womanhood movement that I had experienced growing up, I was still afraid of Scripture," Jennifer says. "I had yet to hear solid interpretations that were contrary to what I had grown up with."

Then Jennifer discovered *All We're Meant to Be* and found these solid biblical interpretations. She expresses concern for the many other millennials who, like her, have been raised with "problematic notions of biblical womanhood, modesty, sexual purity, and restrictive views of sexuality and marriage." Told to be "in the world but not of it," these young Christians never learn "potentially liberating 'worldly' ways of being." Thus, women who wish to live their lives outside of the biblical womanhood model, and LGBTQ young people must either give up their faith or conform to the rules laid out by the church. If they do not conform, they become "outsiders" without "agency to call out the oppression that is happening in the church on a structural level." Jennifer finds *All We're Meant to Be* "incredibly empowering" because it "provides much-needed answers and framework," giving "agency back to these believers so they don't have to abandon their faith." In addressing the rhetoric taught by the church as "truth," the book offers "compelling and liberating alternative interpretations." *All We're Meant to Be* is "timeless in that it still actively stands against traditional evangelical interpretations of Scripture that unfortunately keep returning." Jennifer frequently recommends this book to people in evangelical churches who are seeking answers to questions of gender and sexuality.

At George Fox University Jennifer went on to form Common Ground, the unrecognized Gay-Straight alliance on campus and then to graduate with a double major in politics and philosophy and a minor in women's studies. Later she completed a graduate degree in Religion, Gender, and Sexuality Studies at Vanderbilt University Divinity School. In her application for the Nancy A. Hardesty Memorial Scholarship, Jennifer wrote about her calling as a Christian feminist.

> I am a Jesus Feminist! I desire to be a woman who loves people wholeheartedly, who adventures, seeks God's will, writes, takes walks in fields, pursues a career with the drive God has given me, and to never, ever give up on my dreams. Christian feminism has encouraged me to pursue my gifts, as they are—my drive, my

outspokenness, and my intellect. I have been given many opportunities in these areas: academic conferences, campus debates, etc.
that I would not have taken advantage of before University, moreover, before becoming a feminist. For me, feminism absolutely had
to come first, in order for me to feel comfortable as an academic
voice. Without a doubt, God has given me a unique calling in life
in the realm of Christian feminism, and has blessed me beyond
measure with opportunities and experiences preparing me for the
road ahead. The Christian feminists before me have opened so
many doors, allowing the space for young women like myself to
continue moving dialogue forward.[17]

McKenzie Brown, another young Christian feminist, has entered
doors opened by Letha and others. Letha's influence extended to McKenzie
through her religion professor Kendra Weddle. When McKenzie was at
Texas Wesleyan University, Kendra noticed her interest in feminism and
asked if she would consider working on a student project for the 2014
Christian Feminism Today biannual Gathering. Excited about a feminist
research project, McKenzie immediately accepted this invitation. "New to
the field of Christian feminism and feminist scholarship, I was hungry to
learn. What's more, though I didn't explicitly recognize this at the time, I
was hungry for a community who would encourage me in a field where I
was used to being discouraged."[18] McKenzie says that Christian feminism
had not been available to her up to this point in her undergraduate education, but was often considered just a "niche" topic. One of the most difficult parts of her feminist journey was "finding a place to begin" because
she often saw people who are passionate about feminism being met with
deterrents—conscious and unconscious, subtle and blatant. "Thus, when
Dr. Weddle mentioned the possibility of a project explicitly concerned with
issues in Christian feminism, I saw the opportunity to engage in a community where for the first time, I wouldn't be discouraged from my passion."

At the 2014 Christian Feminism Today Gathering in St. Louis,
McKenzie presented the results of her research in Christian feminism. She
felt the relevance of this research for her own life because at the time she
was in the ordination process to become an elder in the United Methodist
Church. Her presentation at the Gathering explored the historical

17. Newman, "The 2014 Nancy A. Hardesty Memorial Scholarship Recipient," para.
8–10.

18. McKenzie Brown e-mail interview with author Jann Aldredge-Clanton on January
19, 2016. All subsequent quotes from McKenzie Brown are from this interview.

relationship between biblical hermeneutics and female leadership in the church. McKenzie's research for the Gathering nudged her to ask difficult questions about the status of female leadership in institutional church settings. "Though learning about the true nature of the status of women in Christianity was painful, I felt fulfilled in a way I had never felt before."

Although she was nervous about her presentation at the Christian Feminism Today Gathering, McKenzie felt gratified to be in a community that valued what she had to say about women and leadership in the church. She says this Gathering was one of the best experiences of intentional community she had ever had. "Radical hospitality and inclusivity were standard means by which the individuals in this community interacted. I laughed hard and often, and just as frequently was compelled to contemplate the relevance of what I was learning to my life post-Gathering. Good scholarship was appreciated, but even more so were social justice and kindness."

A highlight of the Gathering for McKenzie was the inclusive language used throughout the meeting. For the first time she experienced female divine names and images in story, song, prayers, and scholarly presentations. "Until the Gathering at St. Louis, whether it be in Bible studies or corporate prayer, I always weighed the pros and cons of referencing God as female," McKenzie says. "There was always some stigmatization at stake and, beneath it all, a lingering feeling that what I thought and felt about Christian feminism was flawed or, at worst, unfounded in its assertions." From the time she became aware that she was a feminist, "language was a major sticking point," one that seemed "invisible" to almost everyone she knew. Her church community did not validate her "suspicion of something deeply flawed in masculine God-talk." Any suggestion McKenzie made that "Father was not a fully appropriate signifier for God" made her a "radical feminist" and shifted her to the margins. "I didn't experience physical exclusion in my faith community, but I was a stigmatized person and relegated to the label of angry feminist."

As she became increasingly aware of the "pervasive patriarchy in the Christian faith," McKenzie appreciated the life-giving support of EEWC-CFT. No longer did she feel marginalized as a feminist, but encouraged on her faith journey. "Now I know that I am not alone in my convictions and that feminists are diverse and dynamic. EEWC is a source of solace to me, because I know that there is a community where being a feminist does not by default make me radical or angry." McKenzie affirms her experience with EEWC-CFT as strengthening the role of Christian feminism in her life. "Feminism isn't just a *part* of my life, but something that is woven into the character of who I am and has fundamentally changed how I think, feel, and relate to others. EEWC has aided in the stitching."

Christian feminism kept McKenzie energized as a Christian Studies major at Texas Wesleyan University and contributed to her acceptance in a study abroad program in feminist philosophy at Oxford. "At the introduction of feminist theology to my life, my education took leaps forward," she says. "I had always been a good traditional student in my ability to regurgitate information and offer slightly original, unprovocative research." Christian feminism changed her educational aspirations and helped her ask "subversive" questions. Instead of asking about due dates, McKenzie asked why all of the authors they were reading were white males. She began to consider not only the content her professors were providing, but also "the vehicle and nature of its delivery." McKenzie decided she would rather be "considered subversive than subscribe to patriarchal means of interpreting biblical texts," and she would rather find her "own voice than complacently listen to those entrenched in masculinist traditions that do no favors to the marginalized." Christian feminism has led her "to think more critically, and to self-actualization," enabling her to be cognizant of her privilege and the role that it plays in her relationship to others, and teaching her to "love justice in all of its varied forms and manifestations."

All We're Meant to Be empowered Erin S. Lane,[19] a writer and communications strategist, to become a Christian feminist. "It was one of those rare books that named things I had long thought but not yet articulated about being a Christian feminist," Erin says.[20] "I read it during those pivotal post-college years when idealism runs low and reality runs deep." At the time she was working in San Francisco as a religion book publicist and came across Christian Feminism Today in the list of media outlets to pitch. Erin e-mailed Letha about promoting a book. In the e-mail, Erin also mentioned her interest in Christian feminism. She wrote that she "was starved for real theological engagement with gender" in her local church, and that she was "lonely for Christian women" who struggled as she did in "living at the intersection" of their beliefs and experiences. Letha responded, offering to send Erin a copy of *All We're Meant to Be*. When *All We're Meant to Be*

19. Formerly Erin Lane Beam.

20. Erin S. Lane e-mail interview with coauthor Jann Aldredge-Clanton on November 6, 2015. Unless otherwise noted, all subsequent quotes from Erin S. Lane are from this interview.

arrived, Erin "drank it like water." She highlighted whole paragraphs with "thick pink, orange, and green markers." This book gave Erin "not just the language for biblical feminism but permission to *be* a biblical feminist."

This permission led Erin to earn a master's of theological studies degree from Duke Divinity School. "I enrolled in Divinity School to see if I couldn't make a living calling Christianity to greater gender-fullness," she says. Now Erin works for a Quaker-based nonprofit, the Center for Courage & Renewal, facilitating retreats that help clergy and lay leaders learn to "hear and trust the presence of God within them." She also writes blog posts, articles, and books on how the church can "create spaces of better belonging." She gives *All We're Meant to Be* credit for creating "a space of better belonging" for her during a time when she "could have easily gone adrift." Erin is the author of *Lessons in Belonging from a Church-Going Commitment Phobe*, in which she explores her struggles with being in faith communities; and coeditor of the anthology *Talking Taboo*, in which Christian women under forty address often prohibited topics of faith, gender, and identity.

In an article in *Christian Feminism Today*, Erin writes about how she embraced her calling as a Christian feminist and why she stays in the church.

> The church is only weakened by the departure of strong men and women of faith, and it is strengthened by those who stay and ask questions, working for change. I've seen the powerful harmony that the two ideologies—Christianity and feminism—can wield, both in the enraptured face of my mother and now in the healing hands of my young husband, and I am convinced restoration is at hand. Let us begin baptizing each other in solidarity as faith-*full* feminists, working for full equality in our churches and in our world.[21]

As she has worked for full equality through her writing and through various organizations, Erin has valued Letha as a mentor and friend. Erin serves on the board of the nonprofit Resource Center for Women and Ministry in the South, where she delights in her connection with women across all ages and stages. For three years she served on the EEWC-CFT Council. "Letha was one of the first Christian feminists I met who thought young people like me had as much to teach her as to learn from her," Erin says. "Letha's energy is boundless. Everyone who meets her knows this to be true. Her memory is encyclopedic. Her enthusiasm is infectious. And

21. Beam, "Holy Hellion," 8.

her mentoring is rigorous." Erin expresses gratitude for Letha's "commitment to intergenerational relationships."

Increasing Diversity

Through her writings, cocreation of EEWC-CFT, and mentoring, Letha has inspired commitment to equality so that all can become all we're meant to be in the divine image. The connections continue to expand to include not only people of various generations, sexual orientations, and gender identities, but also people of diverse races, ethnicities, and religious affiliations.

Womanist minister Leslie Harrison reflects on her experience as a member of the EEWC-CFT Council and of Letha as a mentor. "I feel that the organization values and appreciates my voice as an African American womanist. I can say that Letha has given me strength to flex my muscles as a confident, strong African American woman."[22] Letha has empowered Leslie to use her voice so that "more women can be reached to give them self-confidence and affirmation about their decisions to live as single women or women in cisgender or homosexual relationships." Leslie appreciates Letha's encouragement "to be a bold woman." And Letha models boldness as she "stands up for us, affirms us, and encourages us to go forward to be *all* that we are meant to be." Leslie has experienced the EEWC-CFT Council and the entire organization as celebrating the gifts of women, providing an accepting atmosphere for "women to join together to discuss joys and pains," and working "for the good of all."

In EEWC-CFT's online version of the magazine *Christian Feminism Today* Leslie published a review of Monica A. Coleman's book *Ain't I a Womanist Too? Third World Womanist Religious Thought*. Here Leslie writes about her call to take bold stands for justice. "I am also an activist, and Monica Coleman's book helped me to understand that when I fight for justice I am standing on the shoulders of so many who came before me. Each of us may wear different labels at different times, but each of us finds, in our own struggle, a unique path to freedom. We are each but one, but together we are changing the world in the name of *justice and liberty for all*."[23]

---

22. Leslie Harrison e-mail interview with coauthor Jann Aldredge-Clanton on January 22, 2016. Unless otherwise noted, all subsequent quotes from Leslie Harrison are from this interview.

23. Harrison, "Ain't I a Womanist Too?," para. 16 (italics original).

At "Oriented to Love: A Dialogue about Sexual and Gender Diversity in the Church," sponsored by Evangelicals for Social Action, Leslie first learned from Lē Weaver[24] about EEWC-CFT. Lē invited Leslie to the 2014 Christian Feminism Today Gathering in St. Louis. Leslie agreed to attend even though she at first thought she would be an "outsider." But even before she arrived in St. Louis for the Gathering, she felt welcomed as a member of the organization, she recalls. "I knew I would be among friends even though I had met only Lē. The hospitality and generosity of spirit and substance were amazing!" Although Leslie experienced the Gathering as "more inclusive and inviting" than she had imagined it would be and although asked to take part in the Gathering worship service by writing and leading a litany, she still felt "leery" about being accepted. "I was leery because as a 'womanist' I was wondering how my voice would be perceived and accepted in a 'feminist' community. Even upon arrival in St. Louis after accepting the invitation, I still had reservations as I was among strangers, but I was open-minded and ready to allow the Holy Spirit (Sophia) to direct me." Leslie feared she might "experience racial issues" there in "the Deep South," but she was "willing to be vulnerable." When she met Letha and felt the warmth of "her bubbly personality," Leslie knew she was "among friends." All of her fears subsided as she saw Letha as "a wonderful vacation Bible school teacher and friend." Letha's "leather soft hands and soothing welcoming voice" gave Leslie "peace and assurance" that she was going "to learn and grow exponentially."

When Leslie returned home to New Jersey, she read *All We're Meant to Be*. "I could literally hear Letha's voice and feel her passion, commitment, and wisdom," Leslie says. "I realized as I was reading the book that Letha did not necessarily understand the plight of an African American woman, but I found myself in the pages." Leslie felt "affirmed as a single woman with a mission of social justice for all." As she read *All We're Meant to Be*, she could also see how valuable Letha's "leadership and wisdom" have been to "the spirit and direction of EEWC-CFT."

As she serves on the EEWC-CFT Council, Leslie contributes her wisdom to help make the organization more racially diverse. She encourages the presence of EEWC-CFT members at conferences where minorities predominate and on college campuses where young womanists and feminists are looking for information and affirmation as they encounter new ideas and diverse populations. She believes that many young women are

24. See chs. 4 and 5, pp. 110, 130.

confused about the term "Christian feminism," wondering if it is inclusive of women of color. In addition to sharing information on campuses, Leslie wears T-shirts to promote the organization and invites students to apply for the Nancy A. Hardesty Memorial Scholarship and to attend the Christian Feminism Today Gathering. "I hope that my enthusiasm and interest will inspire them to participate," she says. "Exposure and helping women of color understand that their voices are welcomed in EEWC-CFT will be a key to increasing their involvement."

Another reason Leslie believes that some women of color may be ambivalent about joining EEWC-CFT is the organization's stand on LGBTQ inclusiveness. "The other issue facing many women of color is the stigma of sexuality issues (gender identity, partner preference), especially for those who wish to profess Christ publicly." Small groups, such as teas and rap sessions, may "prove essential" to encouraging these women to value themselves in the divine plan. "To these curious, vulnerable, and sometimes suffering women I encounter, I offer Letha's books to increase their self-image, self-confidence and self-esteem," Leslie says. "These books are so affirming and encouraging."

Also, Leslie hopes her presence at freshmen orientation and other campus "meet the community" events proves helpful. "I'm not a 'converter,' but I have been told that I could be considered an 'informational-ist' as I just give out the facts hopefully with little bias but considerable passion." Leslie strongly believes EEWC-CFT is an "important organization for this time in our society." EEWC-CFT empowers "those who have a passion to help those who do not have a voice concerning their gender identity," and provides a safe place for those who are struggling to find that "they are not alone and it is ok to seek information that will bring them peace." Leslie is "excited about what EEWC-CFT is giving to the world!"

Alicia Crosby, cofounder and executive director of the Center for Inclusivity (CFI), also expresses enthusiasm for EEWC-CFT and offers her wisdom for building more bridges to increase diversity. Like Leslie, she encourages the organization to enter into dialogue with more feminists of color and womanists and bring a greater diversity of "voices together for our common mission."[25]

At the Wild Goose Festival in the mountains of North Carolina, Alicia first learned about EEWC-CFT. She describes sitting in the midst

25. Alicia Crosby e-mail interview with author Jann Aldredge-Clanton on August 21 & September 2, 2016. Unless otherwise noted, all subsequent quotes from Alicia Crosby are from this interview.

of seminarians, pastors, and faith leaders speaking about their passion "for what the church could be." Lē Weaver quietly handed Alicia a CFT card and invited her to talk. "I remember that moment so vividly because it was one in which I was encouraged to lean into my sense of vision and give voice to my thoughts."

Alicia says that Lē, Letha, and the rest of the EEWC-CFT family have welcomed her "into their fold with open hearts and open minds." Alicia also appreciates their encouraging her to write, giving her platforms to speak, and supporting her work to grow her nonprofit Center for Inclusivity that strives "to create space where all are welcome." Alicia believes "'welcome' is a good word to associate with CFT because this network of incredible people embodies the Feminine Divine as they foster space where those committed to equity and equality can find a space to belong."

At the 2016 Christian Feminism Today Gathering, Alicia facilitated a workshop titled "Inclusion as Prophetic Action: Creating Spaces Where All Are Welcome." She modeled the inclusivity she advocated by hearing and valuing each voice at the workshop. She asked participants to form small circles to explore these questions: "What is inclusion? What does it look like? What does it feel like? What's the most inclusive community you've ever been part of? What made it that way? What did you find most challenging? What did you learn? What kind of diversity was represented? Who was left out? What do you gain by making a community inclusive? How is building an inclusive space prophetic?" The small circles then came together in a large circle to share insights. For example, participants reflected on inclusive communities as prophetic in that they bring people of varied cultures, faiths, genders, races, and sexual orientations together and give equal value and power to each person.

Grounded in her theology of the sacredness of all persons, Alicia sees the intersectionality of justice issues and contributes to the elimination of sexism, racism, heterosexism, and economic inequality. She works through the Center for Inclusivity to live out her values by uplifting the marginalized, amplifying minority voices, and advocating for equality for all. The Center participates in annual justice events like Transgender Day of Remembrance, Black History Month, and World AIDS Day. The mission of the Center for Inclusivity is "to connect the individuals behind every 'issue,' giving social embodiment and structure to the practice of empathy," and "*to foster healing communities among people of all faiths, genders and sexual orientations with an ethic of inclusion that is locally embodied, sacredly held and widely replicable.*[26]

Through pursuing an MA degree in Social Justice at Loyola University Chicago and through her writing, Alicia also fulfills her prophetic call. In an article titled "Fast of Embodied Solidarity," Alicia laments the treatment a Wheaton College professor received when she took a stand for justice.

> I, like many of you, have been following the situation between Wheaton College and Dr. Larycia Hawkins—the professor repri-manded by college administrators for wearing a hijab in a Face-book photo and quoting Pope Francis that Muslims and Christians worship the same God. I feel that Wheaton's mistreatment of Dr. Hawkins reveals realities of racism, sexism, Islamophobia, and other ways in which the Christian faith has become complicit in oppression and dishonoring the humanity and *imago dei* present in others.[27]

In the article Alicia goes on to invite people to stand in solidarity with "others who are tired of the(ir) Christian witness being used to subjugate others instead of inspiring healing and true reconciliation."[28]

Deborah Jian Lee, author of *Rescuing Jesus: How People of Color, Women & Queer Christians Are Reclaiming Evangelicalism*, interviewed Letha for the book and was impressed by "her deep moral convictions, her lifelong commitment to empowering all women," and her solidarity with other oppressed groups.[29] "A lot evangelical leaders agonize over whether to affirm the LGBT community, but Letha speaks of her support with such peace and confidence, even though she first expressed her support at a time when it was widely unpopular, extremely divisive, and personally costly." Deborah says that many other evangelical activists focused on just one justice issue at the expense of other marginalized people. "On all other is-sues, they had to toe the evangelical conservative party line. Letha radically broke this mold." Through her writing and through the organization, which she cofounded, Letha advocated not only for women's rights but also for

---

26. Center for Inclusivity, "Mission & Vision," para. 3–4 (italics original).

27. Crosby, "Fast of Embodied Solidarity," para. 5.

28. Ibid., para. 6.

29. Deborah Jian Lee e-mail interview with author Jann Aldredge-Clanton on Janu-ary 23, 2017. Unless otherwise noted, all subsequent quotes from Deborah Jian Lee are from this interview.

rights of LGBTQ persons. As a result, "EWC struggled for years and almost shut down."

In *Rescuing Jesus*, Deborah relates some of her own experiences of marginalization as she was growing up. "For much of my childhood I felt like an outsider, always toggling between Chinese and American culture."[30] Her parents, immigrants from Hong Kong via Taiwan, worried that she was assimilating to white America. The "widening cultural distance" between Deborah and her parents "made home life tense at times."[31] She also experienced this tension at school. "I was the kid faking it to fit in. I rarely invited friends over, worried that they'd make hurtful observations about my 'weird' Chinese home (they often did) . . . the habitual drive-by racial slurs (the kind of street harassment that has followed me into adulthood) and one particular assault haunt me to this day."[32]

When she was a teenager, Deborah joined a conservative immigrant Chinese church. There she felt she had found her people who accepted her unconditionally. Soon after arriving at the University of Illinois, Urbana-Champaign, Deborah joined InterVarsity Christian Fellowship, one of the largest evangelical campus organizations in the country. She had mixed feelings about this mostly white group. "Part of me felt at home, with the shared faith language and new friends to bond with. But another part of me felt uneasy: something was off."[33] She became increasingly uncomfortable with the evangelical rhetoric against those they labeled "liberals."

By the time she had graduated from college and started the graduate program in journalism at Columbia University, Deborah had left evangelicalism. One of the reasons she left was that "the patriarchal culture put oppressive limits" on her humanity. "Once I started asserting my whole humanity, including my ethics as a Chinese American woman with LGBTQ friends, I felt sidelined, my loyalty to the faith questioned."[34] She says she wishes she had known about Letha and her work at that time.

When Deborah was doing research for *Rescuing Jesus*, she "was floored to learn that decades ago an evangelical feminist movement had taken flight" through Letha's writing partnership with Nancy Hardesty. In *Rescuing Jesus*, Deborah describes the emergence of this movement.

30. Lee, *Rescuing Jesus*, 3.
31. Ibid.
32. Ibid.
33. Ibid., 4.
34. Ibid., 13.

One key moment in the movement came in October 1969, when Letha Scanzoni, a Christian feminist writer, sat down at her type-writer. A diminutive thirty-four-year-old, with short brown curls and an easy smile, Letha identified with the struggles of many women her age as she juggled the responsibilities of marriage and children with forging a career. For years she had dreamed about writing a book on women's liberation for an evangelical audience, but it wasn't until this fateful October day that she took the first step in doing so. Over the years, Letha had gotten to know an editor at *Eternity* magazine named Nancy Hardesty . . . She had responded positively to Letha's earlier writings about equal-part-ner marriage . . . Letha, sensing she had found a "sister Christian feminist," proposed in a typed letter to Nancy that they cowrite this Christian feminist book.[35]

Letha and Nancy began writing this book that would become *All We're Meant to Be: A Biblical Approach to Women's Liberation*, first published in 1974. Deborah praises Letha and Nancy for their courage in writing *All We're Meant to Be*, "which put the Bible in historical and cultural context and dismantled the toxic gender roles evangelical leaders have reinforced for so long." She gives Letha credit for shaping the evangelical feminist movement also through cofounding EWC. "I was amazed that EWC advocated for the Equal Rights Amendment and that many within the group defended women's reproductive rights and civil rights for gays and lesbians."

Deborah laments that this history of EWC has been silenced by many evangelical leaders. Perhaps if she had known about this evangelical feminist organization and Letha's writings, Deborah would have been able to remain within evangelicalism. She admires Letha for her continued "moral leadership," and hopes that "more Christians hear Letha's story of courage, scholarship, bravery, and leadership."

The evolution of the organization's name from EWC to EEWC-CFT symbolizes the building of more bridges to expand the organization beyond evangelical denominations. In 1990 the organization added "ecumenical," and in 2009 added "Christian Feminism Today." These changes in the organization's name signal the inclusion of all Christians, not just evangelicals.

Catholic feminist theologian Mary E. Hunt[36] celebrates this religious inclusiveness. "I used to think of evangelicals as quite different from my-self until I met Letha, Virginia, and the EEWC-CFT community," Mary

35. Ibid., 50.
36. See chapter 5, p. 127.

says. "I cannot report any uptick in my interest in the Bible as such. To the contrary, after seeing up close the damage that textual tyranny can do, I am less inclined to suggest the Bible for casual reading or prayer." But Mary discovered affinity with evangelicals through her many years of reading *EEWC Update*, "published under Letha's careful editorship." Letha's interviews in the publication "brought alive" for Mary "what might otherwise have been simply names on the page." Letha's reflections and interviews with people whose work Mary admires, including Joan Chittister,[37] Marjory Zoet Bankson,[38] Martha Ann Kirk,[39] and Colleen Fulmer,[40] were "always spot on, capturing the essence of the person as well as letting the person speak for herself." Letha's "Editor's Notebook" entries that "graced the back page of each print journal make a handy reference guide to a movement on the move." As EEWC-CFT grew, "her constant, faithful, insightful words grounded it and made it accessible to the rest of us."

For many years Mary has collaborated with Letha and others in EEWC-CFT, especially through their publications. Letha has done an interview for *WATERtalks: Feminist Conversations in Religion Series*, published on the website of Women's Alliance for Theology, Ethics, and Ritual (WATER), an organization Mary cofounded and codirects.[41] In turn, Mary has written for EEWC-CFT and given a plenary address at an annual Christian Feminism Today Gathering. "I consider Letha a colleague of the first order," Mary says. "As WATER has grown more diverse, EEWC-CFT is a natural ally. Letha and I know one another through the printed page more than in person. She corresponds the way some people breathe, with a fluidity and naturalness that makes her recipient feel as if s/he is the only person in the world. Indeed, that gift of communication is not facile schmoozing but genuine outreach to another who is in Letha's view a peer. I have been the happy recipient of such missives, and have tried to respond in kind as we have come to know one another better over the years. I treasure Letha and find her one of those colleagues who always enlightens me."

Mary also values EEWC-CFT as a "vital and welcome partner in the work of feminist, religiously rooted social change." When she writes a book review or suggests an idea for *Christian Feminism Today*, Mary aspires to

37. Scanzoni, "A Spiritual Heart Transplant," 1–3.
38. Scanzoni, "Answering God's Call to the Soul," 1–3, 9, 12.
39. Scanzoni, "Martha Ann Kirk," 1–4.
40. Scanzoni, "Finding Colleen Fulmer," 1–3, 12.
41. Scanzoni, "Being an Evangelical Feminist Today."

reach the high bar that Letha has set. "Oh to write with her brio and to embrace the Spirit with her enthusiasm. No wonder the organization has strong roots and reputation. Future scholars will comb the archives with excitement as they find the countless contributions that Letha has made to EEWC-CFT and the larger feminist religious community."

Mary and Letha share common cause in their enthusiasm for mentoring future generations of Christian feminists. WATER has an active internship program for students from both national and international seminaries and universities; EEWC-CFT awards an annual scholarship to a college senior or graduate student in religion or theology and includes student presenters at annual gatherings. "I marvel at Letha's focused conversations with younger colleagues, her nurturing of more 'daughters of Sarah' than we will ever know," Mary says. "I learn from her approach, her strategic wisdom in sharing the stories and struggles so that future generations will not need to repeat our efforts."

Because Letha has "never been coopted by evangelical powers," all her work has "an authenticity to it." Mary goes on to commend Letha for never having "siphoned off her feminist energies to make nice with people who finally do not care much about women and others who are marginalized." Above all, unlike "some other evangelicals," Letha "gives the Gospel a good name."

Acknowledging the influence of Letha's work, Mary does not buy into false divisions between feminists. "We are feminists in religion together with no need to distinguish between liberationists and evangelicals since we are all moving in the same direction," Mary says. "I credit Letha with this growth in my understanding. I only wish I had grasped it earlier. As new leaders emerge, and as marvelous publications, conferences, and connections proliferate, I am grateful and humbled to be one of those who can say that Letha brought me along. I look forward to many more opportunities to collaborate."

In her plenary address at the 2014 Christian Feminism Today Gathering, Mary sounds a call for feminists of all faiths to work together. Her presentation, titled "Feminist Faith-Based Social Justice: How Feminists of Faith Can Collaborate to Amplify Our Voices and Deepen Our Collective Impact," outlines strategies for creating a more just and loving world. Among these strategies are to take concrete actions to create change; to say "we," not "they," about one another as feminists of diverse faiths; to encourage more exchanges among young women; and to share theological, liturgical, and ethical resources. Mary expresses her deep respect for the work of EEWC-CFT. "We at the Women's Alliance for Theology, Ethics and Ritual (WATER) read your materials and value our collaboration with you in the development of feminist faith." Alluding to the Gathering theme, "Let Justice Roll On Like a River," Mary closes her address. "We move together without apology and with enthusiasm, confident that, if justice is to roll down like a river, it is because we are in the water together."[42]

Working together with many people to bring justice, Letha continues to make connections to include everyone. Beginning with connecting feminism to evangelicalism, she collaborated with others to widen evangelical feminism to include LGBTQ people. Valuing the gifts of all, Letha continues to expand Christian feminism to include people of many generations, diverse races, and varied faith communities. She has long understood the power of working collaboratively and the power that flows from egalitarian connections. Letha follows Sophia ("Wisdom") in building bridges of justice, equality, and peace.

Resources for Church Groups

This chapter highlights the intersection of justice issues. The stories illustrate ways in which Letha's influence continues to expand to include people of many generations and of diverse races, sexual orientations, and religious affiliations.

» Name justice issues you see as intersecting. Discuss ways they are connected.

» Use online or print reference sources to find biblical stories that illustrate the intersection of justice issues.

» Write and/or share with the group an experience you've had or witnessed of justice issues intersecting (e.g., experiencing discrimination because of gender and race).

» Explore ways of meeting challenges of discrimination from racism and sexism, or to meet the challenge of other injustices.

---

42. Hunt, "Feminist Faith-Based Social Justice," para. 1, 39, 42, 43, 46.

Stories in this chapter demonstrate the value of cross-generational learning and collaboration. Reflect on wisdom you've gained from people of different generations.

» Make a list of people you've learned from who are older than you. Make a list of people you've learned from who are younger than you.

» Identify the benefits of cross-generational collaboration.

» Share stories of mentoring and of being mentored.

Bible Reading: Acts 2

This passage recounts the birth of the church.

» Use online or print biblical reference sources to study the cultural context of Acts 2. Identify unexpected, unconventional ways the Holy Spirit worked.

» Identify ways the first church was inclusive.

Implementing New Ideas

» Encourage your group and your whole congregation to grow more inclusive. Ask your church leaders to teach the biblical basis for inclusiveness.

» Work with your group and your whole congregation to increase connections to include more people.

PART 3

Continuing the Justice Work:
Selected Essays by
Letha Dawson Scanzoni

This section of the book illustrates Letha's ongoing transformational work through two of her essays. These essays provide wisdom for building bridges to accomplish the work of liberation, justice, and peace.

7

Christian Feminism and LGBT Advocacy: Let's Move Away from Slippery Slope Thinking

A s the pianist played the introduction to "Standing on the Promises," the gentleman sharing a hymnal with me leaned over and whispered, "When I saw you had published a book on the Bible and feminism a few years ago, I said to my wife, 'You just watch. Her next book will be on homosexuality.'"

He was a highly regarded evangelical leader from a conservative theological seminary, and this was our first meeting. We were seated side by side on the speakers' platform at a conference on Christians and homosexuality in the late 1970s.

We had been chosen to represent opposing viewpoints. He believed that homosexuality was a sin; I believed the Bible said nothing about a homosexual orientation, that it was a natural human variation like left-handedness, and that committed same-sex relationships could be regarded as no different in principle than heterosexual marriage.

The singing began, followed immediately by his talk, so I didn't have a chance to ask his reason for predicting the topic of my next book. In fact, his comment surprised me. I knew that when Nancy Hardesty and I were writing *All We're Meant to Be: A Biblical Approach to Women's Liberation* (the 1974 Christian feminist book he referred to), neither one of us would have considered writing a book on homosexuality.

He was correct in the long run, of course—as he was well aware that day as we sat side by side sharing the hymnbook—because one of my books published a few years after *All We're Meant to Be* was *Is the Homosexual My*

Neighbor?, coauthored with Virginia Ramey Mollenkott in 1978. But any connection between feminism and homosexuality as I saw these topics was probably different from what he may have been thinking when he made his prediction.

The Widespread Acceptance of the Slippery Slope Argument

His comment to me that day on the speakers' platform introduced me to the slippery slope argument that predicts what the next step will be if an evangelical Christian starts viewing women and men as fully equal in marriage, the church, and the world at large.

Slippery slope ideology teaches that such an acceptance of gender equality—the essence of feminism—is "unbiblical" and therefore "bad," and that once feminism is embraced, advocacy for LGBTQ rights (considered even worse than feminism) will follow next, accelerating a dangerous slide down a slippery slope away from God and Scripture. For evangelicals, this is a scary prospect.

Slippery slope ideologues see *feminism* as the instigator of this downward slide into all kinds of heresy. Mary Kassian says those who consider themselves biblical feminists "may find themselves sliding uncontrollably down the hill, through the red light, and into the intersection, only to discover when they finally stop that their vehicles are headed the wrong way . . . Feminism is a slippery slope that leads towards a total alteration or rejection of the Bible" (in *The Feminist Gospel*, 1992, p. 227). She warns that along the way, as part of the slide, Christian feminists seize the right to define themselves, the world, and even God, including a willingness to see God as "Mother/Father" or even simply as "Mother" and to freely use the pronoun "She" in speaking of God, since God is beyond gender classifications.

Writing on *The Blade Blog* under the name "prasor," Peter J. Razor II suggests that "affirmation of the homosexual lifestyle" is a fourth step needed to go with "Kassian's three-step process." He says that "although it is not logically necessary, it is historically accurate to say that when feminism is affirmed, it eventually leads to the acceptance of homosexuality. Every denomination which has eliminated gender roles has come to accept homosexuality as a valid lifestyle."

Wayne Grudem, in his book *Evangelical Feminism: A New Path to Liberalism,* outlines the steps of the "predictable sequence" that denominations may take in this regard. It begins with abandoning biblical inerrancy, then endorses women's ordination in the church, followed by abandoning "the Bible's teaching on male headship in marriage," with the next step being the exclusion of clergy who oppose women's ordination. The slide continues with "approving homosexual conduct as morally valid in some cases," then "approving homosexual ordination," with the final step being the ordination of homosexuals to high positions within the denomination.

A review essay about Grudem's book on the website of the Council on Biblical Manhood and Womanhood (CBMW) titled, "Sliding the Slippery Slope," asks whether the point of no return may not have already passed. "Perhaps the movement [Christian feminism] has so distorted the clear truths of Scripture that the biblical evangel to which Christians have witnessed for nearly two millennia has become distorted as well." The unnamed reviewer fears that "the slope has already been slid.'"

Another CBMW article wonders what the amorphous link actually *is* between Christian feminism and homosexuality, concluding finally that such a connection is definitely there—but that it's not really clear just what the connection *is*. However, claims the article, our organization, EEWC–Christian Feminism Today, proves the reality of the connection: "Perhaps the most striking example of a parachurch organization drifting from a focus upon women's rights to the endorsement of homosexuality is . . . currently known as the Evangelical & Ecumenical Women's Caucus (EEWC)."

EEWC-CFT, with its total inclusiveness in membership and leadership and its activism for LGBTQ rights, is held up as a warning about what may happen to other Christian groups that begin teaching that women and men are equal. The article concludes: "While many other links between these two ideologies [Christian egalitarianism and homosexual approval and advocacy] likely exist . . . the main reason why some advocates of egalitarianism have been led to endorse homosexuality is that feminist-type arguments so minimize gender identity that once biblical feminism is embraced, it is but a small logical step to accept homosexuality."

Rick Phillips, in his article on the "feminist slippery slope" posted on *Reformation 21*, speaks of drawing a "straight, descending line between the ordination of women and the ordination of homosexuals." He says he is not viewing the slippery slope metaphor in the way it's often used—although the sense of impending doom comes through in his arguments nevertheless. Rather, he claims to be talking specifically about where *feminist methods of biblical interpretation* logically lead. He says that "once the arguments made by the feminists are conceded, fairness and consistency will demand that those same arguments be applied to other similar issues, among them the ordination of homosexuals, but most lamentably that such arguments will have the effect of dismantling the entire doctrinal structure of the Christian faith."

Even a website that's devoted to satire, poking fun at ultraconservatives' constant outrage over social change, has addressed such slippery slope thinking. Using over-the-top language in a screed titled "The Rise in Feminism is Causing a Homosexuality Boom in America," a *Christwire* piece claims Satan has "infiltrated the minds of the naturally weak minded female species since the beginning of the human race."

Amazingly, some Christians are taking such articles on the *Christwire* website seriously, even with lines like these: "In place of the real hot-blooded American male, feminists have put the butch lesbian" who is described as not wearing make-up and daring to "talk out of turn in the presence of men" and causing confusion by "crossing all gender lines." Such behavior, according to the satire, negatively affects "vulnerable Christian men who have not been spending enough time reading the Bible, an activity which naturally raises testosterone levels and protects against the disease of homosexuality." According to the *New York Times,* the *Christwire* website (which uses the tag line, "Conservative Values for an Unsaved World") was set up by two young men who met online and decided to start a website that would not specifically target Christians but rather all those "who do not question what they hear on the news" and who then regurgitate it to others. "It is all one big joke," the article emphasizes. Yet, many people get fooled and believe the website's features are for real.

The Actual Connection between Feminism and LGBT Rights

But it's true that there is a real connection between feminism and LGBT rights. Here's why. It's because both movements *are founded* on *the principle of equality and justice for all people*!

It's as simple as that.

It's as profound as that.

The questioning that gives rise to progressive social change is always about human beings, not abstractions—human beings who are made in the image of God and loved by God but who have been denied that recognition by the dominant "powers that be." The call for change is about acknowledging and honoring the dignity of whole categories of people who have been regarded as "less than" or "lower than" or "unequal to" the privileged groups that determine who benefits from a society's social arrangements and rewards. In other words, justice movements form in order to challenge the hierarchies that have been set up to keep whole groups of people "in their place."

An emphasis on our shared humanity is what links together all such movements—whether the goal has been ending slavery, recognizing the dignity and civil rights of black people, working toward equal rights for women, striving for equality for LGBTQ people, seeking justice for families living in poverty, or any other effort to secure justice and equity for everyone.

Maybe It's Not about Sliding Down a Slope but Moving to a Different Paradigm

Many heterosexual Christians from conservative backgrounds, who were first troubled by the emergence of feminism and its emphasis on gender equality, are now distressed over other changes taking place, including the U.S. Supreme Court's 2013 decision to overturn the Defense of Marriage Act (DOMA) and more recently the legalization of same-sex marriage, not to mention the many other signs of growing societal acceptance of the dignity and rights of those who identify as LGBTQ.

I don't think it's fair (or loving) to label all such distressed Christians as bigots or haters. Many of them are honestly wrestling with the fact that they've been taught by their churches that God calls homosexuality sinful, and they've been warned that interpretations of the Bible that suggest otherwise are wrong. Yet, at the same time, they may be experiencing cognitive dissonance because more and more of them are learning that they know someone who identifies as lesbian or gay—often someone who also identifies as a devoted follower of Jesus Christ. That "someone" may have been in a longtime loving relationship (though perhaps closeted) and may now be legally married to that same-sex partner.

Some thoughtful conservative "straight" Christians, perplexed by the changing attitudes throughout society, may begin questioning the reasoning that's behind the slippery slope argument. Is this really the only way to look at this issue, the only way to be *biblical*?

It may be helpful at this point to think of two contrasting *paradigms*— two different sets of assumptions, each forming a distinct system of understanding the Christian faith. Maybe it's time for a paradigm shift.

Revisiting the Slippery Slope Paradigm

The slippery slope paradigm that we've already examined relies on a simplistic image of the Christian faith as comprising an essential set of beliefs and rules, along with required stances on certain social issues. In this way of thinking, to question any one of these "essentials" can set off a downward slide, knocking over one essential after another, until the whole hill comes tumbling down, along with the questioner. That's why those who take this approach insist on building a fence at the top of the hill, establishing who belongs to the "true faith," and who doesn't ("not a *real* Christian"), as well as anyone who might have once belonged but who is now judged to have strayed away and is not to be taken seriously.

Fred Clark on his *Slacktivist* blog speaks about evangelical "tribal markers," which may vary at particular points in history but always have the purpose of indicating who is "in" and who is "out." Slippery slope ideology helps set the boundaries and spell out the limits, and a person who pushes against the fence and questions the essentials has already begun the slide and is likely to be considered on his or her way out.

The Love Thy Neighbor Paradigm

However, there's another entirely different paradigm that can legitimately claim the term "biblical" in its basic assumptions. In fact, I believe it is more true to the message of the Bible than the more restrictive view embedded in the other paradigm. It is the Love Thy Neighbor Paradigm, which is based on our shared humanity rather than on a set of propositions. It is built upon empathy toward the human beings involved.

It's about relationships rather than rules—relationship with God and others. It's a model of inclusion rather than exclusion. It's the message of God's compassion that Jonah didn't like to recognize. It's the point of the story Jesus told when asked, "Who is my neighbor?" The questioner already knew the two great commandments that encapsulated the law (love God and love your neighbor as yourself), but nevertheless, he appeared to want limits on what neighbor love entails.

Whereas the Slippery Slope Paradigm focuses on a judgmental God and defines sin as the breaking of certain rules and requirements, the Love Thy Neighbor Paradigm focuses on *people*—human beings made in the divine image—and views *sin* as a failure to love others as God has loved us (1 John 4:7–21).

Loving my neighbors means getting to know them, to seek to understand them, to empathize with them. Heterosexual Christians who see their LGBTQ neighbors through the eyes of love and equality will happily accept an invitation to a same-sex wedding, rejoicing in the love the couple shares on this special day (rather than praying that God will break up the relationship, as I have known some Christians to do!).

Loving my neighbor may mean seeking to understand the latest scientific studies on what a homosexual orientation actually is. Or it may mean looking for information on what it means to be transgender. Loving my neighbor means fulfilling the admonition of Romans 12:15 by "rejoicing with those who rejoice" when a lesbian couple welcomes a new child into the family, or when two gay men legally adopt the special needs child for whom they had served as foster parents. Loving my neighbor also means "weeping with those who weep" when a lesbian loses her beloved partner of many years in an auto accident; or a gay male couple mourns a mother's death after the two men had opened their home and cared for her as her health deteriorated, the son-in-law having been just as devoted as her son. These are some of the ways the Love Thy Neighbor Paradigm focuses on our shared humanity rather than exercising the judgmentalism of the Slippery Slope Paradigm with its emphasis on disapproval over supposedly broken rules.

We see these contrasting paradigms in the reactions of some people in Jesus's day as they refused to see his compassion. When Jesus healed people on the Sabbath, the religious leaders closed their eyes, minds, and hearts to the individuals concerned. All that mattered was that a rule had been broken. What rule might Jesus break next on this slippery slide?

Self-righteous religionists could not see the *people*, nor rejoice with them in their new happiness. A man who had been an invalid for 38 years picks up his pallet and walks. As he jumps around for joy, the religious leaders refuse to relate to him as a fellow human being; they see only a broken Sabbath rule. A bent-over woman stands upright and sees the world from a new perspective. The self-righteous religious people refuse to share her sense of wonder and praise to God. They don't see the woman; they can see only a Sabbath violation. A blind man is given sight. Again the religious leaders are outraged and obsessed with what they see as a broken commandment. Dr. Reta Finger has a wonderful discussion of this incident in one of her Bible studies from John's Gospel. ("Who Is Blind and Who Can

See? A One-Act Comedy in Six Scenes—John 9:1–41" https://eewc.com/
blind-can-see-one-act-comedy-six-scenes-john-91–41/)

In Acts 10, we see Peter arguing with God, who had sent Peter a special
vision, a vision that prepared him to break what he thought were ironclad
rules by welcoming into his life a category of people he thought he should
not associate with if he were to be pleasing to God. Instead, he found he was
wrong—that the marginalized group that he had previously condemned
were actually welcomed into God's family and given the Holy Spirit.

But immediately after recognizing this, Peter ran into criticism by
others who saw only boundaries that had been transgressed. "You stayed in
the homes of Gentiles, and you even ate with them!" (Acts 11:3 [CEV])—
equivalent to a shocked statement that might be made today. ("You attended
the wedding of two women! Why didn't you take a stand for God and refuse
to participate in their sin?")

What did Peter do? He didn't apologize or worry about violating the
norms of his religious compatriots, who expected him to separate himself
from a category of people they deemed unholy. Instead, Peter simply told
his story. He talked about what had happened in his own life, including
his struggles and questionings, and how he had changed his mind because
of what God had shown him. "After I started speaking to [the category of
people that his fellow religionists stayed away from], the Holy Spirit was
given to them, just as the Spirit was given to us at the beginning . . . God
gave the Gentiles the same gift that he gave us when we put our faith in
the Lord Jesus Christ. So how could I have gone against God?" (see Acts
11:1–18, CEV).

The Love Thy Neighbor Paradigm has prodded many of us to ask the
same questions Peter dealt with—and then to find the same answers and
come to the same conclusions, assuring us that the Slippery Slope Paradigm
is *not* the only way Christians can approach feminism and LGBT advocacy,
regardless of the continuing stream of fear-based warnings and words of
condemnation issuing from pulpits.

It's something to think about.

Originally published on *Christian Feminism Today (eewc.com)*. © 2015 by Letha
Dawson Scanzoni and Christian Feminism Today. Used by permission.

For links to references, see the article online: https://eewc.com/christian-feminism-
and-lgbt-advocacy-lets-move-away-from-slippery-slope-thinking/.

8

What Can Christians Learn from the "Mystery Dress" Phenomenon?

By now, almost everyone with Internet access has heard about "the dress." It was just an ordinary off-the-rack dress, purchased by the mother of a bride in Scotland to wear at her daughter's wedding. Eager to show the dress to her daughter, she sent her a photo. But when the daughter and her fiancé looked at the photo, they were surprised to find each of them saw the dress in different colors: one saw it as white with gold trim and the other as blue with black trim. How could this be? The couple sent a picture of the dress to friends on Facebook and asked how they saw the color of the dress.

Then, on Thursday evening, February 26, 2015, one of the bride's friends posted a picture of the dress on Tumblr, which then spread to Buzzfeed. Twitter and other social networking sites joined in, as did older forms of mass media, keeping the momentum going all through the night.

Soon people all over the connected world were divided over the color of the dress. Throughout that Friday, millions were joining in to voice their views. There was the blue-and-black team on one side and the white-and-gold team on the other. Some disagreements were intense, even combative. According to some reports, disputes over the dress color even caused some relationships to break up. "This dress is tearing our family apart," the daughter of a *Salon* writer lamented.

People called it "the mystery dress" and described the whole phenomenon as "dressgate." The *New York Times* called it the "dress that melted the Internet." The fashion director of the small UK company that makes this line of dresses was as surprised as anyone else. She reported that sales for the dress had more than tripled the day after the social media posts. There was no evidence this was a publicity stunt, although the company later used it for a good cause when, in March, it created a special version of the dress to auction off for a British charity. In Australia, the Salvation Army featured the dress in an ad calling attention to the plight of abused women.

This explosion of interest and debate could have been just another example of a short-lived web sensation. But something more seemed to be happening. How could so many people look at the same thing and see it in either of two ways?

The Rush to Find Explanations

Ophthalmologists, neuroscientists, psychologists, and other scientists were asked to explain the phenomenon, and scientific theories and explanations multiplied.

Much of the talk centered on how we *perceive* color, with many scientists pointing out that perception involves what our *brains* do with information provided by our eyes. A headline in the science section of the *PBS NewsHour* website went so far as to announce that "color doesn't exist." It's all about perception. Scientists interviewed for that article said color results from constantly occurring complex brain computations that we're not even aware of. Thus, people looking at the same thing can perceive its colors differently.

Seeing different things in a picture is not just about color. Optical illusions of all kinds show how we can view something differently from someone else—or even how we ourselves may see it at different times.

Isn't All This Attention to "Dressgate" a Silly Waste of Time?

As news of the dress enigma proliferated, some critics scoffed at all the attention it was siphoning from more important matters. With so much turmoil and suffering going on around the globe, wasn't it foolish to make so much fuss over *a dress*?

No, says Dr. Pascal Wallisch, a research scientist at the Center for Neural Science at New York University. "While it is true that the world faces many pressing problems, discussing the dress is *not* frivolous." Why?

Because "it's not about the dress—it's about visual perception and human cognition."

He considers this to be the first time that "a powerful stimulus display has been brought to the attention of science by social media," and he considers this highly significant. "Surely, many people have taken overexposed pictures of fabric (the fabric might matter, too) in poor lighting conditions before," he points out. "But without social media to amplify the disagreement (social media seems to be best at that), it would have ended there."

Instead, millions of people worldwide were engaging together in a lively (and sometimes heated) discussion on an important scientific topic: vision and how and why we perceive colors as we do. "So yes," Wallisch concludes, well aware of the serious problems we face in these times, "ISIS is an obvious concern. But that doesn't mean 'the dress' is trivial. It is not. As a matter of fact," he goes on, "I would argue that this could not be more topical. If we can't agree about the color of a dress, how can we hope for world peace? How can we foster tolerance if we don't allow for and don't understand that other people can sincerely see the world differently from us?"

Understanding the Anxieties Awakened through "Dressgate"

It was Wallisch's last point that had similarly struck me immediately upon learning of the dress controversy that Friday morning in February. I wondered if it might have some important lessons for us.

Awareness of differences

The mystery dress jolted many people into realizing that their view is not the only view, that different people can honestly differ in how they see things. This is the most obvious lesson; yet it may be the hardest to accept. If we hear someone say, "I just can't see this the way you do," it probably doesn't occur to us that what they're saying *might be literally true*! That was one of the lessons of the dress. We'd rather believe that someone's inability to see what we see is a deliberate closing of their eyes and minds. Each side may be quick to assume the other is stubborn, biased, or just plain wrong. ("No way!" was a common exclamation among people finding that another person looking at the same picture on the same screen claimed to see the dress in a different color.)

Confusion, cognitive dissonance, and controversy

For many people, what happened next in "dressgate" is what often occurs when people look at the same thing and see it in different ways. It can set up inner turmoil, a sense of uncertainty, a feeling that something is off-balance. How can we trust our own eyes if somebody we care about—somebody we thought we knew very well and assumed shared the same outlook as ours—now looks at the same thing and sees it in a different way? What then?

Determined to hang on to our certainty about what we see, we may not only dispute what the other person reports seeing, but we may begin changing our view of the *person* who is doing the seeing! We had always thought we were on the same page. Now we find that isn't true!

We're experiencing what psychologists call cognitive dissonance. It's as though two musical notes are clashing in discord, spoiling the harmony. People react to such dissonance in different ways, seeking to resolve the discomfort the dissonance brings. Here are two such ways that I'll illustrate from experiences in my own life.

Two Different Reactions

Approach number 1: "I reject your view, and with it, you!"

During the 1960s and early 1970s, when I was an active part of the evangelicalism of that time, the vast majority of evangelicals were convinced the Bible clearly taught male headship and female subordination for all times and places. Because my own study of Scripture, theology, history, and personal experience led me to look at these teachings in a different light, I began questioning that view. I wrote articles (and later a book) emphasizing the equality of women and men in the home, church, and society.

One day, I received a letter from a young woman who said she had considered me her role model from when she had been a 12-year-old camper at an evangelical camp where I was her counselor. We occasionally corresponded over the years after that. She now wanted to let me know she had followed my other Christian writings all through high school and college and had looked up to me as an example of what a Christian woman should be. She had even written a paper about it. Now, as a pastor's wife, she had expected to keep seeing me in that way. But, in a tone of disappointment more than anger, she was writing to tell me I was no longer her role model; my feminist views had destroyed her image of me, and she could no longer see me as an example or mentor. She and her husband decided to discontinue the friendship because, in their eyes, my views on gender equality were unbiblical. They were not open to further discussion. They rejected both my view and me.

Approach number 2: "I'll listen and learn, and then discern"

In this next example, *I* was the one who found it necessary to adjust my way of looking at something that I had not previously questioned or even thought about. At the time, I was one of our church's leaders for a college age discussion group. One Sunday, a visiting speaker told the group about her ministries to various categories of people in a large city. Chief among these ministries, at the time, was meeting with gay men and lesbians. It was 1964, long before the more inclusive term "LGBTQ" was used. (In fact, it was from this woman's talk that day that I first heard the word, "gay.")

This was a time in U.S. history when psychologists and psychiatrists considered homosexuality a mental illness, sociologists spoke of it as deviance, the legal profession and state laws classified it as a crime, and most Christians considered it a sin. The speaker for the college group was no different on this last point, but she had a more humane approach, saw homosexual persons as human beings deserving of God's love and our love, and not as an abstract idea or a class of people to be avoided. She said she was reaching out to them through taking the gospel message to gay bars. But, as an evangelical Christian, she held the traditional "biblical" view and believed gay men and lesbians could be helped to move away from their same-sex sexual expression. The idea of *sexual orientation* was not yet widely considered, although scientists in various fields were beginning to explore it.

After the speaker left to return to her home state, she and I became pen pals, having met in person only that one time. (This was several decades before e-mail became widely used.) In our letters, delivered by the postal service every few months over the next ten or so years, we talked about all sorts of matters relating to the Christian life and Christian service. We talked about prayer, our personal Bible study, reading C. S. Lewis and other books, her ministry of evangelism and student work, her work with persons with addictions, my ministry of writing, as well as other topics, including Christianity and homosexuality.

One day in 1969, I suggested that since the topic of homosexuality was becoming increasingly talked about in the news, maybe she should consider writing some articles about the topic from her Christian perspective. She sent back a postcard and said yes, she had thought about writing sometimes and, in fact, had a stack of letters from Christian magazine editors asking for articles. But she surprised me by saying that if she wrote even a fraction of what she "*really thought* about the topic and the people involved," these magazines would never print it. She said she had met some of the most dedicated, mature Christians she had ever known, and they were living in same-sex relationships. "What's more," she said, "several have both the fruits and the gifts of the Spirit in great abundance."

I wanted to know more about how, when, and why she had changed her perspective on this topic. I didn't want to argue with her but rather to listen and learn and eventually discern what I believed God might want to show me and then develop my own way of looking at the topic. While I listened and learned, I did not hesitate to disagree with her and challenge her. She was listening and learning from me as well, as she saw the reasoning process behind my continuing to hold on to the traditional view. Quite likely she had gone through similar ways of wrestling with such ideas when she, too, had begun seeing through a different lens.

She never insisted I change my views, nor did I insist she change hers. I didn't consider her a "heretic" for leaving the traditional evangelical view; she didn't consider me a "bigot" for holding on to it. As we continued these exchanges off and on over the next three years. I would refer to my understanding of Scripture, theology, and natural law, and she would write back, point to holes in some of my arguments, tell me about new biblical scholarship she had learned was taking place, and would insist that homosexuality was not about sex but about love.

At the same time, I was gathering information on my own through popular media (some talk shows were beginning to talk about the topic by then) and by studying research findings from the Kinsey Institute and other social science studies, including reading about Evelyn Hooker's pioneering work. Yet, I was not sure how everything I was learning through science would fit with my sincerely held traditional biblical interpretation and evangelical faith. So I tried to compartmentalize both my scholarly endeavors and my evangelical beliefs and kept them separate while I tried to sort it all through. All the while, my correspondent and I were sharpening the thinking of each other in the manner of Proverbs 27:17—"Just as iron sharpens iron, friends sharpen the minds of each other" (CEV). It was a dialogue, not an angry debate.

One day in 1972, during one of our discussions by mail, I had an "aha" moment. It occurred to me that she and I were thinking of sexual morality as if it could be defined in two very different and separate paradigms rather than by a single all-inclusive definition that applied to all people and was not dependent on sexual orientation! I typed up a chart and put it in my next letter and asked if it illustrated what she had hoped I would see. It was, and it marked the beginning of a major paradigm shift for me.

A few years later, I expanded that nascent paradigm idea into a longer chart for inclusion in the book I coauthored with Virginia Ramey Mollenkott, *Is the Homosexual My Neighbor?* (first edition published in 1978). Although by then my longtime correspondent had moved overseas and we had lost track of each other, I was able to trace her down to send her a copy of Virginia's and my book. I inscribed it with a note telling her she "had opened my eyes to a different way of looking at the subject."

There it was again—that "new way of seeing" metaphor! It was like looking at one of those optical illusions and suddenly seeing another picture that was hidden within the first view after which you're never able to see it the old way again.

When People See Things Differently

Ideally, it would be best if we could always use the "listen, learn, and then discern" approach when someone else's view differs from our own. We need to be slow to make judgments and accusations. Our patience may be rewarded. Instead of being in a hurry to tell them why we think they're *wrong*, we can say, "Tell me more about why you see this as you do." Both parties are likely to benefit.

On the other hand, if we get upset and angry because their perspective differs from ours, we may need to ask ourselves, "Why do I feel as I do?" Could it be a matter of our own ego being so wrapped up in our particular view that we consider *ourselves* to be under attack when it's our view that is being challenged? That it's all about *us* and not about our view?

Such thinking is why people often slip into the "I reject your view, and with it, *you*" approach. Thus, conflicts break out and escalate—conflicts that might have been avoided by trying to understand why people's perspectives and perceptions differ. We might be surprised to find they (or we) are more open to rethinking something than either of us ever thought possible, even though it may take a long time.

(I need to stress here that I am talking about one-on-one conversations with people with whom we have a relationship—friend, family member or other acquaintance with whom we form some kind of connection and who is open to such an honest conversation—not someone whose mind is bolted shut. For deadbolt-locked minds to display openness to another view can mean a loss of political or religion-based power, money, and prestige in their particular group. Such a person may care only about provocation, self-aggrandizement, and browbeating others through intimidation.)

What the Dress Color Meme Can Teach Us about Different Perceptions and Perspectives

It's helpful to understand some reasons that people may seem so wedded to their own perspective. Going back to the colors of the "mystery dress," scientists who looked for reasons for the different perceptions pointed to a number of factors: (a) the lighting that is perceived—including shadows, and how an individual's eyes adjust to the time of day, (b) the two different ways the dress appeared in relation to the photo's *background*, and (c) slight variations among individuals in the physical structure of their eyes, specifically the photoreceptor cells (rods and cones).

It's possible to think of these same factors (light, background, and the unique composition of an individual) in a *figurative* sense, as well. We can apply them to understanding some differences among people in their thinking and discourse on social, political, and religious issues. Here are some factors to keep in mind when we're discussing sensitive topics.

- What do I know about the *background* against which this person sees this particular issue? Very conservative? Or very progressive? Or somewhere in between? Religious, or indifferent, or anti-religion? Coming from a dogmatic, judgmental church or home, and a view of God as angry and punishing; or coming from a home or church that stressed love, compassion, and empathy toward others? How does this person view and interpret the Bible? Whatever we bring to a topic from our own background is likely to affect how we first see a subject.

- What do I know about the *"time of day"*—metaphorically, the emotional and intellectual "stage of life"—in which this person is viewing or has viewed this issue? Has there ever been a time of openness to change, and is there such openness now? What brought about the change (in either direction) in how the person has looked at this issue?

- What do I know about what defines or makes up *this individual's personality or disposition*—what the person brings to the conversation in a unique or particular way, like the variations in photoreceptor cells in some individuals' eyes? Is he or she fearful, anxious about taking risks, worried about the opinions of others? Does this person tend to be optimistic or pessimistic? Is this person quick to anger when challenged?

- What do I know about the light and shadows in which this person may view this issue? Where is the light perceived to be coming from? What may be blocking it?

Perception and Reality

Among all the online comments people were making about the dress color, someone pointed out that if only we could all be in the same room, we would be able to see the actual dress—not just the *image* of it that we were seeing on our various electronic devices. So true. There was a reality behind and beyond the image. Had we attended the wedding, we would have seen the bride's mother in her blue and black dress.

But in this very divided world today, it's clear that, figuratively speaking, we are not all "in the same room." It is equally clear that even those of us who claim to be followers of Jesus and "one in Christ" are not in the same room either when it comes to our perceptions—as well as the words and actions that are fueled by those perceptions. Thus we hurt each other in the process of making our points.

The apostle Paul said that in this present time there is so much we don't know, so much we can't see, a reality we can't fully comprehend. "For now we see in a mirror, dimly, but then we will see face to face. Now I know only in part; then I will know fully, even as I have been fully known. And now faith, hope, and love abide, these three, and the greatest of these is love" (1 Cor 13:12–13, NRSV).

Beyond our perceptions, we can know this certainty: "God is love" and "God is light" (1 John 4:16; 1 John 1:5). And light is made up of all the colors of the rainbow.

May we make it our goal to walk in that light—the light of love—realizing as the psalmist did, that it is in God's light that we see light (Ps 36:9).

For links to references, see the article online: https://eewc.com/can-christians-learn-mystery-dress-phenomenon/.

Bibliography

Allport, Gordon W. *The Nature of Prejudice*. Doubleday Anchor Books. Garden City, NY: Doubleday, 1958.

Bailey, Catherine. "Summer Council Meeting." *Update: Newsletter of the Evangelical Women's Caucus* 10 (1986) 7.

Bailey, Sarah Pulliam. "From Franklin Graham to Tony Campolo, Some Evangelical Leaders are Splitting over Gay Marriage." Acts of Faith. *Washington Post*, June 9, 2015. https://www.washingtonpost.com/news/acts-of-faith/wp/2015/06/09/from-franklin-graham-to-tony-campolo-some-evangelical-leaders-are-dividing-over-gay-marriage/?utm_term=.cad9980bb12b/.

Baldridge, J. Victor. *Sociology: A Critical Approach to Power, Conflict, and Change*. New York: Wiley, 1975.

Bass, Diana Butler. *A People's History of Christianity: The Other Side of the Story*. New York: HarperOne, 2009.

Beam, Erin Lane. "Holy Hellion: The Rebellion of a Faith-filled Feminist." *Christian Feminism Today* 32/4 (2009) 8. https://eewc.com/holy-hellion-rebellion-faith-filled-feminist/.

Berding, Kenneth. "The Crisis of Biblical Illiteracy & What We Can Do About It." *Biola Magazine* (June 2014). http://magazine.biola.edu/article/14-spring/the-crisis-of-biblical-illiteracy/.

Bieze, Linda, and Alena Amato Ruggerio. "Friends for All Seasons." *Christian Feminism Today* 31/4 (2008) 1–3. https://eewc.com/friends-for-all-seasons/.

Braude, Ann. "Women's History *Is* American Religious History." In *Retelling U.S. Religious History*, edited by Thomas A. Tweed, 87–107. Berkeley: University of California Press, 1997.

Cady, Susan, and Hal Taussig. "Jesus and Sophia." *Daughters of Sarah* 14 (1988) 7–11.

Campbell, Van. Review of *What's Right with Feminism*, by Elaine Storkey and *All We're Meant to Be*, by Letha Dawson Scanzoni and Nancy A. Hardesty. *Journal of the Evangelical Theological Society* 31/1 (1988) 96–98.

Center for Inclusivity. "Our Mission & Vision." https://centerforinclusivity.org/values-mission/.

Christian Feminism Today. "About Christian Feminism Today." *Christian Feminism Today*. http://www.eewc.com/about/.

———. "Origin." https://eewc.com/about/#origin/.

Christianity Today. "The Top 50 Books That Have Shaped Evangelicals." Reviews/Best-Of Lists. *Christianity Today* (October 6, 2006). http://www.christianitytoday.com/ct/2006/october/23.51.html/.

Cochran, Pamela D. H. *Evangelical Feminism: A History.* New York: New York University Press, 2005.

Collins, Gail. *America's Women: 400 Years of Dolls, Drudges, Helpmates, and Heroines.* New York: Perennial, 2004.

Coontz, Stephanie. *A Strange Stirring: The "Feminine Mystique" and American Women at the Dawn of the 1960s.* New York: Basic Books, 2011.

Corey, Benjamin. "Rob Bell: A Symbol of Every Evangelical Who's Been Shunned for Asking Questions." Progressive Christian channel. *Patheos* (December 17, 2014). http://www.patheos.com/blogs/formerlyfundie/rob-bell-a-symbol-of-every-evangelical-whos-been-shunned-for-asking-questions/.

Cottrell, Susan. "Is There Healing for the Church's 'Mother Wound'?" *Christian Feminism Today* (June 2014). http://www.eewc.com/Articles/healing-churchs-mother-wound/.

Crosby, Alicia. "Fast of Embodied Solidarity." Emerging Voices. *Patheos: Hosting the Conversation on Faith* (February 12, 2016). http://www.patheos.com/blogs/emergentvillage/2016/02/fast-of-embodied-solidarity/.

Deaver, Katie M. "The 2015 Nancy A. Hardesty Memorial Scholarship Recipient." *Christian Feminism Today.* https://eewc.com/nahms/katie-deaver-2015-nancy-a-hardesty-memorial-scholarship-recipient/.

Deaver, K. M. "Elsa and the New Roles of Gender Equality." *Café* (February 27, 2015). http://www.boldcafe.org/blog/elsa-roles-gender-equality/.

Dobson, James C. "Foreword." In *Sex Is a Parent Affair: Help for Parents in Teaching Their Children about Sex,* by Letha Scanzoni, i–ii. Glendale, CA: Regal, 1973.

Douglas, Mary. *Purity and Danger.* New York: Penguin, 1966.

Dowland, Seth. *Family Values and the Rise of the Christian Right.* Politics and Culture in Modern America. Philadelphia: University of Pennsylvania Press, 2015.

Eldredge, John, and Stasi Eldredge. *Captivating: Unveiling the Mystery of a Woman's Soul.* Nashville: Nelson, 2005.

Ellwood, Robert S. *1950: Crossroads of American Religious Life.* Louisville: Westminster John Knox, 2000.

Evangelicals for Social Action (ESA). "Chicago Declaration of Evangelical Social Concern." http://www.evangelicalsforsocialaction.org/about-esa/history/chicago-declaration-of-evangelical-social-concern/.

Evans, Rachel Held. *A Year of Biblical Womanhood.* Nashville: Thomas Nelson, 2012.

Finger, Reta Halteman. "A Fish Story: Mother Jesus Serves Breakfast—John 21:1–14." *Christian Feminism Today* (March 2015). http://www.eewc.com/RetasReflections/a-fish-story-mother-jesus-serves-breakfast-john-211–14/.

———. "Gender Remixed: Sophia and Word." *Christian Feminism Today* (May 2013). http://www.eewc.com/RetasReflections/gender-remixed-sophia-word/.

FitzGerald, Frances. *The Evangelicals: The Struggle to Shape America.* New York: Simon & Schuster, 2017.

Friedan, Betty. *The Feminine Mystique.* New York: Norton, 1963.

Furnish, Victor Paul. *The Moral Teaching of Paul.* Nashville: Abingdon, 1979.

George, Kimberly B. "How It All Began." *Christian Feminism Today* (July 2008). https://www.eewc.com/72-27/how-it-all-began/.

Gibson, Dan, et al. *Besides the Bible: 100 Books That Have, Should, or Will Create Christian Culture*. Downers Grove, IL: InterVarsity, 2010.

Gresh, Dannah. *And the Bride Wore White: Seven Secrets to Sexual Purity*. Chicago: Moody, 2004.

Grimsrud, Ted, and Mark Thiessen Nation. *Reasoning Together: A Conversation on Homosexuality*. Scottdale, PA: Herald, 2008.

Hanson. Jeanne. "Climbing the Mountain of Age." *EEWC Update* 27/3 (2003) 2. https://eewc.com/climbing-mountain-age/.

———. "Taking Leaps of Faith." *Christian Feminism Today* 32/2 (2008) 1–2. https://eewc.com/taking-leaps-faith/.

Hardesty, Nancy A. *Inclusive Language in the Church*. Atlanta: John Knox, 1987.

———. "1978 EWC Conference Recap." *Christian Feminism Today*. https://eewc.com/Conferences/women-and-the-ministries-of-christ-1978-ewc-conference/.

Harrison, Leslie R. "Ain't I a Womanist Too? Third World Womanist Religious Thought. Review of *Ain't I a Womanist Too? Third World Womanist Religious Thought*, by Monica A. Coleman." *Christian Feminism Today* (March 2015). http://www.eewc.com/BookReviews/aint-i-a-womanist-too-third-world-womanist-religious-thought/.

Horner, Sue. "Trying to Be God in the World: The Story of the Evangelical Women's Caucus and the Crisis over Homosexuality." In *Gender, Ethnicity, and Religion: Views from the Other Side*, edited by Rosemary Radford Ruether, 99–124. Minneapolis: Fortress, 2002.

Hunt, Mary E. "Feminist Faith-Based Social Justice: How Feminists of Faith Can Collaborate to Amplify Our Voices and Deepen Our Collective Impact." *Christian Feminism Today* (June 27, 2014). http://www.eewc.com/Articles/feminist-faith-based-social-justice/.

Kassian, Mary A. *The Feminist Gospel: The Movement to Unite Feminism within the Church*. Wheaton, IL: Crossway, 1992.

Kent, H. H., and Charles C. Ryrie, "Women in the Church." *Eternity* 14/11 (1963) 12–16, 44.

Kiser-Lowrance, Rebecca L. "God of the Casserole." *Update: Newsletter of the Evangelical & Ecumenical Women's Caucus* 19/2 (1995) 2–3.

Lane, Erin S. *Lessons in Belonging from a Church-Going Commitment Phobe*. Downers Grove, IL: InterVarsity, 2015.

Lane, Erin S., and Enuma Okoro, eds. *Talking Taboo: American Christian Women Get Frank about Faith*. Ashland, OR: White Cloud, 2013.

Lee, Deborah Jian. *Rescuing Jesus: How People of Color, Women & Queer Christians Are Reclaiming Evangelicalism*. Boston: Beacon, 2015.

Linstatter, Anne (née Eggebroten). "A Personal Reaction to Pamela Cochran's *Evangelical Feminism: A History*." Review of *Evangelical Feminism: A History*, by Pamela D. H. Cochran. *EEWC Update* 29/3 (2005) 8–10. https://eewc.com/evangelical-feminism/.

MacHaffie, Barbara J. *Her Story: Women in Christian Tradition*. 2nd ed. Minneapolis: Fortress, 2006.

Marsden, George M. *Religion and American Culture*. 2nd ed. Orlando: Harcourt, 2001.

———. *Understanding Fundamentalism and Evangelicalism*. Grand Rapids: Eerdmans, 1991.

Mock, Melanie Springer. "Even Wikipedia Has a Messaging Problem—A Response: Fearing the Feminine or Embracing Our Mother." *Christian Feminism Today* (May

2013). https://www.eewc.com/FemFaith/fearing-the-feminine-or-embracing-our-mother/.

———. "God's Gift of Motherhood Comes in Different Ways." *Christian Feminism Today* (May 2009). https://eewc.com/gods-gift-motherhood-comes-different-ways/.

Mohler, Albert. "The Scandal of Biblical Illiteracy: It's Our Problem." *Albert Mohler* (January 2016). http://www.albertmohler.com/2016/01/20/the-scandal-of-biblical-illiteracy-its-our-problem-4/.

Mollenkott, Virginia Ramey. "Cochran's Evangelical Feminism—Yet Once More." Review of *Evangelical Feminism: A History*, by Pamela D. H. Cochran. *EEWC Update* 29/4 (2006) 3–4. https://eewc.com/evangelical-feminism/.

———. *The Divine Feminine: The Biblical Imagery of God as Female*. New York: Crossroad, 1983. Eugene, OR: Wipf & Stock, 2014.

———. *Omnigender: A Trans-religious Approach*. Cleveland: Pilgrim, 2007.

———. "Viriginia Ramey Mollenkott." In *Transforming the Faiths of Our Fathers*, edited by Ann Braude, 55–71. New York: Palgrave Macmillan, 2004.

Myers, David G., and Letha Dawson Scanzoni. *What God Has Joined Together: A Christian Case for Gay Marriage*. San Francisco: HarperSanFrancisco, 2005.

———. *What God Has Joined Together: A Christian Case for Gay Marriage*. San Francisco: HarperSanFrancisco, 2006.

Newman, Jennifer. "The 2014 Nancy A. Hardesty Memorial Scholarship Recipient." *Christian Feminism Today*. https://www.eewc.com/jennifer-newman-2014-nancy-a-hardesty-memorial-scholarship-recipient/.

Ogden, Schubert M. "The Church and Homosexual Persons: The Issue of Ordination." *Perkins Newsletter* 13/19 (1980) 7.

"Peggy Campolo Carrier Pigeon Award Recipients 2007–Present." *Open Door Community Church*. http://www.sherwoodopendoor.org/peggy-campolo-carrier-pigeon-award-recipients/.

Quebedeaux, Richard. *The Worldly Evangelicals*. San Francisco: Harper & Row, 1978.

Scanzoni, John H. *Love and Negotiate: Creative Conflict in Marriage*. Waco: Word, 1979.

Scanzoni, Letha. "Biblical Feminism as a Social Movement." *Daughters of Sarah* 10/6 (1984) 18–20.

———. "Conservative Christians and Gay Civil Rights." *Christian Century* 93 (1976) 857–62.

———. "Door Reports." *Wittenburg Door* 31 (1976) 19.

———. "Elevate Marriage to Partnership." *Eternity* 19/7 (1968) 11–14. https://www.lethadawsonscanzoni.com/2010/04/christian-marriage-patriarchy-or-partnership-published-as-elevate-marriage-to-partnership/.

———. "The Feminists and the Bible." *Christianity Today* 17 (1973) 10–15.

———. "God Is at Work in the Women's Movement." *Faith at Work* (August 1976) 8–9, 31.

———. "The Great Chain of Being and the Chain of Command." *Reformed Journal* 26 (1976) 14–18.

———. "The Great Chain of Being and the Chain of Command." In *Women's Spirit Bonding*, edited by Janet Kalven and Mary I. Buckley, 41–55. New York: Pilgrim, 1984.

———. "Homemaking—Prison or Privilege?" *Sunday School Times*. (May 30, 1964) 405–406, 420.

———. "How to Live with a Liberated Wife." *Christianity Today* 20/18 (1976) 6–9.

BIBLIOGRAPHY

————. "Marching On." EWC Conference Plenary Address. Pasadena, June 17, 1978.

————. "On Friendship and Homosexuality." *Christianity Today* 18 (1974) 11–16.

————. "A Patch of Sky Isn't Enough: The Vision of *Yentl*." EWC Conference Plenary Address. Wellesley College, 1984.

————. *Sex and the Single Eye*. Grand Rapids: Zondervan, 1968.

————. *Sex Is a Parent Affair: Help for Parents in Teaching Their Children About Sex*. Glendale, CA: Regal, 1973. Revised and updated ed. New York: Bantam Books, 1982.

————. "Virginia Ramey Mollenkott." In *American Women Writers: A Critical Reference Guide from Colonial Times to the Present*, edited by Lina Mainiero, 3:203–4. 5 vols. New York: Ungar, 1981.

————. *Why Am I Here? Where Am I Going: Youth Looks at Life*. Westwood, NJ: Revell, 1966.

————. "Woman's Place: Silence or Service?" *Eternity* 17/2 (1966) 14–16. https://www.lethadawsonscanzoni.com/womens-place-silence-or-service/.

————. *Youth Looks at Love*. Westwood, NJ: Revell, 1964.

Scanzoni, Letha Dawson. "Answering God's Call to the Soul: An Interview with Marjory Zoet Bankson." *Update: Newsletter of the Evangelical & Ecumenical Women's Caucus* 23/3 (1999) 1–3, 9, 12. https://eewc.com/answering-gods-call-soul/.

————. "Backstory: Elevate Marriage to Partnership." *Letha's Calling* (April 2010). https://www.lethadawsonscanzoni.com/2010/04/backstory-elevate-marriage-to-partnership1968-eternity-article/.

————. "Backstory: Woman's Place—Silence or Service?" *Letha's Calling* (March 2010). https://www.lethadawsonscanzoni.com/2010/03/backstory-womans-placesilence-or-service/.

————. "Back to the Future; Forward to the Dream." EWCI Conference Plenary Address. Chicago, July 20, 1990.

————. "Being an Evangelical Feminist Today." *WATERtalks: Feminist Conversations in Religion Series* (May 2010). https://soundcloud.com/water-womens-alliance/2010-watertalk-with-letha-dawson-scanzoni?in=water-womens-alliance/sets/watertalks/.

————. "Christian Feminism and LGBT Advocacy: Let's Move Away from Slippery Slope Thinking." *Christian Feminism Today* (August 2015). https://eewc.com/christian-feminism-and-lgbt-advocacy-lets-move-away-from-slippery-slope-thinking/.

————. "A Christian Feminist Remembers Elisabeth Elliot (1926–2015)." *Christian Feminism Today* (June 2015). https://eewc.com/christian-feminist-remembers-elisabeth-elliot-1926-2015/.

————. "Editorial: Where We've Been; Where We're Headed." Response to "On Being Evangelical and Ecumenical," by Anne Linstatter. *EEWC Update* 27, no. 2 (2003). https://eewc.com/on-being-evangelical-and-ecumenical/.

————. "*The Feminine Mystique*: Then and Now, Part 1." *Christian Feminism Today* (July 2008). https://eewc.com/72-27/the-feminine-mystique-then-and-now-part-1/.

————. "Finding Colleen Fulmer." *EEWC Update* 28/1 (2004) 1–3, 12. https://eewc.com/finding-colleen-fulmer/.

————. "It Just Keeps Rollin' Along." EEWC-CFT Plenary Address notes. St. Louis, June 28, 2014.

————. "A Long Time Grieving: Recovering from Unwelcome Midlife Divorce." *Daughters of Sarah* 15 (1989) 14–16.

———. "Martha Ann Kirk—Embodying Christ to the World." *Christian Feminism Today* 30/1 (2006) 1–4. https://eewc.com/martha-ann-kirk-th-d-embodying-christ-world/.

———. "My First Encounter with Religious Doubt: The Day I Stopped Believing in Santa Claus." *Christian Feminism Today* (December 2013). https://eewc.com/Articles/religious-doubt-unbelief-in-santa/.

———. "Ordered Order—Conservative Christians' Love Affair with Hierarchy." *Christian Feminism Today* (September 2013). https://eewc.com/ordered-order-conservative-christians-love-affair-hierarchy/.

———. "'Paradigm Lost' and Slippery Slope Panic." *Christian Feminism Today* (October 2010). https://eewc.com/paradigm-lost-slippery-slope-panic/.

———. "Reflections of a Christian Feminist: On Being All We're Meant to Be." *Christian Feminism Today* (December 2012). https://eewc.com/christian-feminism-basics-letha/.

———. "Reflections on Two Decades of Christian Feminism," *Daughters of Sarah*, twentieth anniversary issue (Fall 1994) 7–11.

———. "A Spiritual Heart Transplant: An Interview with Joan Chittister, OSB." *Update: Newsletter of the Evangelical & Ecumenical Women's Caucus* 22/1 (1998) 1–3. https://eewc.com/spiritual-heart-transplant-interview-joan-chittister-osb/.

———. "Welcome Letter." 2016 Gathering Program. *Christian Feminism Today* (October 2016). Letha's Welcome Letter. https://eewc.com/conference-2016/.

———. "What Can Christians Learn from the 'Mystery Dress' Phenomenon?" *Christian Feminism Today* (March 2015). https://eewc.com/can-christians-learn-mystery-dress-phenomenon/.

———. "When Evangelicals Were Open to Differing Views on Abortion." *Christian Feminism Today* (September 2012). https://eewc.com/evangelicals-open-differing-views-abortion/.

———. "Why Should Difference Make Any Difference?." *Christian Feminism Today* (October 2008). https://eewc.com/72-27/why-should-difference-make-any-difference/.

———. "Why We Need Evangelical Feminists." In *New Feminist Christianity: Many Voices, Many Views*, edited by Mary E. Hunt and Diann L. Neu, 64–76. Woodstock, VT: Skylight Paths, 2010.

Scanzoni, Letha Dawson, and John Scanzoni. *Men, Women, and Change: A Sociology of Marriage and Family.* 3rd ed. New York: McGraw-Hill, 1988.

Scanzoni, Letha, and Nancy Hardesty. *All We're Meant to Be: A Biblical Approach to Women's Liberation.* 1st ed. Waco: Word, 1974.

Scanzoni, Letha Dawson, and Nancy A. Hardesty. *All We're Meant to Be: Biblical Feminism for Today.* 2nd ed. Nashville: Abingdon, 1986.

———. *All We're Meant to Be: Biblical Feminism for Today.* 3rd ed. Grand Rapids: Eerdmans, 1992.

Scanzoni, Letha, and Virginia Ramey Mollenkott. *Is the Homosexual My Neighbor? Another Christian View.* San Francisco: Harper & Row, 1978.

Scanzoni, Letha Dawson, and Virginia Ramey Mollenkott. *Is the Homosexual My Neighbor? A Positive Christian Response.* Revised and updated ed. New York: HarperOne, 1994.

Schüssler Fiorenza, Elisabeth. *Wisdom Ways: Introducing Feminist Biblical Interpretation.* Maryknoll, NY: Orbis, 2001.

Smith, Mark A. *Secular Faith: How Culture Has Trumped Religion in American Politics*. Chicago: University of Chicago Press, 2015.

Swartz, David R. *Moral Minority: The Evangelical Left in an Age of Conservatism*. Politics and Culture in Modern America. Philadelphia: University of Pennsylvania Press, 2012.

Taylor, Barbara Brown. *An Altar in the World: A Geography of Faith*. New York: HarperOne, 2009.

———. *Leaving Church: A Memoir of Faith*. San Francisco: HarperSanFrancisco, 2006.

Tucker, Ruth A., and Walter Liefeld. *Daughters of the Church: Women and Ministry from New Testament Times to the Present*. Grand Rapids: Academie, 1987.

Weaver, Lē (née Marg Herder). "The Power of an Unexpected Pronoun." *GodIsNotaGuy .com* (May 2013). http://godisnotaguy.com/2013/05/19/the-power-of-an-unexpected -pronoun/.

Weddle, Kendra, and Melanie Springer Mock. *If Eve Only Knew: Freeing Yourself from Biblical Womanhood & Becoming All God Means for You to Be*. St. Louis, MO: Chalice, 2015.

Weddle, Kendra, et al. "About the FemFaith Blog." *Christian Feminism Today* (June 2012). http://www.eewc.com/about-femfaith/.

Wheeler, David R. "The LGBT Politics of Christian Colleges." *The Atlantic* (March 2016). https://www.theatlantic.com/education/archive/2016/03/the-lgbt-politics-of- christian-colleges/473373/.

Wink, Walter, ed. *Homosexuality and Christian Faith: Questions of Conscience for the Churches*. Minneapolis: Fortress, 1999.

Woods, Richard. "Is the Homosexual My Neighbor?" Review of *Is the Homosexual My Neighbor? Another Christian View*, by Letha Scanzoni and Virginia Ramey Mollenkott. *Library Journal* 103/9 (1978) 985.

Wuthnow, Robert. *The Restructuring of American Religion: Society and Faith Since World War II*. Studies in Church and State. Princeton: Princeton University Press, 1988.

Index of People Interviewed